Texts after Terror

Texts after Terror

Rape, Sexual Violence, and the Hebrew Bible

RHIANNON GRAYBILL

OXFORD
UNIVERSITY PRESS

OXFORD
UNIVERSITY PRESS

Oxford University Press is a department of the University of Oxford. It furthers the University's objective of excellence in research, scholarship, and education by publishing worldwide. Oxford is a registered trade mark of Oxford University Press in the UK and certain other countries.

Published in the United States of America by Oxford University Press
198 Madison Avenue, New York, NY 10016, United States of America.

First issued as an Oxford University Press paperback, 2024

Library of Congress Cataloging-in-Publication Data
Names: Graybill, Rhiannon, 1984– author.
Title: Texts after terror : rape, sexual violence, and the Hebrew Bible / Rhiannon Graybill.
Description: New York, NY : Oxford University Press, 2021. | Includes bibliographical references and index.
Identifiers: LCCN 2020052464 (print) | LCCN 2020052465 (ebook) |
ISBN 9780190082314 (hardback) | ISBN 9780197764114 (paperback) |
ISBN 9780190082345 | ISBN 9780190082338 (epub) | ISBN 9780190082321
Subjects: LCSH: Rape in the Bible. | Bible. Old Testament—Criticism, interpretation, etc. |
Bible—Feminist criticism. | Sex crimes.
Classification: LCC BS1199.R27 G73 2021 (print) | LCC BS1199.R27 (ebook) |
DDC 221.8/3641532—dc23
LC record available at https://lccn.loc.gov/2020052464
LC ebook record available at https://lccn.loc.gov/2020052465

DOI: 10.1093/oso/9780190082314.001.0001

Paperback printed by Marquis Book Printing, Canada

MIX
Paper from
responsible sources
FSC® C103567

"Women are raped in Zion, young women in the towns of Judah."
—Lamentations 5:11

"Dinah, the daughter of Leah, whom she had borne to Jacob, went out to see the daughters of the land."
—Genesis 34:1

Contents

Acknowledgments

In writing this book, I have benefited immensely from many people. First, I am deeply grateful to M. Cooper Minister and Beatrice Lawrence for our ongoing conversations about sexual violence, rape culture, and religion. Many of the ideas expressed here began in our collaborations, including several coauthored pieces and our coedited volume, *Rape Culture and Religious Studies: Critical and Pedagogical Engagements*. I also want to thank the contributors to that volume, Susanne Scholz, T. Nicole Goulet, Gwynn Kessler, Kirsten Boles, Minenhle Nomalungelo Khumalo, and Jeremy Posadas, as well as the Wabash Center for Teaching and Learning in Theology and Religion, who also provided early support for that project, which led to this one.

This book has also been shaped by the work of the Shiloh Project, an international scholarly collaboration around religion and rape culture. Johanna Stiebert, Katie Edwards, Caroline Blyth, Meredith Warren, and others involved with the project have helped shaped my thinking, while also cultivating a real academic community committed to reading the Bible in and against rape culture. I am also especially grateful to Emma Nagouse for inviting me to speak at the 2018 Rape Culture and Religion Conference, sponsored by the Shiloh Project, and for her enthusiasm for the project that became *Texts after Terror*.

This book has also been immeasurably improved by careful and generous readers who have engaged it at many stages. Kurt Beals, Jessica Crist, Lena Salaymeh, Peter J. Sabo, Gwynn Kessler, and Elaine T. James all read significant portions of the manuscript, sometimes multiple times. Steed Davidson, Sarah Emanuel, Mark Leuchter, Dawn Llewellyn, Johanna Stiebert, and multiple anonymous reviewers (both for Oxford University Press and for *The Bible and Critical Theory*, where a version of chapters 1 and 2 was previously published) also read drafts of chapters and offered helpful feedback, as did audiences at the Rape Culture and Religion Conference, Middle Tennessee State University, and the University of Alberta. In addition, Fiona Black, Sarah Bloesch, Kent Brintnall, Sean Burt, Brandy Daniels, Jenna Gray-Hildenbrand, Rachel Havrelock, Lynn R. Huber, Trina Janiec Jones, Alison

Joseph, Nami Kim, Rebekka King, Jennifer Koosed, Maia Kotrosits, Francis Landy, Katherine Low, Joseph Marchal, Kathleen Peters, Erin Runions, Hilary Jerome Scarsella, Robert Paul Seesengood, Sarah Shectman, SherAli Tareen, Linn Tonstad, Jay Twomey, Daniel Ullucci, and Ian Wilson have all supported this project and my work in various ways. At Oxford University Press, Steve Wiggins has been a wonderful advocate for this project, and a skilled and kind editor.

I was able to complete this book because of a sabbatical granted by Rhodes College. Previously, Rhodes also supported this work with a Faculty Development Endowment grant for summer research. The W.J. Millard Rotational Professorship has also provided helpful financial support. At Rhodes, I have also benefited immensely from my colleagues in Religious Studies and in Gender and Sexuality Studies. In particular, I would like to thank Judith P. Haas, John Kaltner, Laura Loth, Steven L. McKenzie, Bernadette McNary-Zak, Joel Parsons, Vanessa Rogers, Sarah Rollens, and Rebecca Tuvel. Christie Arnold and Kenan Padgett also provided valuable support for research and writing. I also want to thank my students at Rhodes, both for their critical engagements with biblical texts and for their passionate advocacy against sexual violence. Many of the arguments in this book are stronger as a result of having been tested (and challenged) in the classroom.

Most importantly, my thanks are due to my friends and family, including Jessica Crist and Turner Graybill; Raphael, Marisa, and Genevieve Graybill; Krista Spiller; Caki Wilkinson; Emily Regier; Emily Wistar; Emily Bulger; Vicky Woo; Tristram Wolff; Corey Byrnes; and especially Kurt Beals. Finally, this book is dedicated to my daughter Dora, who came into the world not long before it, and who has brought so much happiness with her.

Introduction

Reading Sexual Violence

This book, *Texts after Terror*, is a project in imagining new ways of reading and understanding biblical rape stories. The Hebrew Bible is a book filled with sexual violence—we know this, maybe all too well. At times, the very idea of reading or thinking about *another rape story* can feel exhausting, dissatisfying, or simply sad. I remember a friend who told me, while we were in graduate school, that she had a new rule for watching movies and television: She would not watch anything, no matter how critically acclaimed, in which a woman was raped. She was tired of seeing sexual violence displayed on screen, tired of spending what precious free time she had witnessing rape, whether used to advance the plot, to provide a character with a backstory, or simply to fill time on screen. In reading and writing and teaching about the Bible, I have often thought about my friend and her principled avoidance of rape.

I tried, for a while, to avoid the Bible's many rapes, and its other stories of sexual violence. I tried writing about men instead of women (not, it turns out, a solution), I dabbled in horror and horror theory (where the most horrific violence becomes not a problem to be solved but a feature to be celebrated), I flirted with ways of reading that set aside questions of gender, sexuality, and bodies. But I kept finding my way back to the biblical rape stories—in part, no doubt, because of the centrality of sexual violence in contemporary life, in part because of the importance of these stories to the Bible itself: You can't get far in reading Genesis without running into a rape story. Instead of ignoring or rejecting these stories, I began exploring new ways of reading them. From the beginning, the idea of *reading after*, and *reading after terror*, was central to this project. I became interested in finding ways of reading that took seriously the pain and suffering of these texts, and their history of interpretation, without remaining locked in a pattern of what feminist criticism beginning in the 1980s had already done. *Texts after Terror* represents an effort to imagine feminist biblical reading after Phyllis Trible's *Texts of Terror* and other

Texts after Terror. Rhiannon Graybill, Oxford University Press. © Oxford University Press 2021.
DOI: 10.1093/oso/9780190082314.003.0001

similar approaches—what else could a feminist reading of rape stories do? I was also committed to carving out a space for reading *after terror*: that is, not letting the suffering or darkness of the texts consume all the interpretive space around them. In working on sexual violence more generally, I had become increasingly frustrated with the ways in which both scholarship and advocacy frequently repeat a small handful of narratives and predetermined scripts without assessing the degree to which those scripts and stories might limit our ability to talk about sexual violence, even as they also provide a language for it at all.

This is also true of the rape stories of the Hebrew Bible. I use this term, *rape stories*, to refer both to biblical accounts of rape and to other narratives of sexual violence more broadly understood. These include stories about sexual exploitation other than rape, stories where rape is hinted at but not explicitly described, stories of forced sex, unwelcome sex, and unwanted sex, *was it or wasn't it?* stories, stories about forced marriage, stories about sexual trafficking and exchange, stories that assume the same gendered logic as rape without, however, describing rape explicitly. The category of rape stories encompasses both biblical prose and poetry.[1] These rape stories are part of what Nicola Gavey calls the "cultural scaffolding of rape"; that is, they are part of the larger system that makes rape and other forms of sexual violence possible.[2]

The central concern of *Texts after Terror* is with *how we tell biblical rape stories* and *how we might tell rape stories differently*. Throughout this book, I argue that the frameworks we use to talk about sexual violence in the Bible are exhausted, dated, and even unfeminist, and that we need new models for reading and theorizing rape stories. Each of the chapters that follow is an experiment in a different way of reading and telling biblical rape stories. One model that I introduce in chapter 1 and engage throughout the book is a framework for describing sexual violence as *fuzzy, messy,* and *icky*—fuzzy in that it's not always what clear what happened or how it was remembered, messy in its consequences, as well as in the ways that sex and bodies are often messy, and icky in the ways that sexual violence fails to fit into neat patterns of evil perpetrators and innocent victims. To describe rape and sexual violence as fuzzy, messy, and icky goes against many of our closely held beliefs about sexual violence (in general) and feminist biblical interpretation (in particular). These terms introduce ambiguity and ambivalence where moral clarity has been sought and found. And they put pressure on the idea of feminist criticism as a sort of sympathetic witnessing (sometimes explicit, especially in feminist theological responses; sometimes cryptic or submerged, as in other modes of feminist scholarship).

In 1984, Phyllis Trible introduced the phrase "texts of terror" as a way of describing especially violent and terrible stories involving biblical women.[3] The phrase has become a standard shorthand for stories of extreme sexual or misogynistic violence. (It is also used to refer to homophobic or transphobic texts, though not by Trible herself.)[4] But while "texts of terror" furnishes Trible with her title, and is overwhelmingly cited as a phrase, it is only a partial representation of the critical paradigm she describes. *Texts of Terror* opens by outlining three tasks for feminist criticism:

> One approach documents the case against women. It cites and evaluates long-neglected data that show the inferiority, subordination, and abuse of the female in ancient Israel and the early church. By contrast, a second approach discerns within the Bible critiques of patriarchy. It upholds forgotten texts and reinterprets familiar ones to shape a remnant theology that challenges the sexism of scripture. Yet a third approach incorporates the other two. It recounts tales of terror *in memoriam* to offer sympathetic readings of abused women.[5]

The category of "texts of terror" (or as here, "tales of terror") is not a static judgment. It is, instead, a concept that is mobilized through practice: by "recount[ing] tales of terror *in memoriam*"—or in another phrase, which I will return to in detail in chapter 6, by "telling sad stories." Trible's *Texts of Terror* is organized around four examples: the rape of Tamar, the rape and expulsion of Hagar, the gang rape and murder of the Levite's concubine, and the sacrifice/murder of Jephthah's daughter. These stories appear here, as do others. But more than terror, I am interested in the question of the *after*. What comes after sexual violence? What happens to us *after* we read "texts of terror," or *Texts of Terror*? What kind of *afters* are possible? The readings offered here explore these questions. In calling my book *Texts after Terror*, I seek to name my debt to Trible, and to feminist biblical criticism more broadly, while also marking a move beyond it.

One way in which this move occurs is a proliferation of rape stories and reading strategies. I seek to expand the conversation around "what we talk about when we talk about rape," to borrow from Sohaila Abdulali. This includes both the question of which stories count as "rape stories" and how we as readers, especially feminist readers, encounter these stories. I am

interested in what we bring to the scene of reading, as well as what we neglect: or in Abdulali's phrasing, "the questions and assumptions we all carry
around with us," which summon us not just to "talk about rape," but also
to "talk about how we talk about rape."[6] In addition to finding more ways
of talking about biblical rape stories, I will also argue for the importance
of what I will call "unhappy reading"—that is, reading strategies and tactics that do not insist that every act of reading comes to a "happy ending."
A "happy ending," in the case of a rape story, can mean a way of reading that
finds something positive or redemptive even in the ruins of tragedy—for example, arguing that the voices of rape victims speak across texts and time
to demand justice (an argument often made about the raped and murdered
woman in Judges 19, as I will explore in detail in chapter 6). Or it can mean
retelling the story in a way that "saves" its rape victim, whether by imagining
her as a willing partner (as in some retellings of Dinah, explored in chapter 2,
or Bathsheba, discussed in chapter 3) or by describing her as resisting and
even fighting back (an argument that occurs in relation to Daughter Zion,
see chapter 5, and Jephthah's daughter, see chapter 6). A "happy ending" can
even mean the catharsis of a sad story well told—we read the story, we feel
sadness, and we rest contented in that judgment. Against these approaches,
I will argue for "unhappy reading," which holds space for ambiguity, ambivalence, and non-resolution. I will suggest that not every biblical rape story
can be read in a way that brings happy resolution—nor should it be. Our
unhappiness as readers is the point, as much as the rape story itself. Holding
space for unhappiness and unhappy reading, rather than shying away from
it, opens new feminist possibilities in the texts, and in our encounters with
sexual violence more broadly.

Chapter 1, "Fuzzy, Messy, Icky," lays the groundwork for what follows. As
I have already mentioned, one central thread throughout *Texts after Terror*
consists of the fuzzy, the messy, and the icky. The first chapter explains these
terms and their relevance for describing sexual violence in both biblical and
contemporary contexts (here I also sketch the connections between the ancient and the contemporary, which are an ongoing concern of this book). I in-
terweave this analysis with a brief sampling of biblical rape stories, drawing
out their fuzziness, messiness, and ickiness. The other focus of the chapter
is delineating some useful hermeneutic principles for reading rape stories.
Drawing on feminist and queer theory as well as literature, I argue for four
strategies for interpretation: refusing innocence, rejecting paranoid reading,

attending to sticky affect, and reading biblical texts with and through literature as a way of shaking open new meanings.

Chapter 2, "The Edges of Consent," continues the line of inquiry begun in chapter 1, with a focus on how we use consent to narrate biblical rape stories. Consent is often assumed to be the best way of adjudicating whether or not sex is rape, in both biblical texts and modern contexts. However, as this chapter argues, this approach is both insufficient and insufficiently feminist. Three rape stories are central here: Dinah (Gen 34), Tamar (2 Sam 13), and Lot's daughters (Gen 19). That Dinah and Tamar are raped is widely accepted by biblical scholars and readers alike;[7] the story of Lot's daughters, who have sex with their father while he is intoxicated, clearly contains sexual transgression, though *who abuses whom* is a trickier question to answer. But even in these seemingly clear rape stories, things are fuzzy, messy, and icky. The question of *what happened* is a fuzzy one in the story of Dinah, which has persuasively been read as both a rape story and a love story. Things become messy in the Tamar story, as Tamar wishes—or strategically proposes—to marry her rapist and then is excluded from her own narrative. Whatever else the story of Lot and his daughters is, it is certainly icky. My reading explores these ambiguities and complications, while also critiquing the notion of consent more broadly.

In chapter 3, "Narrating Harm in the Bathsheba Story," I take up the question of how we frame *harm* in accounts of sexual violence, using Bathsheba and David (2 Sam 11–12; 1 Kgs 1–2) as a case study. While I follow mainstream feminist criticism in reading 2 Samuel 11 as a narrative of sexual violence and exploitation, I also put pressure on the question of whether Bathsheba is best described as a victim and David as a sexual predator. This model of predation is suggested both by the biblical text (via Nathan's parable, in 2 Sam 12) and by many feminist readers. However, I argue that "predation" (or any model organized around immutable, perverted, and recidivistic "predators" and innocent "victims") is both insufficient and ill suited for describing the forms of sexual and nonsexual harm in this text, and in other biblical rape stories. In place of predation, I employ the category of peremption (the unlimited foreclosing of possibility) to describe the harm of the Bathsheba story, adopting this term from Joseph J. Fischel and his analysis in *Sex and Harm in the Age of Consent*.[8] In reading the Bathsheba story, replacing a model of sexual predation with one of peremption lets us explore female embodiment and subjectivity, as well as the forms of harm Bathsheba experiences, without collapsing these into an essentializing and flattening narrative of victimization.

The intertwined story of Hagar and Sarah (Gen 16, 21) is increasingly recognized as an account of sexual exploitation or outright rape, with Sarah facilitating sexual violence against Hagar. In chapter 4, "Rape and Other Ways of Reading," I use Hagar and Sarah to argue that a feminist theory of biblical sexual violence must take seriously how sexual violence is facilitated, encouraged, or taken advantage of between bodies and subjects, including between women. I focus on two issues: the tensions between how rape stories "ought" to be told versus how they actually unfold, and the question of how relationships between women figure into narratives of heterosexual rape or sexual violence. My discussion here draws both on feminist writings about rape and on recent literary fiction that describes the intersections of sexual violence and female friendship. The literary works I consider index a very different relationship between gender, power, and sexual violence, one in which rape is simultaneously present and secondary. Equally importantly, they press us as readers to take seriously complicated relationships between women without insisting that those relationships are ultimately secondary to the trauma of rape. I will argue that by carving out a space to think about female relationships, over and against defaulting to heterosexual sexual violence as the defining narrative, emotional, or affective event, these novels undertake an important kind of feminist work, which we would do well to consider in relation to Hagar and Sarah, and to the Hebrew Bible as well.

Chapter 5, "A Grittier Daughter Zion," turns to survivors and aftermath. Most biblical rape stories do not tell us much about their survivors. A notable exception is the book of Lamentations, in which Daughter Zion speaks, describing both her sexual violation and her trauma in the aftermath. Though anguished, her speech is also remarkable for giving voice to a victim, as well as allowing her to offer her own perspective on what has transpired. I will turn to Daughter Zion for another, though related, reason: to read her words as a biblical narrative of response to sexual violence, as voiced by a survivor. As such, they are a valuable literary and political resource for theorizing sexual violence without silencing survivors or reiterating tired clichés of how a rape story "ought" to be told. In this chapter, I place Lamentations together with contemporary memoirs and essays about sexual violence to suggest a new way of framing Daughter Zion's words. Daughter Zion can "talk back"— not simply to speak of her own victimization and extreme suffering but also to refuse ostensibly sympathetic narratives that repeat or reinstate trauma.

In chapter 6, "Sad Stories and Unhappy Reading," the argument for un-happy reading, which I sketched briefly earlier in this introduction, unfolds in full. I turn again to Trible and the paradigm for feminist criticism that she outlines in *Texts of Terror*, which still casts a long shadow today. For Trible, one task of feminist criticism—perhaps its most important—is to "tell sad stories" and to offer up interpretations *in memoriam* of female victims of vi-olence and patriarchy.[9] I will argue that while telling sad stories is one part of feminist interpretation, it is not enough: Further, it flattens difficult texts and limits the range of "appropriate" interpretive responses to sadness and grief. By way of example, I consider the story of the rape, murder, and dismember-ment of the Levite's concubine, described in Judges 19. This story, among the most terrible in the Hebrew Bible, has attracted a density of feminist readings, which seek to tell and retell the sad story of the concubine and her death at the hands of one or more terrible men. But while these tellings emphasize the story's sadness, they do so at the expense of its troubling ambiguity. They also treat the death of the woman following her rape as inevitable, an interpretive and ethical error that reinscribes the old rape myth of *rape = death*. After tracing these and other difficulties with "telling sad stories," I will offer as an alternative "unhappy reading," a more flexible interpretive practice that takes seriously the unhappiness of rape stories—as plots, as narratives, as femi-nist problems—without seeking either to "fix" them or to transfigure them into tragic catharsis. Chapter 6 weaves together the threads of the preceding chapters while also offering a new way of approaching the Levite's concubine.

Finally, the book ends with a brief conclusion reflecting on the question of *after*—and what it means to read rape texts *after terror*. *After* is not the same as *instead of*. After trauma, after pain, after terror, we are still touched by it, even after it seems to end. This *after* is filled with feelings—sometimes formal ones, more often fuzziness, messiness, and ickiness. This *after* is at once painful, impossible, and necessary, a space of stillness and possibility. This is the space this book explores.

1

Fuzzy, Messy, Icky

How to Read a Rape Story

In 1985, Margaret Atwood published *The Handmaid's Tale*. The novel is set in a dystopian future in which the United States has been replaced by a Christian theocracy called "Gilead." Infertility is rampant, the birth rate has plummeted, and women of childbearing age are forced to become "handmaids" to powerful men and bear children for them. The novel is narrated by one such handmaid, Offred; it interweaves her everyday life in Gilead with memories of the time before.

Atwood is famous for insisting that her work is speculative fiction and not fantasy or science fiction; nothing happens in *The Handmaid's Tale* that has not happened, or is in the realm of near-immediate possibility. Gilead blends elements of the Religious Right, Iranian theocracy, and the Puritans (Atwood began the novel while living in Massachusetts; she has claimed to be descended from Mary Webster, a woman hanged for witchcraft who nevertheless survived her hanging.)[1] The specific model for the reproductive politics of Gilead is biblical: The "handmaids" are a reference to Bilhah and Zilpah, the slaves who bore children to Jacob and his wives Rachel and Leah when the wives were unable to conceive. Offred and the other handmaids are trained at the "Rachel and Leah Center"; prior to the so-called Ceremony, the account from Genesis is read aloud. The Ceremony itself involves the man of the house having sex with the handmaid while she lies between the wife's legs—a literalizing enactment of the biblical text.

Atwood's novel remains a highly influential text. Protesters for reproductive rights regularly don handmaid outfits (often modeled on the popular television series). References to "handmaids" or "Gilead" offer an easy shorthand for describing the curtailment of women's sexual autonomy, the misogynistic desire to control and punish women, and the manifold ways that women's bodies are trafficked and exchanged. It is widely accepted that *The Handmaid's Tale* is a story about rape, as well as rape culture. With the rise of the novel (and now television show) in popularity and visibility, I no

Texts after Terror. Rhiannon Graybill, Oxford University Press. © Oxford University Press 2021.
DOI: 10.1093/oso/9780190082314.003.0002

longer need to suggest to my students that there is something misogynistic and sinister about the harmless-sounding institution of "handmaids" found in Genesis. Instead, the connections are clear: To be a handmaid, whether in the Bible or in Atwood's novel, is to be raped. And so I was surprised, upon rereading the novel, to discover that this is not in fact how Offred describes her own experience of the Ceremony:

> My red skirt is hitched up to my waist, though no higher. Below it the Commander is fucking. What he is fucking is the lower part of my body. I do not say making love, because this is not what he's doing. Copulating too would be inaccurate, because it would imply two people and only one is involved. Nor does rape cover it: nothing is going on here that I haven't signed up for. There wasn't a lot of choice but there was some, and this is what I chose.[2]

Offred claims she is not raped: This is a disturbing moment, one that unsettles the novel's seemingly clear feminist politics.[3] In fact, she explicitly rejects the term "rape," offering instead a taxonomy of forms of (limited) consent. But at the same time, her explanation seems to contradict what is clear in the novel: that Offred, and the other handmaids, are repeated victims of rape. Could Offred be *wrong*?

It is tempting to suggest that Offred is indeed wrong. Perhaps her mind is muddled by trauma. Perhaps she is experiencing cognitive dissonance. Perhaps she is dissociating. Perhaps this is simply false consciousness, of a particularly pernicious misogynistic variety. And to be sure, the Ceremony is deeply disturbing. It represents a social ritual organized around the sexual exploitation of an enslaved woman by a powerful man. The man who carries out the act—in Offred's case, Commander Waterford—is supported by larger patriarchal structures and a social system predicated on misogyny and the sexual use of women's bodies; other women, with more social power than the handmaids, are complicit in this structure or actively support it (as in the case of the "Aunts" in Gilead).

But at the same time, I am troubled by a reading that dismisses Offred's own analysis, or that suggests, more generally, that women are not able to judge or understand their own experiences. This is perilously close to the old patriarchal and colonialist desire to "save women," or to the old misogynistic line that women are not qualified to speak for or about themselves. Yet I am also unsettled by an intellectual position that allows for rape to be something women "choose," even as I know that many women—many *people*—face precisely such constrained choices. Or in Offred's own words: "There wasn't a lot of choice but there was some, and this is what I chose."

Offred's emphasis on choice, even or especially choice under constraint, challenges our attempts to draw clear distinctions between sex and rape. Atwood, too, insists upon ambiguity and complexity, even against the desires of her readers. *The Handmaid's Tale*'s reflections on constrained and coercive choice offer another way of describing what I term the fuzzy, messy, and icky features of sexual violence. Throughout this book, I will argue that official or technical terms used to discuss sexual violence and rape do not fully capture *what happened* or *how it felt*. Instead of repeating this existing language, I am interested in finding other ways of describing sexual violence that speak to what exceeds or is missed by the formal definitions: the things better captured by flexible and everyday words such as fuzzy, messy, and icky. I will use these terms in a number of ways, associating each with several different ideas and experiences, all of which, however, touch upon sexual violence. The official terms used to discuss sexual violence, although important and perhaps even necessary, do not fully capture either all the nuances or the contours of feeling and felt experience.[4] The alternative frameworks of fuzzy, messy, and icky have the added benefit of speaking to both the biblical texts and contemporary sexual violence. The Hebrew Bible, like the contemporary moment, is dense with misogyny, sexual violence, and rape culture. Furthermore, a close analysis of one can help us to understand and work to deconstruct the other. This goes both ways: The Bible helps us understand contemporary rape culture; contemporary rape culture helps us read and understand rape in the Bible.[5]

One starting point of this book is that the Hebrew Bible, like Offred's Gilead, presents a textual world filled with sexual violence and misogyny. You do not need to look very far or very hard in the pages of the Bible to find suggestions that women are impure, women are dangerous, or women's bodies are leaky and contaminating. Women hold less value than men; a male child is preferable, from birth onward. Women are to be controlled and exchanged by men. And frequently, women are subjected to sexual or sexualized violence. But while these features of the texts are widely recognized, feminist responses to sexual violence do not pay sufficient attention to the fuzzy, the messy, and the icky as they figure in biblical texts. Because these features (which are another way of naming the ambiguity, complexity, discomfort, and disgust of biblical sexual violence) are neglected and undertheorized, the hermeneutic tools we use to read biblical "texts of terror"—that is, texts that display rape, sexualized violence, or extreme misogyny—are correspondingly insufficient. In response, this book offers a feminist theorization of biblical sexual violence that starts from the fuzzy, the messy, and the icky and that adopts interpretive tactics and strategies from feminist and queer theory more broadly. This framework, in turn, makes possible new feminist readings of biblical "texts of terror."

The remainder of this chapter outlines the key ideas, principles, and interpretive strategies that ground the biblical readings that are the heart of *Texts after Terror*. I will begin with the concepts of fuzzy, messy, and icky, setting forth the key features of each while also demonstrating their appropriateness for reading ancient and modern stories of sexual violence. I then turn to a closer examination of rape, rape culture, and sexual violence in the Hebrew Bible, offering a broad overview while also zeroing in on these terms and the way I use them throughout the book. The second half of the chapter turns to the question of how to read a rape story. I offer four key interpretive tactics: (1) refusing innocence, (2) resisting paranoia, (3) attending to sticky affect, and (4) reading through literature. Drawn from feminist and queer theory, these tactics offer new ways of reading texts of terror—or ways of reading texts of terror *after terror*. While the chapters that follow offer extended applications of the tactics, I will conclude this chapter with a brief demonstration of how they help us read a biblical rape story in the form of a poem from the book of Nahum.

Fuzzy, Messy, Icky

Fuzzy, messy, icky. These terms are both descriptive and evocative: They suggest more than they name. All three have a tactile or haptic dimension, sometimes pleasant in the case of fuzzy, less so messy and icky. They are associated with the soft contours of moss, the viscosity of slime mold, the mysterious growth on the refrigerator, the thing we touched and wish we hadn't. This aspect of fuzzy, messy, and icky forces us to remember the body; it also suggests the risk of contamination that these terms, like all language about sexual violence, carries.

Fuzzy, messy, and icky are nontechnical terms; they are familiar from everyday speech. This is intentional: I am interested in the ways that sexual violence, including rape, is talked about and experienced in ordinary life. Here my thinking is aligned with Ann Cvetkovich, who argues for the usefulness of the everyday term "feeling" in doing the work of affect theory.[6] Like Cvetkovich, I find that everyday language, with its imprecisions and casual disregard for fixed definitions, helps to capture something slippery about experience. I am also interested in capturing the ambiguity, ambivalence, and difficulty that sexual violence creates. As such, fuzzy, messy, and icky are not rigid or prescriptive categories; each one represents, instead, a loose collection of related meanings and details. That these terms are informal does not mean that my choice to use them is apolitical or non-ideological; on the contrary, there are good feminist reasons to use ordinary language—both because it speaks to what has been elided from official definitions and because women and other minoritized groups have been excluded from defining terms or from giving voice to their own experiences. I will even go so far as to suggest that the vernacular status of fuzzy, messy, and icky sharpens their feminist edge.

What, then, do fuzzy, messy, and icky have to do with sexual violence? Here is a rough sketch of the terrain covered by each term.

Fuzzy

There are many situations in which it is clear, even straightforward, whether a sexual encounter constitutes sexual violence. Some sex is clearly violent or exploitative; some sex is clearly (even "enthusiastically," to use a term that has gained currency in anti-violence circles) consensual. But as Offred suggests, not all sexual encounters are so easily judged as either "rape" or "non-rape." Sometimes, situations arise that are fuzzy.

One form of fuzziness involves the question *What happened?* It is not always so easy to answer this question. Sometimes, we do not remember what happened, or in what sequence. Chanel Miller, who was sexually assaulted by Stanford swimmer Brock Turner behind a dumpster, describes having no memory of the events of her assault. What happened to Miller was clearly rape, and yet her inability to remember the details was repeatedly and damagingly held against her, as she describes in her memoir:

> I was not only told that I was assaulted, I was told that because I couldn't remember, I technically could not prove it was unwanted. And that distorted me, damaged me, almost broke me. It is the saddest type of confusion to be told I was assaulted and nearly raped, blatantly out in the open, but we don't know if it counts as assault yet.[7]

Miller is hardly alone in this experience: Fuzziness, beginning with the fuzziness (or fuzzy absence) of memory, is frequently experienced by, and used against, victims and survivors.

Alternately, the question *What happened?* may be a way of asking *How should I categorize this experience?* or even *Was this rape?* In *Just Sex?: The Cultural Scaffolding of Rape*, psychologist Nicola Gavey gathers a number of examples of what she calls "consenting to (avoid) rape."[8] A woman she interviews tells Gavey about having unwanted sex because "If I tried it, if I'd resisted, then he might rape me, you know."[9] Another interview subject describes a sexual encounter that she did not want, which left bite marks and bruises for several weeks and which she found terrifying. Nevertheless, the woman resisted classifying her experience as rape, "because I more or less consented" by not fighting back: "I just let him get on with it."[10] Gavey herself observes,

> Many women have talked to me about experiences that they didn't call rape, but which I find difficult to see as just sex. They include stories of situations in which a man applied pressure that fell short of actual or threatened physical force, but which the woman felt unable to resist, as well as encounters where a man was rough and brutish, and the woman described letting sex happen because she felt unable to stop it. They also include stories of situations where a male partner was not directly coercive at all, but where the woman nevertheless found herself going along with sex that was neither desired nor enjoyed because she did not feel it was her right to stop it or because she did not know how to refuse. All of these accounts in different ways point to a complex gray area between what we might think of as mutually consenting sex, on the one hand, and rape or sexual coercion on the other.[11]

A "complex gray area"—or what we might call something fuzzy. Many of Gavey's interview subjects reflect this dilemma. In spite of efforts to draw clear lines between sex and rape, a certain blurriness or ambiguity often remains; this manifests as a disjoint between experience and the language that purports to name it. Studies of sexual experiences frequently uncover significant numbers of "unacknowledged rape victims"—that is, study participants who say they have experienced a sexual act typically understood as rape (for example, nonconsensual sexual intercourse involving force) but, when asked directly, affirm that they have never been raped.[12] Similarly, many victims and survivors report not fully understanding or processing what has happened until retelling it to a friend. Sometimes, we need help finding ways to fit unnamed and unnameable experiences into named categories.

The fuzziness of *What happened?* (in both senses; that is, of actions and of the categories to which they belong) is often compounded by the fuzziness associated with alcohol. This is a difficult topic to raise; activists against sexual violence have fought—rightly—to insist that intoxication is never an excuse for sexual violence. In fact, in the United States, it is not just activists but also government policy that regulates and in some cases prohibits talking about alcohol in relation to sexual assault.[13] Formally or informally, many colleges and universities have similar policies.[14] And yet, as Sarah Hepola writes, "You don't have to look around the Internet long to find women wondering if the sex they had in a blackout was rape."[15] The "blackout" and the "brownout," when drinkers are able to carry on conversations and act relatively normally, but fail to remember anything that has happened, are especially vexing to the question of consensual sex or rape. In the Hebrew Bible, such fuzziness about rape and alcohol is present in the stories of Noah and Ham (Gen 9) and Lot and his daughters (Gen 19).[16] Other passages speak to the stupefying, memory-shattering effects of drink (e.g. Isa 28:7, Hos 4:11).

Another form of fuzziness is caused by trauma. It is now widely recognized that traumatic events can have significant effects on memory. Trauma can sharpen memory, as in Christine Blasey Ford's testimony of her sexual assault by Brett Kavanaugh: "Indelible in the hippocampus is the laughter."[17] But trauma can also interfere with memory, or it may be too painful to re-access or relive experiences of suffering. Or trauma may shatter language, making it difficult to describe what has happened, even if the memory is itself clear.

A final form of fuzziness also involves memory, though not as it relates to individuals. As feminist analyses of structural responses to sexual violence have tirelessly worked to reveal, institutional responses—and institutional policies—are often fuzzy. Institutions champion their efforts at preventing sexual violence, yet when asked about violence that has already occurred the response is often murky. Details are kept confidential; public narratives are vague. Websites are quietly scrubbed. There is, in particular, a vagueness that often attends reporting and official documentation.[18] *Fuzzy*, yet again. Here, Queen Vashti, disappeared from kingdom and from narrative alike after she refuses to show her naked body to King Ahasuerus and his friends (Esth 1:10–22), is one biblical example of such official fuzziness and forgetting.

Messy

Sexual violence is not just fuzzy; it is also messy. This description speaks to the aftermath of sexual violence and the ways that it defies a tidy resolution. Often "things get messy"—a grammatical construction without an actor that neatly reveals how the situation grows beyond a single person, or even a single story.[19] Messy is a consequence of fuzzy, as attempts to clarify fuzziness often collapse into messiness. It is the job of institutional Title IX offices, social workers, counselors, and sassy best friends to either clean up this messiness or shove it under the proverbial rug.[20] (And these actors often work often at cross-purposes to each other: messy, once more.) As I will explore in chapters 2 and 3, the rape stories of Tamar and Bathsheba unfold into larger messy narratives, defying either resolution or catharsis.

Messy can also narrate the complications that ensue when the stories of victims or survivors fail to fit into a tidy, preordained narrative of suffering and recovery.[21] In fact, the term "survivor" represents one attempt to control the narrative around the person who has experienced sexual violence. While "victim" implies passivity and victimization, "survivor" suggests strength, resilience, recovery. "Survivor" points beyond the moment of violence. A victim has things done *to* her; she is powerless, while a survivor is powerful and in control.[22] But both the term "survivor" and its implied politics have also been challenged. While it is intended to empower, it can have the opposite effect. A survivor is understood to be self-sufficient; unlike a victim, she does not need the help of others. If you are the victim of a crime, you may seek help from the police. But a crime survivor? We do not have such a category.[23] In any case: The terminology is messy. In this book, I will use both "victim" and "survivor," as well as such hybrid (or perhaps messy) formulations as victim/survivor, the disruptive slash indicating the disruption to the stability of either category. I am also interested in the tension between "victim" and "survivor" because it speaks to a larger dynamic of the messiness of categories, a theme I explore further in chapters 3 and 5.

Messy can also describe a certain kind of person, nearly always a woman. A woman who is "too much" is messy—in her appearance, her emotions, or both. "Hot mess" is an insult lobbed at women who are too disorganized, crisis-prone, or out of control. With reference to this cluster of meanings, the *messy* of sexual violence and rape also speaks to assumptions about gendered bodies, gender performances, and gender transgression. In the book of Proverbs, the "Strange Woman" exemplifies such a messy woman (especially in contrast to Lady Wisdom and the good wife of Prov 31).

Messy also speaks to the female body. In the Hebrew Bible as in many later cultural moments, including our own, the female body—particularly the leaky, fluid, open female body—is perceived as disgusting, contaminating, or both. Menstruation is particularly a threat on these grounds. It is because of this perceived messiness that the menstruating woman's body is impure in biblical law, and her menstrual flow and vaginal discharges are subjected to such scrutiny—just as contemporary ads for menstrual products are almost obsessive in their imagery of purity and cleanliness. This anxiety over the messy female body is part of the larger structure of purity culture that upholds rape culture and sustains sexual violence.[24]

Icky

Finally, all of this fuzziness and messiness creates something icky. *Icky* is a near-synonym to *creepy*, a common descriptor applied to people and situations when we don't want to rise to the level of official language. At the same time, ickiness suggests what is shameful, disgusting, or "gross"; bodily fluids and sexual shame are often described as icky.[25] *Icky* is the domain of "creeps," "sketchiness," and "weird things" that happen at parties,[26] whether or not these are clearly identified as rape. *Icky* names bad sex, uncomfortable sex, regrettable sex, and sexual encounters like the one described in Kristen Roupenian's short story "Cat Person," which became an internet flashpoint for discussing sex, consent, and #MeToo when it was published by *The New Yorker* in 2017.[27] The protagonist of "Cat Person" is Margot, a college student who works at a movie theater. She meets the older Robert when he buys a package of Red Vines from her; the two have a halfheartedly flirtatious relationship that ends with Margot having extremely unpleasant sex with Robert. When she stops replying to his text messages, he becomes irate. The final lines of the story are a series of his texts, culminating in a single word: "Whore."

The overwhelming sense in "Cat Person"—and in the other stories in Roupenian's debut collection, *You Know You Want This*—is ickiness (a point noted by many reviewers and readers). Robert teeters between pitiable and reprehensible; most frequently, he comes across as a bit creepy. He is a "nice guy," in the way the term is used by Men's Rights activists. On the way to his house to have sex, Margot wonders if, perhaps, Robert will murder her.

Margot both initiates the sexual encounter—she invites herself to Robert's house—and regrets it, even before it happens:

> But the thought of what it would take to stop what she had set in motion was overwhelming; it would require an amount of tact and gentleness that she felt was impossible to summon. It wasn't that she was scared he would try to force her to do something against her will but that insisting they stop now, after everything she'd done to push this forward, would make her seem spoiled and capricious, as if she'd ordered something at a restaurant and then, once the food arrived, had changed her mind and sent it back.[28]

The encounter improves, but only temporarily, as Margot imagines Robert desiring her; the mood is again broken when she laughs at his attempts to be sensitive. The sex itself is terrible. Afterward,

> she thought, brightly, *This is the worst life decision I have ever made!* And she marveled at herself for a while, at the mystery of this person who'd just done this bizarre, inexplicable thing.[29]

Since its publication, "Cat Person" has been hotly debated, especially what it tells us about sex, power, and consent, along with misogyny. I suggest, as well, that it tells us about ickiness. The sexual encounter Roupenian describes is above all icky. It puts pressure on a neat distinction between consent and nonconsent. It raises unpleasant questions about power. And it documents the complication of feelings and outcomes that do not follow a predetermined script (in this case, either the "innocent college student victimized by older predator" narrative or, alternatively, "the temptress who ensnares a decent man").

The specific sexual scenario that "Cat Person" imagines is clearly contemporary; many critics have pointed out that the story's almost immediate viral success reflects the accuracy with which it reflects late 2010s norms of dating and technology, conversations about sex, rape, and power, and so on.[30] But the ickiness of the story has its own echoes in biblical texts, from Lot and his daughters (Gen 19) to the forced exposure and shaming of Jerusalem before her lovers (Ezek 16) to the repeated rape of slaves and concubines as a way of negotiating power between men (Gen 35:22; 2 Sam 3:7, 16:21). *Texts after Terror* explores these resonances.

Rape, Rape Culture, and Sexual Violence
in the Hebrew Bible

From fuzzy, messy, and icky, I want to turn briefly to some other key words and phrases I use throughout *Texts after Terror*, offering a brief explanation and/or elaboration. In order to encompass the breadth, diversity, and ambiguity of sexual violence, especially in its fuzzy, messy, and icky iterations, I will use both the specific term "rape" and the more general term "sexual violence." Using these two terms together underscores that rape is related to a range of other acts of violence and violation; as a concept, "sexual violence" implies not just "rape" but "rape culture." It also signals this book's allyship with activists against sexual violence, who also often use this language.

"Rape culture" is a term drawn from feminist scholarship and activism around sexual violence. It describes the social, cultural, and ideological structures that sustain and nourish sexual violence. The concept of "rape culture" insists that rape is not an act of incomprehensible violence that suddenly ruptures the social fabric, but rather an extreme expression of what is culturally acceptable, salient, even ordinary: It stands on a continuum with other acts of "everyday rape culture." Rape culture is a structure and an ideology that pervades and organizes daily life.[31]

According to Harold Washington, "The prevalence of rape in biblical narrative suggest that ancient Israel might well be designated a rape culture."[32] And indeed, the Hebrew Bible contains many rape stories, and many rapes.[33] Overwhelmingly, these are stories of the rapes of women: Dinah (Gen 34), Tamar (2 Sam 13), enslaved women such as Hagar, Bilhah, and Zilpah (Gen 16, 29–30), women captured in warfare (Zech 14:2), women traveling or forced by others to travel (Judg 19), groups of women celebrating festivals (Judg 21), even women who exist only in the realm of metaphor, such as Daughter Zion (e.g., Lam 1:8–10). In addition to actual rape, the texts contain significant sexualized violence, including the murder of Cozbi (stabbed to death through her womb, Num 25:7–8) and the violence of the Sotah ritual punishing adultery (Num 5:11–31).[34] There are also many accounts of sexual punishment and humiliation, as in the texts of the prophetic marriage metaphor, including the treatment of the feminized Israel in Hosea 2 and Jerusalem, Oholah, and Oholibah in Ezekiel 16 and 23.

The legal texts of the Hebrew Bible also reflect rape culture. As Washington further observes, "Rape cultures are distinguished by a failure of their legal institutions to recognize rape as a crime of violence against women."[35] This is indeed the case with biblical law. As is often pointed out, biblical laws are concerned with the honor of male family members; the rape of a woman represents a harm to her father, brothers, or husband, not to the woman herself. She represents injury, but injury to a masculine economy of power, honor, and the "house of the father." As Deuteronomy 22:22–30 details, the rape of an unmarried woman can be resolved economically (that is, by paying a certain amount and marrying her), while the rape of a married woman is considered to be adultery and is punishable by death for both parties.[36] The marital status of the man does not matter. Rape, like adultery, is an offense of *taking*; it prescribes a proper grammar of *man = subject* and *woman = object*. It likewise emphasizes relations between men, who interact with each other through and against the bodies of women.

Here, I will pause for a moment to consider men and masculinity. While most biblical rape stories involve men inflicting sexual violence upon women, there are exceptions to this rule. Men are sometimes the victims of rape and other forms of sexual violence, as well as its perpetrators. The sexualized humiliation of male prisoners of war by other men is one clear example, attested both in the Hebrew Bible and in other ancient texts.[37] Male characters including Noah (Gen 9), Lot (Gen 19), and the divine messengers to Sodom are threatened with or actually experience sexual violence. Joseph (Gen 39) is subjected to a false rape accusation (at least if we believe him and not his accuser, Potiphar's nameless wife), itself a form of sexual harassment with dire consequences for Joseph. The story of the gang rape and murder of the Levite's concubine, found in Judges 19, is also the story of a rape threat against a man, the Levite himself. Notably, it is not what *actually* happens to the concubine but rather what is *threatened* against her husband that is represented by the text as the true outrage.[38] Other stories use rape threats or forms of sexual humiliation or exploitation as forms of masculine power and domination over other men.[39] And a small subset of the stories of the rape of men raise the possibility of female perpetrators.[40]

These stories are an important part of the larger biblical rape story corpus, but they are not my focus here. The large majority of stories of male rape are stories about the negotiation of masculinity and relations between men.[41] While this is an important topic in its own right, it is not the topic of this book. There is, moreover, a growing—and strong—literature on male rape that engages these issues.[42] More metacritically, as a feminist biblical scholar who began her career writing about masculinity, I have noticed more than once the ways in which masculinity and concern for the masculine often parasitize and displace *both* feminist methods *and* femininity and women as a topic of investigation. Therefore, I have chosen intentionally in this book to focus on a feminist analysis of the rape and sexual violence *against women* in the biblical text. This focus on the rape of women also allows for greater intellectual precision. Just as studies of male rape burrow into questions of masculinity, so too does centering rape stories about women invite us to interrogate female experience, female bodies, and female subjectivity in and beyond situations of sexual violence. This is doubly true when we move beyond an intellectual response that delicately names these stories "texts of terror," performs an observance of grief or horror, and then declares its work complete. In going further in reading rape stories involving women, I draw on the resources of feminist and queer theory. While the violence I describe is almost entirely heterosexual, the frameworks I bring to reading are not. There are both queer theorists and queer literary texts here; chapters 4 and 5, in particular, take up queer approaches to sexual violence. But while varied, the approaches I follow here do largely exclude what Gavey terms "a gender-neutral analysis of heterosexual coercion," an approach I find at best limited in its value.[43] Instead, I intentionally maintain a focus on sexual violence against women and women's bodies.

New Methods, New Tools

If we hope to understand biblical rape stories in a new way, we will need new approaches and new tools—new ways of accessing the fuzziness, messiness, and ickiness of biblical rape stories. This need for something new not really surprising: Audre Lorde famously wrote that "the master's tools will never dismantle the master's house."[44] In the case of biblical criticism, the "master's tools" remain, centrally, the techniques and strategies of the historical-critical method. They cannot provide the tools necessary to understand and dismantle narratives of sexual violence in the Bible. Therefore, we must look elsewhere.

Across *Texts after Terror*, I will sample widely from feminist theory and queer theory, with special attention to places where these two theoretical discourses cross over or entangle each other. Other strands of theory—affect theory, disability and crip theory, postcolonial theory—also appear, sometimes to support feminist and/or queer readings, at other times to challenge them. Throughout, I have also made significant use of literary writing about and around sexual violence, rape, and rape culture, including novels (especially in chapters 2 and 4), memoirs (chapter 5), and short stories (here and chapter 4), as well as film (chapter 3). I am less interested in allegiance to a single approach than in what tactics, insights, or moments we might borrow from texts and bring to the reading of biblical rape stories.

Refusing to Claim a Position of Innocence

The first interpretive tactic I will pursue across *Texts after Terror* is *refusing to claim a position of innocence*. There is no innocent starting point, interpretive or otherwise, from which we enter the fray. This is an idea that I adopt most directly from feminist theorist Donna Haraway, though it has many related iterations in feminist and queer theory.[45] As Haraway argues forcefully in a number of famous essays, including "Situated Knowledges" and "A Manifesto for Cyborgs," there is no master vantage point or innocent subject position from which the world can be judged.[46] Interpreters and situations are never innocent; we are always implicated in situations, texts, and spaces of interpretation. Knowledge of sexual violence, like all knowledge, is situated knowledge. We are neither omnipotent nor pure. Nor are we innocent: "Acquiring knowledge is never innocent," she writes in *When Species Meet*.[47] Elsewhere, I have argued that a hermeneutic of flourishing vis-à-vis the biblical text requires us to abandon claims to the position of innocence.[48] Now I want to suggest that this is essential in the case of interpreting texts about sexual violence.

Abandoning the posture of innocence takes multiple forms. It begins by rejecting reductive historicizing oversimplifications, such as the suggestion that if women are not legal subjects with the ability to consent, then "unwanted sex" is not rape. Dropping the posture of innocence means being wary of sloganeering applied to the past, even when such slogans speak a feminist truth to the present moment. In place of simplicity or certainty, a non-innocent reading practice pursues complexity—a process Haraway terms, elsewhere, "staying with the trouble."[49] "Staying with the trouble" entails reading these stories as stories of sexual violence, without erasing their ambiguities and complexities, without assuming that we know what Dinah or Tamar or Bathsheba wanted,[50] or that the dynamics of victim and victimizer are both clearly marked and unchanging (an assumption that the Lot story, for example, puts pressure on). Refusing innocence means holding open a space for ambivalence, ambiguity, and unknowing, even when we wish for clarity and closure.

Resisting Paranoid Reading

The hermeneutics of suspicion remain highly influential in feminist biblical studies. The second interpretive tactic, *resisting paranoid reading*, directly counters this approach. The notion of "paranoid reading" comes from queer theorist Eve Kosofsky Sedgwick, in an essay entitled "Paranoid Reading and Reparative Reading, or, You're So Paranoid, You Probably Think This Essay Is About You."[51] Drawing on a thick diagnostic description of paranoia, Sedgwick argues that the hermeneutics of suspicion, that cornerstone of so much feminist and queer work, shares the structure of the paranoid subject position. She traces out five key parallels:

Paranoia is *anticipatory.*
Paranoia is *reflexive* and *mimetic.*
Paranoia is *a strong theory.*
Paranoia is a theory of *negative affects.*
Paranoia places its faith in *exposure.*[52]

As with paranoia, so, too, with paranoid reading. As an "anticipatory" form, such readings are constantly "looking forward to and preparing for bad news."[53] (*Everyone knows the Bible is terrible for women; why would this text be any different?*) Paranoid readings offer strong theories. (*Everything in the Bible can be explained by misogyny.*) Paranoid readings are organized around negative affects—that is, they are invested in "forestalling pain," at the expense of "seeking of pleasure."[54] (*I won't let the Bible hurt me anymore.*) And paranoid reading practices believe that exposing X will somehow lead to its being changed. (*If only we realized the Bible was misogynistic, everything would be different!*)

Much feminist work on the Hebrew Bible has as its starting point a suspicious or paranoid reading position.[55] Sedgwick's reading, which is grounded in queer but also feminist commitments, invites us to open up texts, even texts of sexual violence, to other ways of thinking. She challenges the seeming monopoly that paranoid reading holds and calls for it to be joined by "reparative reading" open to contingency, pleasure, and play. Especially useful is her reminder that "to be other than paranoid" is not to deny injustice or oppression. Thus:

> For someone to have an unmystified view of systematic oppressions does not intrinsically or necessarily enjoin that person to any specific train of epistemological or narrative consequences. To be other than paranoid ... to practice other than paranoid forms of knowing does not, in itself, entail a denial of the reality or gravity of enmity or oppression.[56]

Sedgwick's comment is generative in reading texts about sexual or sexualized violence. In the case of sexual violence and the Hebrew Bible, we can do more than simply compile lists of rapes, or lists of scholars who do not sufficiently acknowledge, or properly respond to, these rapes or murders. A nonparanoid reading of sexual violence is a reading that is open to fuzziness. Paranoid readings, like paranoia, demand strong theories and eschew ambiguities of all sorts. A nonparanoid reading also leaves space to attend to the differences between, and within, various stories of sexual violence and rape in the text. It does not impose a single master theory; instead, it lets us encounter each rape narrative on its own terms. Without "entail[ing] a denial of the reality or gravity of enmity or oppression," a nonparanoid reading position also opens space for feminist reading, including feminist readings of rape stories, to do something other than view the text with suspicion or anger.

Tracing Sticky Affect

The reparative reading that Sedgwick calls for as an alternative to paranoia privileges the local, the specific, and the contingent over the grand "theory of everything"; it is also attentive to a variety of affects. Both of these features of reparative reading overlap with the third tactic of fuzzy, messy, and icky reading: paying attention to affect and following its sticky traces. Affect theory asks us to attend to sensations, to feelings, to emotions, to what lurks at the edges of our responses to texts and other things in the world. While affect theory takes many forms, my thinking in this project is especially informed by queer feminist theorist Sara Ahmed and her work on affect in *The Promise of Happiness*.[57]

Happiness is an affect; like other affects, it is "sticky." As such, it can be passed between objects or bodies. Sometimes, it attaches to objects (which include people, bodies, national groups, and stories) without their consent or even awareness. The stickiness of affect means that happiness or unhappiness can be transmitted *between* objects. Elsewhere, I have written about how institutional responses to sexual violence often inadvertently treat survivors as unhappy objects, because they serve as reminders that violence prevention campaigns have failed.[58] Survivors can also become unhappy objects when their stories fail to conform to certain preordained narrative trajectories. Just as the woman who "overreacted" to sexual violence was once scorned, in the present moment there is a criticism of survivors who fail to narrate their experiences properly (even as this demand is itself grounded in the imperative to "tell your story"). The invitation to share stories can also become a command and/or a compulsion.

Sticky affect offers a way of reading biblical rape stories that enters into the complexity of relationships, as well as the fraught dynamics of what comes *after*. The story of Tamar's rape (2 Sam 13), in particular, shows the way sticky affects reach far beyond the scene of rape itself. Sticky affect also offers a way of understanding how biblical rape stories touch us as readers, maintaining an uneasy hold even when we would rather move on or set them aside. The cross-contamination of rape stories to each other, and to other, non-rape stories, is one such effect of this stickiness: Thus, Tamar's rape recalls Dinah's; Bathsheba's victimization foreshadows other sexual violations in the David story; the sexual abuse and exploitation of female bodies recurs across the prophetic literature. All of these texts are sticky, even as they stick to each other.

Reading through Literature

The final interpretive tactic I will introduce is likely familiar; in beginning with *The Handmaid's Tale*, I have perhaps already tipped my hand. Simply put, I will argue throughout *Texts after Terror* that we gain new and vital perspectives on biblical rape stories when we read these texts with and through other literary works. I understand "literature" broadly: fiction and nonfiction, prose and poetry, traditional memoir and more experimental works. While I will occasionally consider works that retell or reimagine biblical rape stories, most of the texts I discuss in connection with the biblical texts have little or no connection to biblical characters or stories. What they do offer are alternative ways of narrating sexual violence, rape, consent, harm, desire, and ambivalence. These works, which range across genres, offer perspectives on sexual violence that are otherwise sidelined, especially within the relatively constrained space of feminist biblical studies. At times, the stories they tell are painful (as in Carmen Maria Machado's searing memoir of domestic abuse, *In the Dream House*, or Chanel Miller's *Know My Name*). At other times, they cause discomfort through their refusal to conform to our expectations and desires.[59] When these texts, and others like them, are brought in contact with biblical rape stories, something important happens. As Gayatri Chakravorty Spivak observes, "Texts open when you talk to groups of others."[60] So too do texts crack open when they are made to talk to other texts.

An Example: Nahum

As a foray into the new forms of reading I am proposing, I want to consider a passage from the book of Nahum. Nahum 3:4–7 is a "rape story" in miniature; it inventories a series of terrible fates promised to the personified city of Nineveh, including her rape. I have chosen this passage because of its ordinariness: It offers a typical example of the sort of representations of sexual violence found across the Hebrew prophetic texts. While it is poetry, it is also a "rape story," insofar as it offers a literary representation of sexual violence.[61] Nahum 3's rape story is brief but repellent:

> Because of the whorings of the whore, graceful and alluring, a mistress of
>   witchcraft,
>   who betrays nations in her whorings, and families with her witchcraft,
> Look, I am against you (an oracle of Yahweh of hosts),
>   I will lift up your skirt over your face,
>   I will show nations your nakedness, and kingdoms your shame,
> I will throw filth at you and disgrace you,
>   and make a spectacle of you.
> All who see you will run away from you and say,
>   "Nineveh is ruined, who will comfort her?"
>   Where will I seek comforters for her? (Nah 3:4–7)

The poem is not subtle. It is also not an especially skillful work of art; it reuses conventional images and even repeats terms without variation. The effect is one of intensity, not of artistic innovation. But the text is clearly a rape story: Sexual violence is everywhere in the passage. Furthermore, this point is widely recognized by commentators; it needs no additional teasing out here.[62] Instead: how else might we read this text from Nahum? And, more specifically, how might the tactics outlined earlier in the chapter contribute to this reading?

We begin by *refusing to claim a position of innocence*. One form of innocent reading insists that because Yahweh is a good and just God, his action must be justified, here as elsewhere in the biblical text: *Nineveh would not be punished without reason*. A second form of innocent reading focuses on Nineveh, insisting on her victimhood while carefully sanitizing her character. Refusing to claim the position of innocence means refusing both of these easy solutions, both of which allow us to fit the text into the framework we already bring to the practice of interpretation. In chapter 5, I will describe what Barbara Johnson calls the "already-read text"—the text we think we know even before we read it—as a persistent threat in interpreting rape stories. That is present here as well. Rejecting claims of innocence is linked closely to *resisting paranoid reading*. One key feature of paranoid reading is its faith in exposure: If we expose the violence in a text (or in the world), surely that will change everything. Indeed, we see a glimmer of this same paranoid logic in Nahum 3:5–6: By (literally) exposing the woman's genitals, Yahweh aims to (metaphorically) expose her shame and thus bring about her destruction. But just as we are suspicious of this act of exposure when it occurs in the text, so too should we be suspicious about the exposure of violence as an interpretive strategy. It is obvious that there is sexual violence in Nahum 3—and yet what would writing another article, or bit of a chapter, exposing this violence achieve?[63] Instead, I am more interested in what a nonparanoid reading might find, even in a text as seemingly one-dimensional and violent as Nahum 3:4–7.

Sedgwick urges us to look for the small and local readings that are "curled up" in larger paranoid metanarratives.[64] There is the possibility of a different story here, nestled uneasily in the larger frame of violence. One way of drawing out this story is to pay close attention to what the text describes, and to what degree our reading of the rape story is touched by sticky affect— more specifically, the sticky affects of other biblical rape stories. This passage in Nahum rubs up against, and draws some of its power from, other parts of the book, where rape is described explicitly (such as Nah 1:12, "though I have raped you, I will rape you no more"),[65] as well as other scenes of more general sexualized violence. And, of course, there is the larger context of the "marriage metaphor," the passages of violence and, occasionally, love between Yahweh and feminized nations and cities (chiefly Israel and Jerusalem but also Babylon, Nineveh, and Assyria). These texts form a sticky corpus; they touch and contaminate each other. It is often difficult to speak of one such text without the others creeping in. I cannot read Nahum 3 without being reminded of the similar scene of violent exposure and punishment in Ezekiel 16, for example, though that text describes not a foreign power but Jerusalem.

But what if we read differently? What if, instead of the other rape stories of the prophetic books, we followed the fourth tactic and *read with literature*? In particular, I propose reading this biblical rape poem through Roupenian's short story "Cat Person," which I have already referenced briefly earlier in the chapter. "Cat Person" is a masterwork of fuzzy, messy, and icky sex; it also speaks sharply to the power dynamics that circulate in and around many rape stories, including Nahum's. Consider the basic dynamics of the biblical text: A more powerful man (or male God) lashes out at a woman (or feminized city), excoriating her promiscuity and her betrayals while also expressing an entitlement to her sexuality. This man/male God is still attracted to the woman, even as he rages against her. More than anything, he wishes to humiliate her, and to humiliate her publicly. This dynamic is not Nahum's alone: It is found as well in such texts as Hosea 2 and Ezekiel 16 and 23. It is also found in "Cat Person," between the older Robert and the younger Margot.

I have already described the terrible sex of "Cat Person"; I want now to speak briefly of its aftermath. Margot breaks off her relationship with Robert, who responds with anger, grief, and harassment. She is disgusted; he becomes even more obsessive. In the story's final scene, Margot is out with her friends when she accidentally runs into Robert in a bar. Her friends quickly escort her out; Robert, however, has seen her and sends a series of text messages to her phone, ending with these:

> *I felt like we had a real connection did you not feel that way or . . .*
> *Maybe I was too old for u or maybe you liked someone else*
> *Is that guy you were with your boyfriend*
> *???*
>
> *Or is he just some guy you are fucking*
> *Sorry*

> *When u laguehd when I asked you if you were a virgin was it because*
> *youd fucked so many guys*
>> *Are you fucking that guy right now*
>> *Are you*
>> *Are you*
>> *Are you*
>> *Answer me*
>> *Whore.*[66]

Set aside for a moment their modern idiom, and Robert's words are not far
from Yahweh's. And Margot's response, like Nineveh's, is absent. No prophet
is required here; the glowing text bubbles now play that role. Many of the
same observations we might make from reading the biblical text are available
here as well: male entitlement to the female body, jealousy, excessive violence,
"whore" as a slur. "Cat Person" does not describe a rape, strictly speaking, but
it captures the larger economy of sexual violence and rape stories. Reading
Nahum 3 through "Cat Person" likewise does not take away the sexual violence of the biblical passage, the lifting of the skirts and the throwing of
disgusting things. But it does put pressure on the biblical text, changing the
ways we encounter it. It deflates the character of Yahweh: His fantasies of terrible violence and misogyny do not elevate him above banality. What would
it mean to take seriously Yahweh as a version of Robert, "a nice guy, sort of," "a
little dorky," "a little melodramatic," someone who "had really done nothing
wrong, except like her, and be bad in bed, and maybe lie about having cats"?[67]

This deflationary representation of the angry, sexually frustrated man
opens onto other ways of reading a text such as Nahum 3. Margot's experience with Robert is not so far from the rape-by-a-friend that lies at the heart
of Patricia Lockwood's poem "Rape Joke," or the sexual abuse within a relationship that Machado describes in *In the Dream House*, or the acquaintance
rapes that pop up in novels such as Sally Rooney's *Conversations with Friends*
and Lara Williams's *Supper Club*.[68] What unites these varied stories is not the
way they answer the question *But was it rape?* but rather their willingness
to explore how sexual violence, and sexual ickiness, might be represented.
Together and separately, these rape stories challenge the insinuation that
bearing witness to trauma, or comforting traumatized victims, is a sufficient
affective, political, or literary response to sexual violence and rape culture.
Even as "Cat Person" captures Robert's rage and entitlement, the focus on
Margot and her responses also subtly challenges the kind of overwrought

imagery we find in the Nahum poem—the alluring prostitute, the seductive sorcery, the flipped-up skirts and tossed filth. Instead, we have something more everyday: familiar, exhausting, prickly, irreducible to the category of tragedy. And also: fuzzy, messy, icky.

Not all biblical rape stories show the heightened rhetoric or gleeful misogyny of Nahum 3 (though some do, especially in the prophetic literature). Instead, we find a range of rape stories. Some are flatly told; some occur only in parenthetical comments (for example, the rape of Bilhah, Gen 35:22). Others are cloaked in drama, as at various points in Lamentations, where sexual violation is accompanied by corpses, looting, and cannibalism.[69] But the vast majority of these responses fail to draw out the fuzzy, the messy, and the icky—whether in a celebration of sexual violence, such as Nahum 3, or in a text that takes it for granted, such as the handmaid stories in Genesis 16 and 30. They also fail to consider the possibility that a story such as "Cat Person"—or a novel such as *Supper Club*, a film like *Doubt*, a memoir, or even a fairy tale—might illuminate biblical rape far better than hermeneutic models organized around witnessing, mourning, or repeating familiar platitudes, however feminist their origins or intentions.

In *The Handmaid's Tale*, women are forbidden to read; the Bible itself is kept locked away. Offred reflects, "It is an incendiary device: who knows what we'd make of it, if we ever got our hands on it?"[70] Our world is not Offred's; the Bible is widely available to read and reread, to question and to examine. But we have not done enough to take its rape stories into our own hands. These texts, more than almost any others, are treated with delicacy; they are carefully labeled "texts of terror" and made available only to a limited inventory of critical responses—historical inquiries into rape, lament over female suffering, postures of witnessing. Other ways of reading are still waiting to be explored; the stories remain to be taken into our hands. It is time for reading such "texts of terror" *after terror*.

2

The Edges of Consent

Dinah, Tamar, and Lot's Daughters

Does consent have "edges"? And what does it mean to invoke the "edges of consent"? An edge is not quite a margin; it evokes not a *between* so much as a border or limit. Edges also suggest brinks, drop-offs, uncertainties, borderlines. It is discomfiting to think of *consent* as a concept with *edges*—and yet also, I will suggest, essential.

This chapter expands upon the argument for biblical sexual violence as fuzzy, messy, and icky while also putting pressure on the notion of consent. Consent has become the primary framework for talking about sexual violence, rape, and rape culture. It has likewise become a rallying point in feminist activism against sexual violence, especially on college and university campuses. Consent discourses also dominate discussions of rape in the Hebrew Bible. As we have already seen, the text is filled with narratives of sexual violence and rape, and a common feminist response to these stories begins by foregrounding the issue of consent.

Consent is an attractive notion for many reasons. It offers a framework for sexual relations that is easy to understand and to enact. Consent discourses and consent education programs provide an accessible language for talking about sex and for framing and understanding experiences. Consent must be "freely given" and "given at every stage"; the best consent is "enthusiastic." According to a popular YouTube video, consent is much like a cup of tea[1]— freely offered, freely refused, and always off limits for unconscious people. More than anything, the great appeal of consent lies in its simplicity and clarity: *Consent is always a necessary precursor to sex; sex without consent is rape.*

Just as colleges, universities, and other social and public health bodies have turned to consent education as an easy solution to sexual violence, so too is it tempting to use the framework of consent to understand and respond to sexual violence in the Bible. To the question often lobbed at "texts of terror"—*But was it rape?*—the framework of consent offers an easy shortcut

Texts after Terror. Rhiannon Graybill, Oxford University Press. © Oxford University Press 2021.
DOI: 10.1093/oso/9780190082314.003.0003

to an answer: *Did she consent? Was it verbal? Enthusiastic? Noncoerced?* The problem with this response is equally easy to determine: It neglects what I have termed the fuzzy, messy, and icky features of sexual violence, in the Hebrew Bible as in the world beyond it.

My argument throughout the chapter reflects the larger argument of the book: Sexual violence in the Hebrew Bible is fuzzy, messy, and icky, and a feminist response to the Bible's "texts of terror" demands that we take this seriously. Instead of appealing to the framework of consent/nonconsent— already a troubled notion, but doubly so when we attempt to apply it to ancient texts[2]—we must formulate new hermeneutical tools and strategies. After demonstrating that a framework of consent is both *insufficient* and *insufficiently feminist* to read three key rape stories—the accounts of Dinah (Gen 34), Tamar (2 Sam 13), and Lot's daughters (Gen 19)—the final portion of the chapter explores the application of the alternative principles for a fuzzy, messy, icky hermeneutic set forth in the previous chapter: refusing innocence (following Donna Haraway), resisting paranoid reading (borrowed from Eve Kosofsky Sedgwick), tracing sticky affects (associated with Sara Ahmed), and reading through literature (exemplified here by Meredith Minister, in her reading of Octavia Butler). The critique of consent throughout the chapter brings together arguments *within* biblical studies (concerning the translation of specific terms, the question of personhood in ancient Israel, and so on) with more sweeping challenges to consent from *beyond* biblical studies, with specific reference to feminist and queer theory.

It is important to underscore here that I am not calling for the thoroughgoing rejection of consent. In fact, I am persuaded by Joseph J. Fischel's argument for affirmative consent as the "least-bad" standard for sexual assault law and campus policies alike.[3] At the same time, this chapter, and *Texts after Terror* more broadly, answers Fischel's summons to "screw consent"—that is, to put pressure on consent and its dominance over imagining sexual subjectivity and practice—as part of a feminist practice of sexual politics and sexual justice.[4] My goal, like Fischel's, is a more feminist, more egalitarian, and more just sexual politics and sexual culture. But getting there requires us to look critically at consent.

It has become common to describe consent as an idea as simple as a stoplight: Green ("yes!") means go, red ("no!") means stop, yellow means proceed with caution.[5] But sex is not a traffic pattern, and neither is rape. The fuzzy, the messy, and the icky haunt sexual violence in both the biblical text and the world; we ignore this at our peril. Thus, instead of relying on a theory of traffic signals, this chapter takes on the fuzzy, the messy, and the icky to com-plexify our readings of biblical rape and rape culture.

Rape and Consent in the Hebrew Bible

The pervasive sexual and sexualized violence of the biblical text is undeni-able. Still, a remarkable number of critics have resisted identifying rape in biblical stories, even in narratives such as the stories of Dinah or Tamar (David's daughter). One problem concerns terminology: As is often noted, there is no unambiguous term for rape in the Hebrew Bible.[6] Instead, the text presents a range of terms, including the verb 'innâ (to overpower or to rape) and the noun něbalâ (outrage, often with a sexual sense). However, each term also has a range of meanings that extend beyond sexual violence, at least as it is narrowly understood. Thus, while sexual violence clearly occurs, the very terms that are used to describe it in the Hebrew Bible are themselves both fuzzy and messy.

A second difficulty concerns a larger methodological question: Is it pos-sible to speak of rape in the case of persons who are not treated as subjects? Robert S. Kawashima, for example, addresses the problem of "Could a Woman Say 'No' in Biblical Israel?" by reconstructing ancient legal episte-mology.[7] Kawashima's answer to the question his title asks is no. He insists that it is illegitimate to use the word "rape" in reference to forced sexual acts in ancient Israel:

> If I am correct, this verb ['innâ] should never be translated as "rape," as it often is. Inasmuch as biblical legal thought recognized the basic person-hood of all people, neither women nor girls could ever be reduced to pure objects. But neither did it recognize them as full subjects, and so they could never constitute victims of a legally prosecutable crime.[8]

Because women in the Bible are not agents capable of consent, what happens to them cannot properly be called rape.

From a legal-historical perspective, Kawashima may well be right. It is clear from the biblical text that women and girls are not considered fully empowered subjects; they cannot always—perhaps cannot ever—"consent" in a modern sense. However, I am unwilling to follow Kawashima in his ar-gument that the absence of possibility of consent implies the absence (or meaninglessness) of "rape" as a category.[9] Sandie Gravett offers a clear statement of the opposing position:

> Although Hebrew lacks a legal or technical term for rape, biblical writers
> nonetheless make the necessary accommodations by impressing a wide
> range of words and phrases to describe violent, non-consensual sex . . . even
> though the cultures which wrote and passed down the Hebrew Bible con-
> ceived of sexual assault differently from our own, "rape" remains the pri-
> mary term we use in English for such violence.[10]

Kawashima rejects the term "rape" on technical legal grounds; Gravett argues for it on the basis of everyday usage. Here, I am inclined to follow Gravett, while also noting that English has its own complex vocabulary of sexual violence, including ambiguous poetic terms like "ravish," technical legal terms, and a robust vocabulary of slang. What I find most compelling in the call for translating 'innâ as "rape" and not, for example, social sexual shaming is the way this translational choice aligns with recent feminist notions of "rape culture," which push back strongly against attempts to define the parameters of "real rape" or to suggest that some acts of sexual violence are more real than others.[11]

While I disagree with Kawashima that it is a mistake to speak of rape in the Hebrew Bible, I do find interesting the way his argument puts pressure on consent discourses. Kawashima asks, "What is the modern legal subject and how does it differ from the entity found in biblical tradition?"[12] Many of these historical differences hinge on consent, when it may be given, and by whom. Similarly, when he writes about 2 Samuel 13, the rape of Tamar, "we must conclude that Tamar had no power of consent and that her violation did not constitute a forcible rape," we can read this statement in at least two ways.[13] First, that Tamar was not really raped (a reading I find troubling), and second—and more usefully—that even a biblical rape story as seemingly clear-cut as the rape of Tamar is typically, and problematically, read through assumptions of consent.

Furthermore, Kawashima's legal reconstruction, even as it denies the strict historical existence of the category of "rape," converges with what I have been calling the fuzzy, messy, and icky problem of reading rape and consent in the Hebrew Bible in other ways. There is an epistemological fuzziness in attempting to reconstruct clear legal principles based on the patchiness of biblical evidence. The reconstruction that Kawashima provides is also messy: While women are supposed to be under the control of patriarchal familial authority, in practice this depends upon the power of various male figures. And, of course, the end effect is icky, particularly in the suggestion that there are at least some women in the Bible's pages (and thus perhaps outside of them as well) who cannot say "no."

Arguing for the impossibility of consent and the categorical nonexistence of rape also runs into another difficulty: It compresses the Bible as literary text into a transparent reflection of its historical contexts. Stories of rape in the Bible certainly stand in relation to the time in which they are set, as well as when they were written; at the same time, the text is a literary creation. Biblical characters do not necessarily act in accordance with ancient Israelite law. Thus, Israelite laws and legal norms cannot be taken as the *ne plus ultra* for adjudicating biblical stories of sexual violence. All this introduces another degree of fuzziness to the attempt to reconstruct who can and cannot say "no."[14]

Problems with Consent

While disagreeing with Kawashima that it is illegitimate to speak of rape in the context of the Hebrew Bible, I am interested in the ways in which this critique—which I read as opening onto, if not necessarily offering, a critique of consent—aligns with work *within* feminist and queer theory. Having set forth the biblical arguments, I turn now to the contemporary. I will briefly summarize each position before returning to the biblical texts to trace their resonances. My focus is not on specific moments of consent or nonconsent but rather on the way we talk about and use the idea of consent more broadly; I will thus refer to "consent discourses" as a way of describing this larger constellation of ideas, practices, and ideology.

Critique 1: Consent Discourses Assume a Liberal Enlightenment Subject; This Assumption Prevents a Complex Analysis of Rape Culture

A fundamental issue with consent concerns the type of subject that discourses of consent assume. The consenting subject is the liberal Enlightenment subject, the subject we encounter in Kant and Locke. As we know from a lengthy tradition of feminist critique, this subject, while putatively universal, is often coded: as male, as White, as adult, as owning property, as able-bodied. Therefore, there is at the very least an irony in predicating a feminist theory of sexual violence on the very figure feminist theory has so vigorously critiqued.

The subject who consents (or withholds consent) is further assumed to be self-contained, knowable, and self-aware. When I am asked to consent, there is the assumption that I understand what I am being asked, and believe myself capable of answering. This means knowing what I want, and knowing myself. This notion of the self may seem familiar, even banal. However, this notion of the subject is constructed on assumptions antithetical to poststructuralism and postmodernism—in Nietzsche's famous judgment, put to much use in poststructuralist and postmodern theory, we are strangers to ourselves.[15] Furthermore, the kind of self-contained subject that consent assumes is unable to accommodate the shattered subject of sublimity, trauma, or religious experience.[16]

An understanding of rape defined against consent and predicated upon the idea of a subject who is self-contained, self-known, and able to choose whether to give or withhold consent has unintended consequences. One such consequence is the perpetuation of ableist discourses.[17] Another is the potential to erase rape as a category when we are talking about non-modern and/ or non-Western contexts.[18] This is a vulgar version of Kawashima's thesis but a frequent line of reasoning around rape stories in the Bible: Because women were not empowered as subjects to consent, it is meaningless to talk about consent, and without the language of consent, it is meaningless to speak about rape. While this argument can be critiqued on many grounds, I suggest that by relying on a model of rape that itself assumes a liberal understanding of the subject, we undercut our own efforts to name and understand *both* sexual violence in the Hebrew Bible *and* the phenomenon of rape culture more broadly—a term coined, in fact, to speak to the fuzziness and messiness of sexual violence.

Critique 2: Consent Discourses Ignore More Subtle Techniques of Power, Such as Discomfort

The model of all subjects as equally empowered to give consent ignores the weight of our personal histories, as well as the contingencies that attend any given sexual interaction. The assumption that subjects can simply give or withhold consent also neglects the influence of more subtle forms of pressure, as well as discomfort.

This is a point that Ahmed has analyzed incisively in *Willful Subjects*. As the title suggests, *Willful Subjects* explores the theme of willfulness, including how the accusation of acting "willfully" is used to control resistant subjects, especially women and children. Taking up the fuzzy/messy/icky problem of "how women willingly agree to situations in which their safety and well-being are compromised" and "the cases in which yes involves force but is not experienced as force," Ahmed draws out the power of *discomfort*: Discomfort constitutes "a polite strategy or technique of power (the capacity to carry out will without resistance, or with the will of others)."[19] The significance of discomfort, and its role in leading victims/survivors to compromise their own wishes or will, is a point made again and again in contemporary accounts of rape culture.[20]

Critique 3: Consent Discourses Neglect Intersectional Analysis, Especially Concerning Race, Sexuality, and Disability

The right to say "no" has been historically denied to many categories of people. This persists today; research on bystander intervention shows, for example, that bystanders are more likely to intervene to help a White woman than a woman of color, and a straight-presenting woman rather than a visibly queer person.[21] In this situation, "intervention" is a recognition of "hearing" the "no" (whether or not this "no" has been uttered). In addition to race and sexuality, the question of who can say "no" also raises serious questions around the issue of ability and disability.[22]

Consent discourses are also informed by troubling racialized assumptions surrounding sexual violence. In the contemporary United States, as well as Canada, Europe, Australia, New Zealand/Aoteorea, and elsewhere, the victim of sexual assault is imagined as a White woman; rape is figured as a threat not just to women but also to Whiteness. In this way, representations of rape offer another iteration of cultural narratives protecting (and policing) White womanhood, such as panic over "White slavery" and sex trafficking of White women.[23] Furthermore, the imagined Whiteness of the ideal rape victim is bound up with the implied Blackness or Brownness of the imagined rapist. Protecting (White) women from rape means protecting them from (Black and Brown) men.[24] Consent discourses and consent education initiatives often perpetuate these racist assumptions without challenging them. In particular, the appeal to consent often ignores the ways in which consent runs up against race, sexuality, and other vectors of identity. In the context of the biblical stories, ethnicity is a key concern, especially given the biblical text's repeated association of ethnic difference with sexual transgressions and general lasciviousness.

Critique 4: Consent Is a Legitimized Form of Subordination

Another serious concern with consent discourses is the way in which they inscribe and reify relations of subordination.[25] This is especially the case with respect to gender: The framing of consent assumes that sex or rape is something done by one person to another; these positions, moreover, are typically gendered. In *States of Injury*, Wendy Brown makes this point clearly. As Brown writes:

> If, in rape law, men are seen to do sex while women consent to it, if the measure of rape is not whether a woman sought or desired sex but whether she acceded to it or refused it when it was pressed upon her, then consent operates both as a site of subordination and a means of its legitimation. Consent is thus a response to power—it adds or withdraws legitimacy—but is not a mode of enacting or sharing in power.[26]

As Brown draws out, discourses of consent assume power relations: Consent is something that the more powerful (typically male) partner seeks from the weaker (typically female). While recent public campaigns around consent have fought to challenge gendered assumptions—consider the significant increase in consent posters, videos, and training modules featuring same-sex couples, as well as female aggressors and male victims—this does not address the larger issue of power and the structures, implicit or explicit, that sustain it. Consent does not share power so much as it reiterates relations of domination.

Critique 5: Consent Risks Becoming Colonialist

The power relations that Brown describes in consent discourses play out, as well, in questions of colonialism and power. Consent is often used as part of a hermeneutic practice of "saving" women.[27] This is especially clear in the literature on Dinah and on Tamar, which is almost obsessive in its desire to remember, recover, and especially re-voice. However, this desire to recover women, while grounded in feminist commitments, is uncomfortably close to the desire to "save" women that postcolonial feminist theory has so soundly critiqued. If colonialism is "white men saving brown women from brown men," as Gayatri Chakravorty Spivak has remarked, then this saving certainly involves saving from rape.[28]

This desire to save women and girls from sexual violence may be well intentioned; it also risks slipping into colonialist sentiments—indeed, this is a common critique raised against neoliberal and imperialist forms of feminism. Saving women is big business, even as the "plight" of women—and, more recently, of LGBTQ people—is a frequent point of appeal used to justify intervention abroad.[29] That this intervention also serves the imperialist and financial motives of the governments advocating for it passes largely without comment. Women's rights provide a convenient cover for other forms of global intervention (not to mention the generation of capital). Consent, far from reducing exploitation, can increase it, especially when we fail to attend to (post)colonial contexts and colonializing assumptions about who knows what's best.

Critique 6: Consent Is a Low Bar

Finally, consent discourses are insufficient to the task of addressing the full complexity of sex and rape, beginning with, but not limited to, the fuzzy, messy, and icky.[30] When the framework of consent is the only framework we have to assess sexual culture, other questions and problems and possibilities become impossible to consider. In particular, consent discourses risk evacuating the question of sexual pleasure from sex. As Kelly Oliver writes, "Affirmative consent should not be conflated with desire. Just because a woman submits to sex, does not mean that she wants it, especially in a culture where women feel pressured to please men."[31] The limitations that consent places on sexual culture are not limited to specific sexual encounters; the question concerns not simply individual sexual pleasures—though those too, I would insist, should matter to a feminist theory of sexual violence—but also broader social and intellectual horizons.[32]

Or even more clearly, as a college student activist told feminist writer Rebecca Traister, "Seriously, God help us if the best we can say about the sex we have is that it was consensual."[33]

To this, I will only add that we might say the same about sex in the Bible.

In Sum: Consent Discourses Fail
to Accommodate Complexity

The framework of consent, while sometimes useful in describing and diagnosing sexual violence in contemporary culture, is insufficient and indeed inadequate in addressing sexual violence in all its fuzziness, messiness, and ickiness. It also suggests a limited horizon of creativity and critical engagement—which is a key feature of feminist and queer critique. I want now to turn to three biblical stories of sexual violence to demonstrate that the framework of consent is not only flawed *in general* but also insufficient to the reading of biblical rape texts *in particular*.

Fuzzy: The Rape of Dinah

Perhaps the most famous rape story in the Bible is also its fuzziest: the rape of Dinah, found in Genesis 34. The story begins with Dinah going forth to visit "the daughters of the land" (Gen 34:1). Her visit, however, is quickly curtailed by violence: "When Shechem, the son of Hamor the Hivite, the prince of the land, saw her, he took her, lay with her, and forced himself on her. His soul was drawn to Dinah the daughter of Jacob. He loved the young woman and spoke tenderly to the young woman"[34] (34:2–3). Following this encounter, Shechem seeks to marry Dinah; her father Jacob agrees, but Simeon and Levi, Dinah's brothers, object ("because he had defiled Dinah, their sister"; 34:13). They insist that Shechem and his men be circumcised; as the men are recovering, the brothers carry out a massacre against the Hivite men. When Jacob protests, they reply, "Should our sister be treated like a whore?" (34:31). Dinah herself is never heard from in the text; her fate is unknown, even as her silence becomes the subject of much reflection in feminist responses to the story.

The narrative is fuzzy on several levels. These include the semantic (how to translate the sequence of verbs describing what is done to Dinah

by Shechem), the narrative (what Dinah wanted or how Dinah felt; her silence leaves only questions), and the literary (whether it is in fact possible
to clarify the questions of meaning and narrative, or whether the text makes
intentional use of ambiguity, as is sometimes suggested). An additional
level of fuzziness, which I will not consider here, concerns the textual; text
critics suggest that the Dinah story in Genesis reflects multiple strata of text
redacted together.[35]

Dinah's story also makes clear the difficulties with appealing to consent to
adjudicate biblical sexual violence. First, of course, is the question of whether
a woman, including Dinah, would even be able to consent; insofar as consent assumes a modern idea of the subject, this possibility seems foreclosed
(this correlates with Kawashima's argument). Other scholars attempt to answer the question of "Was Dinah raped?" through linguistic analysis of the
text of Genesis 34. The key portion of the verse comes in 34:2: *wayyiqqaḥ*
'ōttāh wayyiškab 'ōttāh wayĕ'annehā. The first two verbs in the sequence
are clear: "he [Shechem] took her [Dinah] and he lay with her." The third
verb, *wayĕ'annehā* (from the root *'innâ*) is more controversial, as its range of
meanings includes "humiliate," "oppress," and "do violence to," including in a
sexual sense. The full phrase could be translated, *pace* Kawashima, "he seized
her and lay with her and raped her." However, the translation of *wayĕ'annehā*
as "and he raped her" is not universally accepted. Ellen van Wolde tracks a
number of definitions of the verb, including rape, make love, have sexual intercourse with, have illicit sex with, and abuse, and concludes that it is "not
acceptable" to translate the verb as "rape" or "sexual abuse."[36] Alison Joseph
argues for "forced sex" and "social shaming" in place of "rape."[37] Other critics
disagree; Yael Shemesh titles her article on Dinah "Rape Is Rape Is Rape,"
announcing her argument at the outset.[38]

I do not intend to offer a definitive statement on the meaning of *'innâ* here,
though I incline, like Shemesh and Gravett (quoted earlier in the chapter) to
read rape in the text. Instead, I want to highlight how the question of whether
the text describes what Whoopi Goldberg infamously called "rape-rape" is
at once unsolvable and distracting.[39] The fuzziness is built into the semantic
fields of the language itself.

The definitional fuzziness surrounding *'innâ* is linked to a larger narrative
fuzziness in the Dinah story. Because the Hebrew Bible does not differentiate between willing premarital sex and premarital rape—both are punished
with a fine and a marriage (Deut 22:28–29)—it is possible to argue, based on

the information presented by the text, that Dinah is a willing partner. Dinah could have consented; the narrative, which privileges the viewpoint of male authorities such as Dinah's father and brothers, would have been told in the same way. This is what makes possible a reading such as *The Red Tent* (Anita Diamant's novel, adapted into a film), which retells the narrative of Dinah as a love story.[40]

The openness of the text to such readings gains further support from Dinah's silence. *We do not know what Dinah wants, or would have wanted.* Todd Penner and Lilian Cates offer a helpful analysis of the silence in the Dinah story:

> It has been tempting, particularly in feminist scholarship, to focus on this "silencing of women" as providing grounds for "recovering" the lost female voice behind the text and hence, in many respects, also history. The problem, however, is that, aside from the momentary glimpse of agency opened up in the first verse ("Dinah went out"), Dinah does not actually exist in this text apart from the male gaze—even female experience becomes difficult to conceptualize let alone talk about given the parameters of the narrative.[41]

I share the assessment of ambiguity in the text. I would suggest, however, that the ambiguity in the representation of Dinah is not wholly reducible to male authorship and the male gaze. Instead, it accurately represents the ambiguity and fuzziness that attends many reports of sexual violence, ancient and modern alike. Such fuzziness is, as the contemporary expression has it, "a feature, not a bug," of the Dinah story, even if it is ill accommodated by consent discourses, which seek clear distinctions.

While we cannot determine *what Dinah wanted*, the desires of the male characters in the text are clear. Shechem desires to marry Dinah; Jacob supports marrying off his daughter to the prince of the land. Simeon and Levi desire blood and vengeance (whether for their sister's honor or their own is less clear). In this framework, including in Jacob's consent to the marriage of his daughter, the dynamics of consent as a "legitimized form of subordination" are obvious. Marriage, like sex or rape, is something done by one party to another; the party who is acted upon is overwhelmingly female. The narrative logic of Genesis 34 thus replicates the problematic logic of consent.

I have also suggested that appeals to consent often neglect intersectionality, ignoring the significance of race, ethnicity, disability, and other vectors of identity. The Dinah story also raises troubling questions when read with this perspective in mind. While Genesis 34 is frequently read as a narrative of interethnic encounter, the specific *colonial* context of the encounter is often downplayed or glossed over. This is taken up by Musa Dube in her recent study of Dinah "at the contact zone" (that is, the zone of contact between colonizing and colonized cultures), where she foregrounds the imperializing move that the promise of the "promised land" makes.[42] As Dube analyzes, Shechem occupies the place of the colonized man who targets the body of the female colonizer. That Shechem represents the colonized subject does not mean that he is not a rapist. But it does mean that we need to accommodate a more complex analysis that also accounts for ethnicity and coloniality. A simple appeal to consent is not enough.

Messy: The Rape of Tamar

As famous as the rape of Dinah is the rape of Tamar at the hands of her brother Amnon. Amnon is obsessed with his sister Tamar; on the advice of his friend Jonadab, he pretends to be sick so that Tamar will come to care for him. David commands her to bring food to her brother. Amnon ensures that the two are alone, then tells her to bring her cakes closer to him, then rapes her: "He would not listen to her and, being stronger than she was, he forced himself on her and lay with her" (2 Sam 13:13).[43]

More than any other biblical rape story, the narrative of Tamar describes a clear absence of consent. When Amnon solicits sex with "Come, lie with me, my sister," Tamar verbally refuses him: "She said to him, 'No, do not force yourself on me, for such a thing is not done in Israel! Do not do this disgraceful thing! And me—where can I carry my shame? And you would be an infamous scoundrel in Israel. But now, speak to the king, for he will not withhold me from you'" (2 Sam 13:11–12). Following her rape, Tamar goes away weeping to her brother Absalom's house. Absalom tries and fails to comfort her.

As critics both feminist and non-feminist have pointed out, the story of Tamar's rape is narrated in a way that makes it fundamentally a story about men. Tamar is secondary, even in the account of her own rape.[44] And for these men, the aftermath of the rape is messy. Indeed, the rape itself is at once central to the narrative and secondary to it; it is not Tamar, the raped daughter, but Absalom, the wronged brother and beloved son, who is the emotional focus of the passage. As a common feminist slogan about sexual violence has it, "Women have a past, men have a future"—and so it is the futures of Amnon, Absalom, and the Davidic monarchy, not the future of the daughter herself, that receive attention from the text (and it is Absalom, not Tamar, who receives a pillar; 2 Sam 18:18). William Propp even goes so far as to suggest that the rape itself is a distraction from the larger questions in the story:

> Because our society is too familiar with sexual abuse and violent crime, we are liable to miss a deeper meaning of the passage. The story is not just about atrocities supposedly committed within the royal family; more broadly, it probes the ambiguities in the network of obligation and taboo that defines Israelite kinship—not as a theoretical exercise, but to make a theological point.[45]

But it is precisely the "atrocities supposedly committed within the royal family" that I wish to stay focused on here, in relation to my critique of discourses of consent.

For now, consider another messy detail of the story: Tamar's desire to marry her rapist. Prior to the rape, she begs Amnon, "Speak to the king,[46] for he will not withhold me from you" (2 Sam 13:13); after the rape, she describes Amnon's expulsion of her from his house (and thus refusal to marry her) as a greater harm than the rape itself: "This evil in sending me away is greater than the other that you did to me" (v. 16). In expressing this desire, Tamar fails to act as a victim of sexual violence "ought" to act. She does not display proper self-actualization, or a Tarantino-esque desire for vengeance. Her failure to conform to expectations is not only a modern perception; Absalom urges her not to fuss: "Now, my sister, keep quiet; he is your brother—don't take this to heart" (v. 20). Tamar, however, is acted upon, or nudged to act as she does, by the force of discomfort that Ahmed describes.

While the specific advice that Absalom gives Tamar is different from what a modern reader might desire—silence instead of vengeance or self-actualization—it expresses a similar sense that Tamar should not marry her rapist. And yet there is a sort of gaslighting here, via the suggestion—first articulated by Absalom, but echoed by contemporary interpreters—that Tamar cannot possibly know what she wants, or what is in her best interest (neglecting, as well, that Tamar is a literary character). My interest is not in what Tamar "should" do but rather in how Tamar's deviation from what she ought to want to do leads to her criticism (both in the narrative and by interpreters) and eventual narrative death. It is a messy feature in an already messy family narrative. It does not fit with what the characters in the world of the story want, any more than it fits with what we as contemporary feminist readers want. Of course, what survivors of sexual violence want is also not always what we want them to want.

The critique of consent discourses speaks to this difficulty by drawing attention to more subtle techniques of power, such as discomfort. This story presents at least two modes of coercion: one explicit, one more subtle. To quote again from Ahmed and her critical assessment of consent in *Willful Subjects*:

> We certainly need to hear the violence that converts no into yes. My additional suggestion is modest: we also need to hear the cases in which yes involves force but is not experienced as force, when for instance a woman says yes to something as the consequences of saying no would be too much . . . If being willing does not mean the absence of force, then we need to account for the social and political situations in which yes and no are given.[47]

If the first episode of the Tamar story is "the violence that converts no into yes," then what follows—when Tamar expresses her desire to marry Amnon, even as she mourns the rape—offers an instance of "say[ing] yes to something as the consequences of saying no would be too much." Thus, the Tamar story is one case study in why "women willingly agree to situations in which their safety and well-being are compromised"—a situation that consent discourses, in their rigid and positivistic formulations, are unable to accommodate. Perhaps this is why so much feminist reflection on Tamar focuses on the rape itself or on mourning with/for Tamar, and not on the question of why Tamar might marry her rapist. The fuzzy/messy/icky possibility that Tamar might be acting willingly, or in her own best interest—or that her own best interest is not accommodated in a rigid form of will—is rarely taken up here, a silencing that consent discourses, in their rigidity, can inadvertently encourage. As with the fuzziness in the Dinah story, the messiness in the Tamar story is not secondary, but essential to the narrative.

Icky: Rape and Lot's Daughters

The third rape story involves Lot and his two daughters. After the divine destruction of Sodom, the three take refuge in a cave in the hills. In a bid to ensure their survival,[48] the daughters take drastic action:

> The firstborn said to the younger, "Our father is old and there is no man
> on earth to get us pregnant in the manner of the whole world. Come, let's
> get our father drunk on wine and lie with him, so that we can preserve off-
> spring through our father." They made their father drink wine that night.
> The firstborn went in and lay with her father, and he did not know when she
> lay down or when she got up. The next day, the firstborn said to the younger,
> "Look, yesterday I lay with my father. Let's make him drunk on wine again
> tonight and you lie with him, so that we can preserve offspring through our
> father." They made their father drink wine again that night. The younger
> came and lay with him, and he did not know when she lay down or when
> she got up. Both the daughters of Lot became pregnant by their father. (Gen
> 19:31–36)

This is clearly a story of sexual transgression, though of what sort is not immediately clear.[49] One obvious reading is that the daughters rape their father
in order to produce children—or, perhaps, as revenge for his earlier offering
them to the would-be rapists in Sodom (Gen 19:8). This reading gains intertextual support from its parallels to Genesis 9:20–27, where Ham sees his
father Noah's nakedness and perhaps sexually abuses him. Another possible
reading suggests that the daughters are in fact victims of their father.[50] One
articulation of this position comes from Ilona Rashkow, who argues that the
text presents the incestuous desire of the father and then covers up this desire
by making the daughters into responsible agents.[51] J. Cheryl Exum offers a
similar reading, arguing that the text, as the product of male authors, cannot
but display male fantasies, extending to the fantasy of incestuous rape.[52] Still
other readers propose, for example, that the characters act in a courageous
way to increase human survival, or that the point is not the daughters at all
but rather the incestuous children to whom they give birth (who happen to
be the neighbors of the Israelites).

What is undeniably clear about this story is its ickiness (let the reader who
doubts me teach this story to a room full of eighteen-year-olds and then report back). The story draws much of its icky power from the violation of

the incest taboo. It also has an icky setting: Nothing good happens in a cave in the Hebrew Bible, but many morbid, perverse, or disgusting things do, involving dead bodies, excrement, dangerous animals, and of course incest.[53] The story becomes even ickier through the presence of excessive drinking (suggesting uncomfortable parallels to sexual violence on college and university campuses) as well as its repetition of sex acts. In the Lot story, intoxication is entangled with knowledge; In Hebrew, the verb *yada'*, "to know," frequently carries heavy sexual implications. The story is also connected, intertextually, to a number of other icky moments, from Ham and Noah (Gen 9:18–25) to Jephthah and his daughter (Judg 11:29–40). That the daughters are nameless and semi-interchangeable is a final icky touch.[54]

The story of Lot and his daughters also resonates with the critique of consent discourses in a number of ways. The "low bar" of consent is obvious here—whether or not the daughters consented, or Lot consented, hardly matters to the ickiness of the story.[55] The story also foregrounds a difficulty that appears with uncomfortable regularity in contemporary discussions over consent: how to judge the situation in which *no one* is legally or philosophically able to consent.[56]

I would also suggest that attempts to apply the principle of consent to narratives such as Genesis 19 also risk becoming colonialist—both because they involve the ethnic other (Lot and his daughters being the ancestors of the Moabites and the Ammonites) and because they assume a posture of "knowing what's best." This is the position that Mattias Rudolf critiques:

> To ask, as consent theorists are wont to do, about who can consent to what and under what circumstances and what counts as consent is merely to refine the lines of demarcation that separate the permissible from the forbidden and prescribe *who* can consent to *what* under which circumstances. It is also to push a particular "universal" model of subjectivity and personhood—one uniquely qualified to quantify the relative value of wrongs insofar as they can be articulated in terms of the body—on communities that have good reasons, economic and otherwise, to reject the model of rational self-interest and human dignity it advocates.[57]

While Rudolf's specific concern is with contemporary pharmaceutical test subjects, his words speak, as well, to Lot's daughters. Believing themselves (and Lot) the sole survivors of unthinkable apocalypse, hidden away in a cave with a father who previously offered them up to be raped, they may well have their own "good reasons . . . to reject the model of rational self-interest and human dignity" that consent discourses advocate or simply assume.

Toward a Fuzzy, Messy, Icky Reading of Dinah, Tamar, and Lot's Daughters

Even a brief consideration of the rape narratives of Dinah, Tamar, and Lot's daughters makes clear that consent is not just a problematic framework but one that is insufficient to address the complexity of actual biblical rape stories. The rape of Dinah is fuzzy in the ambiguity that surrounds the story. The rape of Tamar is messy, both in its consequences for the family and in the messiness of what Tamar herself wants. The sex/rape encounter between Lot and his daughters is icky in its incest, as well as the difficulty of determining the "true" victim (Lot? The daughters? The sons born to the daughters? Everyone? No one?). Of course, each of the terms—fuzzy, messy, icky—applies to the other stories as well. The daughters' icky story is fuzzy and messy. Tamar's messy story is fuzzy and icky. And Dinah's fuzzy story is messy and icky as well.

Furthermore, all three stories show the weakness of consent as an explanatory model for biblical sexual violence. The liberal Enlightenment idea of the subject, which so many appeals to consent assume, is missing in all three texts, and indeed across the Bible as a whole (critique 1). While all three texts contain shocking violence, they also exhibit what I have called, following Ahmed, "subtle techniques of power, such as discomfort" (critique 2). These appear across the story of Tamar's rape, from David urging her to visit her ill half-brother to Absalom's instructing her not to fret after the rape. Tamar's protests that Amnon should seek permission from David to marry/rape her, and her desperate attempts to regain her dignity and family status after the rape, further demonstrate the power of discomfort in the narrative. Turning to Dinah with this dynamic still in mind, we might perceive discomfort as a driving force in Jacob's acquiescence to Dinah's marriage to her rapist (and perhaps infer such discomfort to Dinah as well, before or after the rape). That sex and rape alike inscribe relations of subordination (critique 4) is also clear in both stories: The fact that marriage is proposed as a remedy to rape by Shechem and his father (Gen 34:8–12), by Tamar (2 Sam 13:13), and by biblical law (Exod 22:16–17) simply points to the lack of substantive distinctions between consensual sex and rape.

The framework of consent also ignores intersectional analysis (critique 3), while also risking becoming colonialist (critique 5). Questions of ethnicity and alterity, or of "Israelites and others," are prominent throughout biblical narrative. Dinah is literally the daughter of Israel (Jacob); the story of her rape is also a story of a family seeking to make their home in a land not their own, where they can be read as colonizers. Shechem, meanwhile, is cast as an ethnic other. Lot's daughters are the matriarchs of two foreign nations, the Ammonites and the Moabites. The association of non-Israelites with sexual perversity and deviance is well documented, as is the way that difference becomes doubly marked as sexualized and racialized. These assumptions are retrojected onto the story of Moab and Amon's origins. However, a narrow focus on "did the daughters consent?" risks ignoring the intersections of ethnicity, sexuality, and alterity in the text. There is also the risk that, in surveying this and similar stories, we will presume that our modern, consent-inflected perspective allows us to know *better* what ought to have been done. This is a perspective that reflects the desire to "save biblical women"; as should go without saying, this—like other discourses of "saving women"—is deeply colonialist.

Finally, consent is a low bar (critique 6). This is clear across the stories. As creative reimaginings of Genesis 34 as a doomed love story suggest, Dinah's consent would still be meaningless at preventing the massacre that her brothers undertake in the name of her honor. Tamar urges Amnon to seek David's consent, implying that under these circumstances, his desires would be acceptable. This is a low bar indeed. Tamar's acquiescent instincts are critiqued within the text even by her brother, Absalom, who maintains a kind of heroic status, in spite of his doomed rebellion against David. And in the story of Lot and his daughters, consent does nothing to ameliorate the incest taboo—just as pointing out that father–daughter incest is not included in the biblical incest laws does little to increase its palatability. The ickiness remains strong.

The bad news is that the notion of consent is insufficient to address the complexities of biblical narratives of sexual violence, as even a cursory examination of these three stories shows. The good news is that there are other interpretive options available to us, beginning with the four tactics introduced in the previous chapter: refusing to claim innocence, resisting paranoia, tracing sticky affect, and reading with literature.

Refusing Innocence and Staying with the Trouble

We begin by setting aside claims to innocence. As Donna Haraway has demonstrated again and again, there are no innocent vantage points from which to view the world and its stories, just as there are no innocent women, or animals, or cyborgs, or cats, or bacteria, or trees. Instead, everything is interconnected, and everyone is implicated. Knowledge, too, is always positional and partial. Rather than seeking a single truth, or staking a claim to a neutral or innocent position from which judgments can be issued, Haraway insists on the presence of multiple "situated knowledges."[58] Furthermore, knowledge itself "is never innocent"; it is always implicated in relations of power.[59]

Instead of mourning for innocence lost (which may never have existed at all), Haraway suggests that we should work at "staying with the trouble."[60] This describes a practice of embracing complexity and ambiguity, while refusing simplicity and stridency alike. In the case of Dinah, as we have seen, the text is plagued with perhaps irresolvable ambiguity over *what happened*—how to translate the verb ʿ*innâ*, and whether to understand it as referring to rape, to some other form of sexual transgression, or to consensual but socially unacceptable premarital sex. In this case, refusing innocence does not mean rejecting the suggestion that Dinah was innocent. But it does summon us to "stay with the trouble," including the troublesomely broad range of meanings grouped under ʿ*innâ*. We should linger here and consider what this collocation of meanings, encompassing rape, sexualized humiliation, political oppression, and even masochism, tells us, not just about Dinah but about the broader understanding of gender and power the text reflects.

Haraway's repeated admonition that "acquiring knowledge is never innocent" also calls for a more rigorous examination of the colonial dynamics of the text. One of Dube's key insights is that colonizer/colonized relationships, even with the gender script flipped, as it is here, "serve the interest of the colonizer." In this case, this happens after the rape, when Shechem is represented as a "good native" who wants to do right by Dinah after the rape.[61] His desire, Jacob's response, and Simeon and Levi's violent actions all converge around the same point: telling a story that serves the interests of the colonizer. Though their specific actions oppose each other, they are all in the service of the same ideology.

The ethnic dynamics of the Dinah story also push back against the normative biblical move of constructing a binary between good and bad women, where "good" is also "Israelite" and "sexually pure," while "bad" is collocated with both "foreign" and "sexually loose."[62] Across the Hebrew Bible, there is a tendency to associate promiscuous sexuality with foreignness, and foreign women in particular, as in representations of Moabite and Midianite women (e.g., Num 25; see also Deut 7:3–4, Josh 23:12). The flipped script, as in the Dinah story (Dinah is "a woman from the colonizer's camp," who goes out to visit "the native women of the land"), seems to promise an alternative narrative.[63] However, it instead resolves in favor of the colonizers/Israelites. The colonizer always wins; sometimes consent discourses are used to cover over or distract from this truth.

As with Dinah, so too with Tamar. Like the patriarchal history in Genesis, the books of Samuel tell a story about families and power. Though Samuel lacks the colonial context that Dube identifies in Genesis, it is nevertheless a narrative about political and familial power, as well as the obligations people hold toward each other (recall the quote from Propp). Refusing innocence in this context does not mean dismissing the violence and trauma that Tamar suffers at the hands of her half-brother. But it does mean attending to the intergenerational complexity of this trauma. As Sarah Schulman draws out in detail in *Conflict Is Not Abuse*, family trauma is rarely a one-off event.[64] Instead, events bleed into each other. David's toxic masculinity and cavalier attitude toward women—a theme I return to in the next chapter—are implicated in the familial and sexual trauma of his children. Even David is not innocent of what happens.

Refusing the position of innocence seems, at first, easier in the case of Lot and his daughters. No one seems to be very innocent here: The plan is clearly the daughters', but Lot is in many ways an undesirable character, from his shoddy hosting of the divine messengers to his earlier offering up of his daughters to be raped. Perhaps everyone is a bit to blame? However, I suggest that in the context of this story, refusing innocence means refusing to claim an innocent exterior position from which we can judge the events of the cave above Zoar. Refusing innocence is linked, as well, to the refusal of purity. Just as there are no good or "pure" options available to Lot's daughters, who believe themselves and their father the sole human survivors, so too should we refuse easy judgment. And in this story, as in Dinah's visit to the contact zone, it is crucial, as well, to remember the costs of knowledge for the characters in the story. Here, the Haraway-inflected reading position of *refusing innocence* echoes with the postcolonial critique of presuming to know what is best for others, or what they want.

It is tempting to demand that Dinah, and Tamar, and Lot's daughters, and the many other sexually victimized and violated women of the Bible add their voices to the #MeToo movement. And such efforts can be powerful, for survivors and religious communities alike. However, refusing a position of innocence means insisting, as well, that the messy contours of these stories exceed scripted soundbites. There is a complexity here. "Staying with the trouble" means reading these stories as stories of sexual violence, without erasing their ambiguities and complexities, without assuming that we know what Dinah wanted or that the dynamics of victim and victimizer are both clearly marked and unchanging (an assumption that the Lot story, for example, puts pressure on). Refusing innocence means holding open a space for ambivalence, against purity and security alike.

Venturing beyond Paranoid Positions

Refusing innocence leads to the related second interpretive tactic of a fuzzy/messy/icky hermeneutic: resisting paranoid reading positions. As Sedgwick describes, paranoid reading is at once anticipatory (*Bad things are coming!*) and mimetic (toward its own contexts).[65] Its central concern is with avoiding negative affects (or bad feelings). Paranoid reading offers a "strong theory"—there is nothing that it cannot explain. And it places great faith in exposure: If violence or misogyny would only be *exposed*, then it could be transformed.

Of course, violence and misogyny are rarely truly secrets; in the words of artist Jenny Holzer, "Abuse of power comes as no surprise."[66] Neither should the sexualized violence and pervasive misogyny of the Hebrew Bible come as a surprise; this extends to the three rape stories I have considered in detail here. Dinah's rape fits a larger pattern of sexualization and violence at the "contact zone" between cultures; her brothers' genocidal rage over the slight to their male familial honor fits a larger pattern of violent biblical masculinity. So too does David's refusal even to acknowledge his daughter's rape and suffering fit with the larger dynamics of the so-called David story (even the name bespeaks its masculine orientation). And Lot and his daughters are the ancestors of the Moabites and the Ammonites; given everything the Bible has to say about dangerous and perverse foreign sexuality, the sexual transgression and perhaps rape of Genesis 19 is hardly surprising. The sexualized violence in Sodom that precedes the cave episode similarly primes us to expect sexual violence in its aftermath.

So, if a reading of Genesis 34, or 2 Samuel 13, or Genesis 19 is to resist paranoid reading, what does this mean? Sedgwick offers the alternative of "reparative reading," which seeks, in place of suspicion or paranoia, flexibility, openness, the amelioration of pain, and even pleasure. Instead of exposing what is (purportedly) hidden, reparative reading is "additive and accretive"; it is local and context-specific, rather than making sweeping claims.[67] Importantly, for Sedgwick the paranoid and the reparative are *positions*, not people; it is possible to move from one to another.[68]

A reparative reading of the three rape stories considered here resists the urge to make sweeping generalizations that encompass all three stories, or rape as such. Reparative reading does not dismiss the pain of these stories but instead opens the possibility of imagining an *after* to such pain. Paranoid reading sets limits on the *after*, allowing trauma to determine the limits of the imaginative horizon. It suggests that after rape, nothing is ever the same. Reparative reading, in contrast, suggests that we can imagine an *after* to sexual trauma in the Bible without erasing that trauma itself. Instead, this is simply a practice of finding space—as Ahmed reminds us in *The Problem of Happiness*, an "aspiration" is, originally, a space to *breathe*.[69] To be otherwise from paranoid is not to deny suffering, pain, or tragedy—it is simply finding space to breathe, for the texts, for their characters, and for ourselves.

Sticky Affects and Icky Stories

As I have already discussed, affect is "sticky": It clings to objects and is transmitted between them. This stickiness is similar to an idea of contamination but is also a more flexible and open metaphor: Instead of casting blame on an original bad cause ("Patient Zero"), it focuses our attention more broadly. Stickiness also suggests that affects can be passed back and forth repeatedly, as between sticky hands, or in the affective dynamics of an unhappy family (such as David's).

The stickiness of affect is clearly apparent in the three rape stories considered here. As I have described in the previous chapter, the victim/survivor of sexual violence often becomes an "unhappy object." Not only is she understood to be contaminated by the sexual violence she has experienced, but she threatens to bring this contamination into the community. Further, the survivor is an unhappy object insofar as she serves as a reminder of the breakdown of social norms and systems. In the case of the survivor who refuses to narrate her experience using the terms and framework prescribed by those in authority, her very presence is an unpleasant reminder that prevention efforts have failed. (Consider the wealth of campaigns organized around the rough principle of "All of us can prevent sexual violence!" It sounds lovely, but if *she* has been raped, then *we* have all failed, which is not always pleasant to contemplate.) In the case of the biblical narrative, the presence of the survivor/victim is a reminder that something has failed. The "trouble" (Gen 34:30) that Simeon and Levi bring on Jacob is the consequence of their response to Dinah who, from this perspective, has become an unhappy object to the Israelite family/community.

These dynamics are even clearer in the story of Tamar, who functions as an unhappy object in multiple ways. This becomes immediately clear in Amnon's reaction to her; after the rape, he is filled with loathing toward her. Tamar is also an unhappy object, though differently, to her brother Absalom; he rejects her desire to marry Amnon and by extension her narrative of the events, urging her instead to be silent and calm. Absalom, too, finds Tamar an unhappy object; he attempts to correct her unhappiness by setting her on a different trajectory. In *Queer Phenomenology*, a precursor to *The Promise of Happiness*, Ahmed suggests that certain objects are queer because their orientations or potential trajectories are improper; disciplinary processes seek to "fix" and "straighten" such trajectories.[70] For Absalom, Tamar's desire to marry her rapist half-brother is a queer desire indeed (and here recall the affective overlap of "queer" and "unhappy"); his words are an attempt to force her on a less unhappy path.

Affective stickiness or contagion also offers another model for thinking about the way that Tamar's rape spreads bad feelings and trauma throughout David's family, and Dinah's rape through Judah's family, without reducing either story to a simplified "argument between men over a woman." This is a move that both nonfeminist and some feminist critics make but that has the effect of hedging in the text and foreclosing other feminist and queer ways of thinking, while constraining Tamar to the exclusive position of victim.

Sticky affect also offers a model for the story of Lot and his daughters. It is sometimes difficult to trace the origins of stickiness (consider: *Wait, why are my hands sticky?*), even as its remarkable powers of transfer between bodies and surfaces are unmistakable. Sticky affect and the stickiness of sexual violence explain why the sexual transgression or rape that immediately precedes the birth of Lot's (grand)sons Moab and Ben-Ammi contaminates the Moabites and the Ammonites more broadly. Do the daughters contaminate their children, and the children the people who are named after them? Or does stickiness work the other way, from the deviant Moabites and Ammonites to the daughters? And how does all this relate to the events in Sodom that precede it? What matters is less the directionality than the economy of contamination and transfer between texts and bodies that touch each other.

Reading with Literature: "Sex and Alien Encounter"

In the previous chapter, I have introduced the strategy of "reading through literature" as a way of opening and disrupting biblical rape stories by confronting them with and through contemporary literary analogues. This strategy is especially useful for querying consent. Here, I will turn to literature and to nonconsensual sex in feminist science fiction, in particular, in order to put pressure on consent and open a space for considering compromised pleasures. This is a reading strategy I adapt from M. Cooper Minister and their work on "sex and alien encounter." Engaging feminist science fiction pioneer Octavia Butler, Minister explores Butler's descriptions of sexual encounters between aliens and non-alien beings. These include Butler's story *Bloodchild*, in which benevolent aliens can reproduce only by gestating their eggs in humans (either women or men) and the *Xenogenesis/ Lilith's Brood* trilogy,[71] in which another species of aliens engage in sex—not always fully consensually—with humans and eventually create a new hybrid species with them. Minister uses these stories to put pressure on received ideas of consent, autonomy, and "the bounds of the self," offering a theory of "compromised pleasure" that challenges us to "engage questions around language and communication, the bounds of the self and individual autonomy, and the nature of pleasure."[72] This touches on both communication and consent.

First, while consent discourses typically emphasize the verbal,[73] Minister notes the challenges that Butler's fictions pose to this norm. The aliens in *Xenogenesis* communicate primarily through touch; in another of Butler's stories, "Amnesty," communication occurs through light. Minister uses this to explore responses to sexual violence that are not dependent upon ability. She also problematizes a binary understanding of consent/nonconsent, suggesting it fails to do justice to the complexity of the narrative. Of Butler's fictions, she writes:

The word consensual cannot describe the human-alien encounters in the *Xenogenesis* series, "Bloodchild," or "Amnesty." Butler, however, does consistently describe these encounters as pleasurable. And the pleasure of these encounters between humans and aliens often exceeds the pleasures of sexual encounters between humans. While the compromised nature of communication and the lack of clearly definable individual boundaries do not excuse the overt forms of violence sometimes exerted by the aliens against the humans, it can help explain why the encounters between the humans and aliens can be described as both coercive and pleasurable. There is, Butler's stories seem to suggest, a crossing between pain and pleasure.[74]

Minister further suggests using Butler's work to open up conversations about sexual violence and sexual pleasure that move beyond the liberal model of the subject and the binary formulation of consent/rape.

Minister's reading of Butler opens the biblical text in a number of ways. The Bible, it is generally accepted, lacks aliens; however, divine and other non-human creatures are frequently present. Though the Hebrew texts lack the narrative pattern of rape-by-a-god that is prominent in, for example, Greek myth, there are occasional divine sexual encounters with humans, in which consent is not clear (Mary's impregnation is the marquee example, in the gospels of Matthew and Luke;[75] consider also Sarah's impregnation in Gen 21:1). In Genesis 6:1–4, the "sons of God" have sex with mortal women, who give birth to "heroes of renown." Consent or nonconsent is never addressed in the story; there is, however, the suggestion of transgression, insofar as this sex seems to be an instigating factor for the world-destroying flood that follows. Reading this narrative fragment as an account of "sex and alien encounter" offers a new way of understanding both the encounter and its consequences.

Yahweh's sexually inflected "opening" of the bodies of his male prophets offers another such example of nonconsensual but pleasurable "alien encounter." As I have argued in a previous work, prophecy "opens" the male body; this process is both painful and pleasurable.[76] It is also largely nonconsensual; Jeremiah, in particular, protests against the prophetic word entering his body (though he also describes it as a source of pleasure). The most clearly sexual description comes in Ezekiel's swallowing of Yahweh's scroll (Ezek 3:1–3); while Jeremiah protests, Ezekiel remains silent, and at times is made mute by Yahweh. It is a common tenet of consent discourses that consent must be verbal, thereby positioning the silent Ezekiel outside of the very possibility of consent. Minister's work on ability, disability, and cripping consent suggests interesting possibilities for interrogating these assumptions. It also opens new ways of reading the larger scene of divine/alien—prophet/human relation. Jeremiah has even been read as a victim of rape, though also as a participant in a (consensual) BDSM scene.[77] The parallels with Butler's *Xenogenesis*—violence, coercion, but also pleasure—speak to these moments in the prophetic literature as well. Of course, Yahweh also opens women's wombs, also without their consent. This suggests an additional frontier for thinking about compromised consent and alien encounter.[78]

Applied to the biblical rape texts, Minister's work also directs attention to alterity. We find this in the Dinah story: Dinah and her family are foreigners in the land of Canaan. As many feminist critics have pointed out, we do not know how Dinah responded to the rape; at least one midrash speculates that Dinah enjoyed sex with Shechem and had to be dragged from his home (*Genesis Rabbah* 80:11).[79] While most modern readers, including nearly all my students, find this suggestion repulsive, Minister's theorization of sex and alien encounter opens a space to consider it, and the question of pleasure more broadly, without the sort of romanticizing rape erasure that *The Red Tent* undertakes by presenting it as a love story. We might think similarly, if carefully, about Tamar, or about the various "non-rape" arranged marriages in Genesis and the Deuteronomistic history.

I do not perceive much pleasure when I read the stories of Dinah, Tamar, or Lot's daughters, even compromised pleasures, such as Minister describes. But positioning these stories in conversation with the complex and nonconsensual sexual encounters of feminist science fiction challenges our easy assumptions about the stories. More than anything, reading the texts with science fiction, and with science fiction's complexity surrounding sex and rape, encourages us to think beyond the moment. The first sexual encounters between the aliens and Lilith, the heroine and matriarch of the *Xenogenesis* trilogy, have clear overtures of rape. Were we only to read to here and stop, we would have a very different perception of the text. But the book continues, the series continues, and the sexual encounters become something more complex. While the biblical narrative is of course different, reading with this in mind urges us to think beyond the tragedy of the moment. We can commemorate, but we can also think beyond simply a posture of grief, even to imagine new forms of flourishing.[80]

The aliens in Butler's work are literal (if fictional) ones; Minister's concern is with how science fiction narratives of sex and rape might help us put pressure on our received assumptions about both categories, as well as the boundaries that distinguish between them. The critique of consent that I have constructed throughout this chapter draws on different sources and forms of knowledge; my conclusions, however, resonate with Minister's: The consent/nonconsent binary is insufficient to the complexities of both sexual violence and sex itself, more broadly. As Minister writes of sex in Butler's alien fictions, "there is . . . a crossing between pain and pleasure"[81] that remains unspoken and unspeakable when consent is the only language available.

Postcards from the Edge of Consent

Consent, it seems, does have edges. This can be understood in two ways: as the points where consent falls off or fails, and as the zone of possibility for a more complex understanding of sexual violence. The edges of consent are sometimes fuzzy, sometimes messy, often icky. They threaten to wound us. But they also suggest a possibility of a beyond, to pain and trauma and grief.

Rape and rape culture remain challenging and sometimes shattering matters, in the biblical texts and even more so in the world. In pushing back against consent discourses, my aim has been not to reject consent itself, which plays an important role in contemporary understandings of sexual encounter and sexual violence, but to summon us as feminists to think beyond the limitations of consent. Consent discourses flatten and erase the fuzzy, the messy, and the icky. They impose anachronistic and, more importantly, antifeminist notions of the liberal subject onto ancient texts. They ignore discomfort and subtle forms of coercion. They neglect race, ethnicity, and other questions of intersectionality and risk slipping into a colonialist project of saving women. They legitimize subordination. And they set too low a bar, foreclosing questions of pleasure. And yet we also have alternatives, as this chapter has begun to explore.

3

Narrating Harm in the Bathsheba Story

Predation, Peremption, and Silence

In *Why Stories Matter*, Clare Hemmings stakes a claim for the importance of stories and storytelling. In particular, Hemmings argues that how we describe the history of disciplines and ideas—in her case, how we narrate the history of feminism—is a crucial part of how these ideas are produced and sustained. The object depends upon its telling. Along with charting several major trajectories in the way that feminist theory narrates its history to itself, Hemmings explores the possibility of renarration as a way of destabilizing dominant narratives and uncovering suppressed resonances. The focus of renarration is not on telling entirely new stories but rather on telling stories *differently*: or, as Hemmings puts it, "I am interested in experimenting with alternative ways of telling feminist stories (rather than telling different feminist stories as such)."[1]

This focus on "the telling" and on what is assumed or elided is not unique to Hemmings; instead, it resonates with many articulations of historiography and metacriticism.[2] Nietzsche's famous argument about genealogies is also an argument about (re)tellings.[3] Feminist rewritings of myths and fairy tales cast classic stories in new light, summoning us to consider what is emphasized and what is elided in more traditional tellings. Even psychoanalysis can be understood as a practice of finding ways to tell stories differently. And closer to home in biblical studies, feminist scholars have drawn our attention to how the history of the field is narrated, often in ways that elide non-male scholars and voices. The question of "the telling" also speaks to my central concern here: *how to tell rape stories differently.*

This chapter explores how to read a specific rape story differently. The key text is the story of Bathsheba (2 Sam 11–12; 1 Kgs 1–2). The crucial incident occurs in 2 Samuel 11, when David sees Bathsheba bathing and desires her. Sex and complications quickly ensue, leading to pregnancy, murder, and divine intervention. While often treated as either a royal intrigue or a compelling love story, the account is increasingly recognized as a narrative of rape.

Texts after Terror. Rhiannon Graybill, Oxford University Press. © Oxford University Press 2021.
DOI: 10.1093/oso/9780190082314.003.0004

This view is not only held by scholars but also increasingly present in pop-ular accounts of David and Bathsheba.[4] I agree with the upsurge of readers—feminist and popular alike—who read this story as a rape story. But I also want to insist that in reading and retelling Bathsheba's story, it is important—and important for specifically feminist reasons—not to gloss over or mini-mize its fuzziness, messiness, and ickiness. Bathsheba's story resonates with so many contemporary stories of sexual violence *because* of its ambiguity, as much as because of its violence.

My reading will also put pressure on how we frame harm in the Bathsheba story. To this end, I take up the question of whether Bathsheba is best described as a victim, and David as a sexual predator. This model of predation is suggested both by the biblical text (via Nathan's parable in 2 Sam 12) and by many feminist readers. However, I argue that just as "consent" is an in-adequate framework for reading the rape stories of Dinah, Tamar, and Lot's daughters, so too is "predation" (or any model organized around immutable, perverted, and recidivistic "predators" and innocent "victims") both insuf-ficient and ill suited for describing the forms of sexual and nonsexual harm in this text. In place of predation, I will employ the category of *peremption* to describe the harm of the Bathsheba story. I adopt this term from Joseph J. Fischel and his analysis of adolescent sexuality in *Sex and Harm in the Age of Consent*. For Fischel, "peremption" identifies the "*uncontrolled disqualifica-tion of possibility*"—in particular, the disqualification of certain forms of sex, sexuality, and sexual subjectivity.[5] The root of the word, the Latin *perimere*, means to utterly kill or destroy; in the U.S. legal system, a "peremptory chal-lenge" is a type of objection that requires no explanation. With respect to sexual harm, "peremption" describes the way that certain future possibilities, including possible forms of sexual subjectivity and being in the world, are peremptorily foreclosed. Fischel uses the term with specific reference to ad-olescent sexual subjectivity. In contrast, my focus here, as throughout *Texts after Terror*, is on women, in this case Bathsheba. In reading the Bathsheba story, replacing a model of David as sexual predator with one of Bathsheba as perempted lets us explore female embodiment and subjectivity, as well as the forms of harm Bathsheba experiences, without collapsing these into an essentializing and flattening narrative of victimization.

Bathsheba, moreover, is perempted in multiple ways. She is first and foremost "*perempted by narrative*"[6]—that is, the pull of the story, and the compulsory forms of narration and identification with the ostensible pro-tagonist, David. In addition, she is *perempted by masculinity*—in this case, by the performance of masculinity that David exerts throughout the narrative. Even as the David story opens space for alternative imaginings of masculinity and of how to inhabit a masculine body and self, it perempts its women, Bathsheba first among them. The issue of masculinity opens, as well, onto the question of ethnicity, which is only hinted at in the Bathsheba story but which plays a significant role in scripting biblical narratives of sexual violence and sexual harm.

Beyond tracking Bathsheba's peremption, this chapter asks the question: *What does Bathsheba want?* To conceive of Bathsheba as a desiring or wanting subject pushes against the dominant thrust of the narrative, as well as many feminist hermeneutic moves that seek to protect or shelter Bathsheba from either the predations of rape or antifeminist critical scrutiny. Moreover, the text provides no easy answer to this question: What details we do receive, in the form of Bathsheba's actions toward Abishag (2 Kgs 1–2), further complicate the question of a feminist reading of Bathsheba. And yet I will suggest that asking this question is nevertheless essential. Furthermore, it leads us to link Bathsheba's peremption to the peremption of women more broadly: Abishag the Shunammite is herself perempted by Bathsheba. The chapter thus concludes by tracing a broader picture of sexual harm, moving both forward and backward from the events with Bathsheba in 2 Samuel 11–12 and opening onto Bathsheba's treatment of Abishag and the larger question of peremption.

Enter Bathsheba

The first encounter between David and Bathsheba is both one-sided and scopophilic. It begins while the Israelite army (including Bathsheba's husband, Uriah) is away at battle; David, however, has remained at home. The incident unfolds quickly:

> It was evening. David got up from his couch and went up on the roof of the king's house. He saw a woman bathing on the roof; the woman was very beautiful. David sent and inquired about the woman. The answer came,[7] "Isn't that Bathsheba, daughter of Eliam, wife of Uriah the Hittite?" David sent messengers and took her; she came to him, and he lay with her. She was purifying herself from her uncleanness. She returned to her house. The woman became pregnant. She sent and told David, "I'm pregnant." (2 Sam 11:2–5)

This pregnancy presents a complication: Bathsheba is already married to Uriah, who is absent; thus the unborn child cannot be passed off as his. David recalls Uriah from the front and tries, unsuccessfully, to persuade the loyal soldier to have sex with his wife. When he fails, David arranges for Uriah to be killed (11:14–18). After a period of mourning, Bathsheba joins David's household as his wife. Her child dies as a punishment for David's sin; the infant's death is ordained by Yahweh and foretold to David by the prophet Nathan (2 Sam 12:14). Bathsheba is not included in this scene—or, at least, her response is not documented by the text. The episode comes to an end when Bathsheba bears another son: Solomon, David's eventual successor.

Readers frequently note the laconic narration, as well as its ambiguities and silences. For critics seeking to establish the artfulness of such style, and thus of biblical narrative more broadly, the text is a favorite. 2 Samuel 11 is the crucial text for Menachem Perry and Meir Sternberg's theory of "gaps" in biblical narrative.[8] Gale Yee takes up Erich Auerbach's famous description of biblical narrative as "fraught with background" to offer a comprehensive reading of ambiguity in the text.[9] And Robert Alter praises the "cultivated ambiguities of motive" and general artfulness of the story, which he calls "orchestrated with a richness that scarcely has an equal in ancient narrative."[10]

I concur with these related assessments of the narrative, but I am inclined to describe the fraught background or productive ambiguity differently—as fuzziness, accompanied by messiness and ickiness. The narrative is fuzzy, first and foremost, in its representation of Bathsheba. As with Dinah in Genesis 34, we do not know what Bathsheba wants, and whether her desires are confirmed or contradicted by the outcome of events. Bathsheba never verbally consents;[11] indeed, in the initial incident, she never speaks at all. 2 Samuel 11 has been read in a range of ways by critics: Some suggest that Bathsheba invited David's attentions or even sought to seduce him by bathing on the roof;[12] others read the story as one of coercion or rape. Richard M. Davidson offers a full seventeen arguments for reading the incident as an example of "power rape"; the bulk of evidence he compiles is largely convincing.[13] Still, as with Dinah, there is a pervasive fuzziness—we know what the male protagonist wants, and what the men around her want. But we do not know what she wants, only what happens to her. This fuzziness around sexual violence is not a failure to understand the text clearly, but rather a key feature of the narrative.[14]

The intentionality of the fuzziness around rape becomes even more persuasive when we consider what follows. David recalls Uriah from the front and tries to persuade him to sleep with his wife; Uriah refuses, insisting that he cannot enjoy this privilege while other men are still away at battle. David then tries alcohol, but Uriah continues to refuse, and sleeps at David's home rather than his own. Unable to prevail over his loyal soldier, David sends him back to the front with a letter that instructs Joab to "set Uriah in the forefront of the hardest fighting, and then draw back from him, so that he may be struck down and die" (2 Sam 11:15). Joab complies and Uriah is killed. As Perry and Sternberg draw out extensively, the episode thematizes questions of knowledge and ignorance.[15] Does Uriah know what has transpired? Does Uriah understand what David wants, and why? And does David really know what Uriah knows, or simply think he knows? Then there is the matter of the letter—does Uriah realize that David is sending him to his death? Does David correctly deduce what Uriah believes is happening? And so forth. This thematization of knowledge and ambiguity highlights the ambiguity—and fuzziness—in the prior scene with Bathsheba. Does Bathsheba recognize that she can be seen on the roof, and by whom? Does David know what Bathsheba knows? Questions beget further questions.

The Bathsheba story is also messy. There is the messiness, both figurative and literal, of the murder of Uriah, killed in cold blood. There is the messy narrative of the birth and death of David and Bathsheba's child, followed by a second replacement child. There are shades of ickiness here as well— a God who kills innocents, as well as the suggestion of the interchangeability of children, which recalls other pairs of living/dead children in the Deuteronomistic history, such as the children of the prostitutes in 1 Kings 3:16–28 and of the cannibal mothers in 2 Kings 6:24–31. Bathsheba's body also introduces another narrative level of messiness: When the story begins, she is bathing. In addition to catching David's eye, this detail has attracted the attention of commentators, who have fiercely debated its significance. One reading, advocated by Perry and Sternberg, Alter, and the translators of the New Revised Standard Version, among other readers, is that Bathsheba is washing herself following her period.[16] This detail teases a larger narrative significance: Because Bathsheba has recently had her period, she must not be pregnant at the time David sees her (and has sex with her).[17] Thus, the child conceived in the sexual encounter is inarguably David's child, a fact that David, having watched the bath and discerned its significance, would also acknowledge. This also explains David's urgency in recalling Uriah and trying to persuade him to have sex with Bathsheba, to provide a cover for the king's previous sexual activity.

But the meaning of the Hebrew phrase *wĕhî mitqaddešet miṭṭumᵓātāh*, roughly "and she was purifying herself from her uncleanliness," is not as clear as these translators suggest. The term *miṭṭumᵓāh*, "uncleanliness," is not only used for women; it appears in reference to men rendered unclean through touch (Lev 5:3, 7:21), skin disease (Lev 14:2–19), and genital discharge (Lev 15:13), swarming things (Lev 22:5), corpses (Num 19:13), and an unclean spirit (Zech 13:2). Usages involving women do not clearly differentiate between the *miṭṭumᵓāh* caused by menstruation, sex, or rape and the blood or other discharges that each may cause. Something is unclean; but it is not clear what, or why. So while it is possible, and perhaps even the simplest reading, that Bathsheba is purifying herself following menstruation, this is not the only interpretation the text sustains. And it may be too instrumentalizing, too quick to write off the messiness of both body and text. Without suggesting that the bath is a calculated attempt to catch David's eye,[18] I want to hold open a space for the ordinary.[19] I would even suggest that we hold open a space for pleasure—perhaps Bathsheba is simply enjoying the water. Perhaps she enjoys feeling it drip down her hair, over her skin. Perhaps there is a cool breeze on the rooftop. Perhaps there is even pleasure here, even if it is momentary or risky or compromised pleasure.

But pleasure or no pleasure, the story of Bathsheba is icky in multiple ways. There are the familiar ickinesses that feminist reading draws out: David acts without seeking Bathsheba's consent; Bathsheba never speaks, aside from "I'm pregnant" (*hārāh ᵓānōkî*, just two words in Hebrew); it is deeply unsettling to be observed, without your knowledge, while in the bath. There is the extreme ickiness of David ordering Uriah's murder and of Yahweh killing David's child. And there is the icky implied logic of "like father, like son," as David's actions with Bathsheba are followed, two chapters later, by his son Amnon's rape of Tamar—a repetition of trauma that suggests an uneasy logic of inevitability.

Another source of ickiness, at least for modern readers, is the way in which the text encourages us to consider Bathsheba a victim of sexual violence while also rebuffing that reading. We find ourselves in the uncomfortable position of choosing between identifying Bathsheba as a victim (and thus assuming she has no agency in what happens, and possibly denying her desires as well),[20] describing Bathsheba as the instigator and perhaps even mastermind of the liaison with David (and thus risking blaming the victim and perpetuating tropes of "she wanted it"),[21] or simply skipping over a clearly troubling biblical chapter or refusing to determine its meaning (hardly a feminist approach of "staying with the trouble."[22]) But ickiness does not excuse us from exploring the question, and so I want to consider, briefly, some of the ways that scholarship has answered it.

Is Bathsheba a Rape Victim?

There are many readings of Bathsheba that straightforwardly present the story as rape. Susanne Scholz directs attention to consent and power, two points that recur in a number of readings: "Since the power differential between the king and his subject could not possibly be greater, the woman obeys her king's command. Since her consent does not matter, his action equals rape."[23] For Scholz, the power differential renders it impossible for Bathsheba to say "no"—or, perhaps, for her "no" to be heard by David, or in the narrative. Echoing this point, many of the arguments for Bathsheba as a rape victim stress her lack of agency, as she is consistently *acted upon* by others: seen, summoned, sexually used, sent home.[24] Her vulnerability is also indicated by Bathsheba's initial nakedness, which increases the power differential between her and the (presumably clothed) man watching her.[25] Both nakedness and female beauty are typically viewed in the Hebrew Bible as signaling sexual availability: To be beautiful is to be *asking for it*. This is the case even in a manifestly innocent bath, such as Bathsheba's (a point Caryn Tamber-Rosenau draws out by contrasting Bathsheba's modest actions with Judith's flamboyantly performative and provocative ones[26]). There are also specific linguistic clues in the text that point to rape. Jennifer Andruska analyzes the syntax of the crucial verse, 2 Samuel 11:14, and finds key resemblances to other biblical accounts of rape, including the rape laws in Deuteronomy (Deut 22:25, 28) and the rape of Dinah (Gen 34:2).[27] She buttresses her reading with reference to the Bible's earliest interpreters, noting that while they fault David for his acts, they never spread the blame to Bathsheba.

In contrast, scholars who reject reading the story as coercion, exploitation, or rape often emphasize Bathsheba's agency. This argument takes a number of forms: Bathsheba and David were in love; Bathsheba went to David willingly; Bathsheba made the best of a bad situation; Bathsheba sought to seduce David to improve her own life or social standing; Bathsheba seduced David out of her own cunning or desire for power; David, not Bathsheba, was the story's real victim. Often, these arguments place significant stock in the act of Bathsheba's bathing, as well as the location of her bath, which is, according to the text, visible to David "on the roof" and thus is treated as a public or semipublic space.[28] By bathing here, the argument goes, Bathsheba sought to catch David's eye. Her near-silence in the text thus conceals not a victim but rather the mastermind behind the chapter's events. Interpreters who read Bathsheba in this way do not always criticize her for her actions. George G. Nicol describes her as a "clever and resourceful woman," praising her ability to "achiev[e] her goals."[29] Kristine Henriksen Garroway similarly describes Bathsheba as a woman who acts out of informed self-interest: "Bathsheba weighs her options and makes a daring decision for the sake of fulfilling her deepest desires. Her decision to seduce King David via a carefully timed bath thwarts both the law and the patriarchal system . . . with cunning and intention."[30] Other readers are less kind, treating Bathsheba's actions as entrapment or even representing David as the true victim.[31]

A third reading strategy attempts to chart a middle path between Bathsheba as passive victim and Bathsheba as empowered actor and initiator. Seeking to balance these possibilities, some readers turn to what I call the "strong survivor" narrative: Bathsheba was indeed a victim of David in 2 Samuel 11, but as time passes and the narrative progresses, she becomes a strong character in her own right.[32] In the Bathsheba story, we see this clearly when Bathsheba returns at the beginning of the book of Kings, first to intercede with David to secure her son Solomon's inheritance of the throne of Israel, then to nudge Solomon to dispose of his half-brother and rival, Adonijah. David J. Zucker and Moshe Reiss offer a clear iteration of this reading, calling Bathsheba in Kings "very politically astute" and "someone who knows how to make her way through the corridors of power."[33] I do not deny that Bathsheba displays political astuteness and even power in the events of 1 Kgs 1–2. But I also find in these readings a movement familiar from much contemporary advocacy against rape culture: the conversion of the victim into a survivor. Claiming the identity of "survivor" is a way of taking control of one's own story. This reading suggests that Bathsheba does the same.

Frustratingly, but in accord with what I have called the ickiness of the story, all of these readings are possible based upon the information the text itself provides. The rich ambiguity of the narrative, so often praised on literary grounds, here produces a lingering indeterminacy on matters of plot. This is further complicated by the wide-ranging questions of consent, female autonomy, and the ability to say "no," as discussed in detail in the previous chapter. As in the case of Dinah, my own feminist reading commitments and my immersion in the literature of sexual violence incline me strongly toward reading the Bathsheba story as an account of a rape. But the text itself—insistently, vexingly—does allow space for other readings. This is clearly a "rape story," in the broad sense I have used the term. But its specific negotiation of consent/coercion, sexual politics, and sex itself can be, and has been, read in multiple ways.

Raped by the Pen; or, Is Nathan a Feminist Interpreter?

Confronted with this dilemma, some feminist interpreters choose to focus their attention elsewhere: not on the story itself, but on its modes of constructing meaning and its trajectory of interpretation. J. Cheryl Exum, for example, famously describes Bathsheba as "raped by the pen," specifying that "the rape of Bathsheba is something that takes place not so much in the story as by means of the story."[34] For Exum, the real matter of concern is not what David does or does not *do*, but rather how those events are *represented* "at the hands of the androcentric biblical narrator." In her reading, Bathsheba is doubly victimized: *both* by her silencing in the narrative *and* by her treatment by commentators and interpreters, who tend to read the text in line with the androcentric and misogynistic tendencies of its narrator.[35] Bathsheba's silence is crucial to the construction of harm in the narrative. This silence allows patriarchal and misogynistic ideologies to be read onto the text: "By denying her subjectivity, the narrator symbolically rapes Bathsheba, and by withholding her point of view, he presents an ambiguous portrayal that leaves her vulnerable to the charge of seduction."[36] Thus the way the biblical text is narrated encourages (or compels) a certain mode of reading and interpreting. "Rape by the pen" is not simply an event within the narrative; it is also a process engaged in, and brought to completion, by readers and interpreters.

Exum presents Bathsheba's "rape by the pen" as a sort of gang rape, accomplished by the collusion of the androcentric narrator and his sympathetic interpreters. Though she explicitly brackets the question of David's complicity, there are suggestions that he, too, is in on it.[37] But what Exum's reading underplays is the degree to which Bathsheba's violation is already narrativized and critiqued by the text itself. In particular, the prophet Nathan makes an appearance in 2 Samuel 12 and offers a critical assessment of the situation that, to a notable degree, resembles Exum's. The prophet offers a parable in which Bathsheba is compared to a lamb:

Yahweh sent Nathan to David. He came and said to him, "There were two men in a certain city, one rich and one poor. The rich man had very many flocks of sheep and herds of cattle, but the poor man had nothing at all except for one little lamb, which he had bought. He raised it, and it grew up together with him and with his children. It would eat from his morsels of food and drink from his cup and lie in his lap, and it was like a daughter to him. A traveler came to the rich man; he was unwilling to take from his flocks or his herds to prepare for the guest who had come to him. He took the poor man's lamb and prepared it for the man who had come. (2 Sam 12:1–4)

When David reacts with anger at the rich man's unjust actions, Nathan replies that David himself is the man; as punishment, the child born to Bathsheba will die. While the specific workings of the parable are much discussed, the representation of harm at the heart of Nathan's metaphor is clearly one of predation.[38] The rich man preys on the poor man's lamb, just as David has preyed on Bathsheba. As Ken Stone writes, "a basic comparability between the woman as sexual object and the daughterly lamb as edible object is what allows Nathan's parable and oracle to make sense."[39] Like the lamb, Bathsheba is here represented as belonging to a man—in her case, Uriah the Hittite, her husband. The specific use of a lamb and not some other symbol of property reinforces the sense of Bathsheba (and of female sexuality) as prey, as even a brief canvasing of the Bible's many references to ewes and lambs makes clear.

Is Nathan a (proto-)feminist interpreter? Insofar as Nathan's parable condemns David's actions and highlights Bathsheba's innocence—a status reinforced by the associations of the lamb—it seems to do a certain kind of feminist work in the text, at least opening space for a form of feminist critique, whether or not this critique is pursued. (The representation of women as male property, and the association of female sexuality with edible animals, both pose challenges to this reading, though critical feminist animal studies offers some intriguing possibilities in framing the latter.) But if we take seriously Exum's description of the mechanisms by which Bathsheba is "raped by the pen"—and I would suggest that we should—then reading along the lines set forth by Nathan's parable should give us pause.

Here we can note a striking point of confluence between (1) Exum's "rape by the pen," (2) the conventional feminist rape/exploitation reading (*Bathsheba was raped*), and (3) the text's own metadiscursive commentary on the events, which takes the form of Nathan's address to David. All three of these interpretations represent Bathsheba as a *victim of predation*: David's sexual predation, in the case of the rape reading; misogynistic victimization by narrator and interpreters, in the case of Exum's "rape by the pen"; and literal predation, in the terms of Nathan's metaphor of stolen lambs/women. Both the rape reading and Nathan's interpretation treat David as a (sexual) predator; Exum brackets David to emphasize the predatory function of an androcentric and misogynistic narrator and textual ideology. This view of Bathsheba as victim and David as predator is further buttressed by the narrative representation of David across the books of Samuel. David is introduced with descriptors including "a man of valor and a warrior" (1 Sam 16:18); he brags to Saul about his prowess in killing lions and bears (1 Sam 17:34–36); and his first significant narrative action is to kill Goliath (1 Sam 17:48–51).[40] The account of David's rise in 1 Samuel alternates between increasingly impressive military feats (some of them, we might note, mercenary ones) and personal entanglements with the house of Saul: Merab, Michal, Jonathan, and Saul himself. These features of the David story are connected by the central metaphor of predation: Thus, Walter Brueggemann, Carolyn J. Sharp, Baruch Halpern, and the novelist Geraldine Brooks each describe David as a "predator."[41]

Notably, even those readings that defend David's actions toward Bathsheba tend to assume a basic model of sexual violence as predation. However, these readings operate in the opposite direction: By reading the sex between Bathsheba and David as consensual and/or desired, if not necessarily licit, they aim to redeem David by removing him from the category of "sexual predator." Or, in the case of Nicol's "cunning woman" or Garroway's "daring decision for the sake of fulfilling her deepest desires," the roles are flipped, with Bathsheba cast as the active initiator—an implicitly predatory role, though not one for which she is condemned by Nicol and Garroway.[42] In both cases, the harm that Bathsheba experiences is neatly written out of existence: If David does not prey on Bathsheba, then Bathsheba must not experience harm. But this reading, too, is limiting: It does not allow a space to consider harm beyond the harm of being *preyed upon*.

Thus, upon surveying the breadth of readings of sexual violence in 2 Samuel 11–12, we find, overwhelmingly, the structure of predation. The text represents David as predatory, both in Nathan's speech and in many of the other key narrative events in the David story. Readers who understand 2 Samuel 11 as a story of rape treat David as predator, Bathsheba as victim, and the sexual encounter as one of predation and exploitation. Defenders of David reject the specific description of David as predator, either arguing for consensual sex (thus, no predation) or placing Bathsheba, not David, in the predatory role. However, they do not challenge the general model of rape/ sexual exploitation as a predator/prey paradigm. Similarly, to treat Bathsheba as "survivor" is to reframe the narrative as an account of Bathsheba's transformation from victim to active and empowered subject—that is, from prey to non-prey. And a reading such as Exum's that emphasizes the ideology of the text still assumes predation, but on behalf of text, author, and/or readers, rather than characters. Yet, in the face of such overwhelming agreement, we would do well to be suspicious. In particular, if we take seriously the androcentric and misogynistic orientation of the text—as we should—then a feminist reading built on the text's own ideological foundations (sexual violence = predation) should raise questions. As Exum herself writes, feminist reading "can only be done . . . by stepping outside the androcentric ideology of the biblical text."[43] This extends, I suggest, to stepping outside of the ideology of predation.

Predation is a flawed model, one that limits our ability to perceive harm, including the harms of sexual violence and rape culture. I will suggest that *any* reading of the story that frames sexual violence in terms of predation, let alone women as beloved and violated lambs, should give us pause. My argument is not with the animal as a category—there is a great deal of useful feminist work being done in and with the discipline of animal studies—but rather with the specific language of predation that the animal metaphor here entails. Pushing a bit further, I want to resist a model of sexual harm as sexual predation in the text. I resist for several reasons, which I detail here.

From Predation to Peremption

Predation offers a basically static model of the harm of sexual violence. As its central metaphor, which is borrowed from the animal kingdom, suggests, there are clearly distinguished "types" of people; these include predators and prey—or, in language more familiar from sexual violence, "perpetrators" (or "offenders") and "victims." While not every potential victim becomes a victim, the possibility is always close at hand. In this model, identities do not change; they are, instead, consistent and characterological: "once a predator, always a predator," or, as Nietzsche writes in a well-known passage from *On the Genealogy of Morals*,

That lambs dislike great birds of prey does not seem strange: only it gives not ground for reproaching these birds of prey for bearing off little lambs . . . To demand of strength that it should *not* express itself as strength, that it should *not* be a desire to overcome, a desire to throw down, a desire to become master, a thirst for enemies and resistances and triumphs, is just as absurd as to demand of weakness that it should express itself as strength.[44]

As in Nietzsche's extended metaphor, there are also clear differences between predators and those they prey upon; the victims of predation are constructed as simultaneously innocent, threatened, and tempting.[45] In the case of sexual violence, this means a model of lurking potential rapists and unwitting, inviting, and always-already-threatened victims—not unlike the opening sequence of any film or television episode in which a woman enters an empty parking garage or walks home alone at night. The framework of predation also makes a strong case for acts (and indeed potential or interrupted acts) as identities: here, the rapacious, sexually predatory king and the innocent bathing woman.

But this representation of sexual harm, though it offers a clear plot and characters, is both flattening and ideologically suspect from a feminist perspective. While predation directs attention to David as an *agent* of harm in the text, it has the effect of rendering the *object* of predation (here, Bathsheba) a passive victim and an acted-upon object. Like the poor man's lamb to whom she is compared, Bathsheba's fate is understood to lie in the hands of others. She becomes someone to whom others do things: either victimized, in the case of David/the rich man, or simply possessed (and ostensibly protected), in the case of Uriah/the poor man. There is no space for her identity to expand beyond the way it is framed in the logic of predation. Often, victims and survivors of sexual violence speak about the experience of being subsumed by the category of the "victim."[46] Others describe the way the category seems to exclude their own experiences. Both of these problems associated with the category of the victim/survivor are particularly a risk, I suggest, in models of sexual violence that emphasize predation and preyed-upon victims.

Beyond the representation of victims and perpetrators—or of Bathsheba and David—a model of predation limits the forms of harm we are able to see in the text. If you have a hammer, everything looks like a nail; if you have hermeneutics of predation, every form of sexual harm looks like being preyed upon. But this neglects other forms of harm, including limitations on sexual flourishing, the limiting of autonomy, and the foreclosing of possibility. While the model of predation seeks to protect victims, it ends up impoverishing them.

Instead of predation, I will turn to *peremption* as a richer description of the harm in the Bathsheba story, and indeed beyond it. I adopt this term, and its uses in describing sexual harm beyond consent and victims, from Fischel and his book *Sex and Harm in the Age of Consent*. Fischel's specific concern is with the sociological and legal fictions that sustain our own contemporary discourses about sexual violence and, insofar as they place limits on our ways of understanding harm, limit our ability to address or respond to it in new feminist ways. As his title suggests, "consent" is one such fiction that is called upon to uphold the sexual order. Consent is itself predicated on (or, in Fischel's language, "subtended by") other fictions, including the child, the sex offender, and the good homosexual.[47] The problem with these fictions is not their fictiveness so much as the ways that they overvalue consent, while also rendering it impossible to perceive other forms of harm.[48] (Here, I use "fiction" not in the sense of something false—"fiction" as opposed to "truth"—but rather to mean something *invented*, as from the Latin *fingere*, to invent or contrive.)

In response, Fischel offers two proposals that can be made to speak, as well, to biblical narrative. The first involves reconfiguring how we view adolescent sexuality: Fischel suggests focusing on "a desiring, volitional subject" rather than "an always endangered, passive one."[49] Second, Fischel rejects predation as a model for the sexual harm that children, adolescents, and other legally incompetent subjects face, offering instead *peremption*, a term he describes as

> denotative of sexual harms irreducible to predation, that is, irreducible to the sex offenses committed by the legal fiction of the sex offender. I define peremption as *the uncontrolled disqualification of possibility*; for my purposes, I want to move our attention to the peremptory narrowing of *sexual* possibility. Peremption names a set of conditions that restrictively channel young people's desires, that disable young people not simply from achieving their interests but also from developing them.[50]

Peremption limits our futures, rendering some possibilities impossible before they can even begin. When people are perempted, their sexual futures are limited, without explanation. They experience forms of harm that cannot simply be explained as *being preyed upon*. This more expansive framework emphasizes that "relations, rather than bad persons," are often the source of harm, as they "constrain . . . and disqualify possibilities for more successful, less damaged modes of intimacy."[51]

Peremption does not require "a doer behind the deed"; it can also describe "the force of a norm or the collateral of enculturation."[52] Thus we can speak of peremption without assuming a contemporary idea of the subject, which is then anachronistically retrojected into the biblical text. Furthermore, because peremption is a framework specifically developed to describe sexual harms experienced by a category of persons who cannot legally consent to sex (adolescents), it is easily adapted to fit another such category (biblical women). The question "Could a woman say 'no' in ancient Israel?", discussed in detail in the previous chapter, no longer hamstrings our ability to describe sexual harm in the text, because harm is no longer limited to either predation (the focus of this chapter) or the violation of consent (the focus of the previous chapter). And it allows us to explore forms of harm in the text without first determining unambiguously whether or not Bathsheba is a "victim"—because the scope of harm is not limited to being preyed upon or victimized. More than anything, peremption allows us a fuller, richer picture of harm. The goal of this intervention is to empower subjects and to qualify a wider range of possibilities for sex and intimacy.

But how do we move from models of predation to models of peremption? One step is to change how we focalize sexual stories and assess sexual harm. Fischel undertakes this work through close readings of three films that offer alternate portrayals of the "gendered adolescent."[53] Reflecting on the questions that these films surface, Fischel writes,

> If instead the law asks not *what will young people accede*, but *what do young people want*, it acknowledges agency, hedging against the sexualizing of socially imagined childhood innocence or blankness the law had previously codified.[54]

So too do I want to ask not *what does Bathsheba accede*, but *what might Bathsheba want*. This, in turn, opens onto how we might consider harm beyond framing Bathsheba as a passive violated victim.

Perempted by Narrative in *Doubt* and the Bathsheba Story

Exploring the question *What might Bathsheba want?* presumes an understanding of how she is perempted. The first form of peremption in the

Bathsheba story is peremption by narrative. Throughout this chapter, I have emphasized the importance of how we narrate stories, including stories of sexual violence. Peremption by narrative describes the compulsory structuring of stories surrounding an event, scene, or experience. Fischel describes peremption by narrative as resembling "the discursive structures and compulsory affect of a sex scandal."[55] Rape stories, too, are narrated with compulsory structures and affects. These structures, moreover, are peremptory: They are imposed without explanation or justification; they are not able to be questioned.

Fischel builds his description of peremption by narrative around a reading of the film *Doubt* (2008). Based on John Patrick Shanley's play *Doubt: A Parable*, the film centers on a charismatic priest, Father Flynn, who develops a close relationship with a young Black student named Donald (the first Black student admitted to the all-White school; the film is set in 1964).[56] The school's principal is the steely Sister Aloysius. Following a report from an eighth-grade teacher, Sister James, Sister Aloysius becomes concerned that Flynn is pursuing an inappropriate relationship with Donald. A power struggle ensues; eventually, the priest is promoted and transferred to another school. The question of what, if anything, happened between the priest and Donald is never resolved: Is Father Flynn a pedophile? a mentor? a sympathetic closeted gay man mentoring a young closeted gay teenager? some mixture thereof? something else? The questions surrounding the priest also touch on another set of questions involving Donald's possible queerness or gayness, which the film hints at but never confirms. (The closest confirmation comes in a conversation between Sister Aloysius and Donald's mother, in which as much is left unsaid as said aloud.)

As the question of Father Flynn's guilt (and the attendant "doubt" of the title) becomes increasingly central, Donald himself recedes more and more. Indeed, as Fischel points out, the "'did he or didn't he' binary plot" (a phrase equally well suited to describe 2 Sam 11–12) actually distances us from Donald, the purported victim:

> [W]e are ultimately twice removed from the protogay child and his desire for anything: sex, love, support, whatever. Donald is perempted by narrative, by the discursive structure and compulsory affect of a sex scandal. He and his sexual possibilities are disqualified because he is a pretextual prop, and the pretext of his abuse effaces any deeper inquiry into the conditions and constraints of his sexuality.[57]

Such peremption by narrative offers a powerful way of framing harm that also redirects our attention to the otherwise elided Donald. The boy never appears in the play; in the film, he is on screen for only about five minutes. (This is not so different from Bathsheba, who appears only briefly, even in the biblical chapters that are ostensibly about her.) It is Father Flynn, like David, who draws all the air in the room, who becomes the focus of interpretive debates. But as a consequence, Donald is perempted. The story that is told about him is a story that is narrated without attention to how he, the purported victim, experienced it; furthermore, his feelings and desires *now* are silenced or ignored, the better to follow the contours of "the discursive structure and compulsory affect of a sex scandal."[58]

Donald, moreover, is prevented from flourishing. As Fischel teases out, the film hints at his (proto-)gayness or (proto-)queerness, without, however, ever fully allowing it to emerge. Donald's mother, Mrs. Miller, comes closest to naming this feature of her son's experience, but the narrative she attempts to set forth is forcibly overridden by Sister Aloysius, who vocally and affectively rejects Mrs. Miller's attempts to speak. Furthermore, the film does not allow space to tease apart questions of Donald's sexuality, whether stable, emerging, or in flux, from questions of the harm he may have experienced. Or in the terms of this book, Donald is not allowed to be fuzzy, messy, or icky: instead, he is reduced to an instrumentalized object, a point of cathexis for the desires of others and a tool for catalyzing judgments against a powerful, charismatic man, who is apparently favored by God.

Bathsheba has a greater narrative presence than the almost-absent Donald, but she too is forced into the shapes of a compulsory narrative. Aside from the inconvenient fact of her pregnancy, Bathsheba begins to disappear from the text almost from the moment she enters it. In Nathan's narration, which functions much like Sister Aloysius's in *Doubt*—that is, it advances the dominant narrativizing of the events, along with their interpretation—she is reduced to a mute animal. David, meanwhile, achieves the more authoritative position in Nathan's parable, even as he is the object of its condemnation/correction. But to be corrected is also to be the focus of the narrative script; the aim of this correction, moreover, is David's future flourishing, which the birth of the second child confirms. As the significance of the incident is narrated in relation to David, Bathsheba is further perempted, the harm of the initial encounter amplified by her disappearance from the narrative following the birth of the second child, which signals David's renewed approval in the eyes of Yahweh.

Bathsheba's relative and persistent silence across the narrative also signals her peremption. Her failure to speak is crucial to understanding the forms of harm in the text—and not simply because we as readers never hear her say "yes" to David. Instead, Bathsheba's silence connects to her larger *silencing* in the narrative. Aside from "I'm pregnant," she never speaks in 2 Samuel 11 or 12. We do not know how she feels, what she wishes, whether she is afraid. Even the death of the child is framed entirely through David's response, with no reference to Bathsheba. 2 Samuel 12:24 reassures the reader that "David comforted his wife Bathsheba"—but *why she is comforted* remains absent from the text. Attending to stickiness, especially the stickiness of anger and grief, we would do well to note that Bathsheba's own response is missing here—as, indeed, it is a chapter prior, when David has Uriah murdered in battle. The report there, too, is opaque, and again oriented toward David: "When the wife of Uriah heard that her husband was dead, she made lamentation for him. When the mourning was over, David sent and brought her to his house" (2 Sam 11:26–27a).

The silencing of Bathsheba extends to the silencing of her future narrative, beyond the minimum necessary for the text's masculine reproductive and dynastic politics. We do not receive an account of what happens to her after the birth of Solomon; instead, she disappears entirely until it is time for her to reappear and help install him as David's heir, many years later. There is, presumably, a foreclosing of possibility for Bathsheba as she joins the royal household, though even this foreclosure goes unremarked upon. But this narrowing of the horizon of possibility itself represents another form of peremption in the text. Like Exum's "rape by the pen," such narrative peremption limits our ability to see Bathsheba, or to imagine a space of possibility beyond that which the text itself exhibits. Instead, our narrative attentions are redirected to David, and to the narrative logic of the David story. At best, Bathsheba becomes a kind of ancient Israelite "Manic Pixie Dream Girl," the woman whose luminous, quirky presence attracts the attention of the male protagonist and whose relationship with him ultimately transforms him.[59] This is the role Bathsheba plays in many film versions—transformative love object.[60] At worst, Bathsheba becomes either the scheming seductress or the innocent victim who leads to the protagonist's undoing—note the unfolding tragedy of the house of David that consumes the remainder of 2 Samuel.

Like Donald, Bathsheba is perempted by the events into which she is drawn; they overshadow and encompass her. Both David's woman and

Father Flynn's altar boy are perempted in their own stories, unable to flourish. There is some ambiguity surrounding the initial harm in each story—was Bathsheba raped? was Donald preyed upon?—but the structures of narration refuse our attempts to linger with these moments, to explore how they might be read or experienced. Instead, the question of "what happened" is forced into the shape of a "sex scandal," and narrated accordingly. The force of norms weighs heavily on both Donald and Bathsheba, precluding an ability to think seriously about the forms of sexual harm, the structuring of interests, and the foreclosure of flourishing that each text presents.

Perempted by Masculinity: David and "David's Women"

A second form of peremption across the books of Samuel and Kings involves *peremption by masculinity*. More specifically, the so-called David story presents a remarkably rich account of masculinity, its complexities, internal contradictions, and ongoing negotiations. But this comes at the expense of Bathsheba, and of the representation of women more broadly. Nor is this secondary to the text. Instead, the peremption of female characters, Bathsheba foremost among them, is a strategy in the narrative's efforts to reconceive of masculinity in and around the character of David. But the complexity of David's masculine performance across the books of Samuel and Kings comes at the expense of the women in his orbit—including Bathsheba.

Masculinity in the David story has been much discussed by scholars; indeed, David was an early focal point for masculinity-oriented approaches to biblical texts.[61] Early work in this area emphasized David as a masculine paradigm, associating Yahweh's favored king with what the sociology of masculinity terms "hegemonic masculinity." I am increasingly unpersuaded that David represents any sort of ideal or paradigmatic masculinity, or that we can describe a stable mode of hegemonic masculinity in the biblical texts.[62] I do think that masculinity plays a crucial, if unstable, role throughout the David story and is frequently contested and renegotiated between men—most centrally David, Saul, Jonathan, and Absalom, but also figures such as Samuel, Nathan, Joab, and Uriah.[63] David's masculinity is also articulated through and against Yahweh, whose masculine performance is pronounced and perhaps even hegemonic in these texts. Interestingly, as queer scholarship has drawn out, the David story holds open space for homosociality and perhaps even queer desire: between David and Jonathan, between David and Saul, even (or especially) between David and Yahweh.[64]

But homosociality and even homoeroticism do not preclude either misogyny or homophobia. To the contrary: Homosociality can in fact sustain certain forms of both misogyny and homophobia. Similarly, homophobic violence is frequently facilitated by homosocial bonding (consider the many fraternity hazing scandals, or the biblical narratives of Gen 19 and Judg 19) or other modes of fraught eroticism and fear. In the David story, David's persistent homosocial entanglements with other men coexist with and even draw sustenance from his relations with women. Thus masculinity becomes a mode of peremption: Homosociality and masculine exceptionalism, which occur throughout the David story, come at the expense of female flourishing. The very emphasis of the narrative on masculinity, and on masculinity as negotiated between men (and male characters such as Yahweh), presents a second mode of peremption in the text. In the case of 2 Samuel 11–12, the Bathsheba story quickly transitions from a scene of fleeting encounter between David and Bathsheba to a series of negotiations between David and other men: first Uriah, then Joab, then Nathan (and Yahweh as mediated through Nathan), then David's sons: first a dying child, then a living one. David's relations with Bathsheba, with the exception of the sex/rape itself, are mediated through other men. There are no other named female characters; there do not even seem to be any other women present. Often, paintings of the bathing scene add a maid, perhaps seeking, if unconsciously, to redress the striking gender imbalance of the text.

The peremption by masculinity that this scene reflects resonates with other modes of peremption by masculinity across the David story. Bathsheba's story is an imperfect repetition of Michal's; it likewise anticipates Tamar's. Merab stands further behind Michal; Abigail and Abishag also populate the text's horizons. Saul uses his daughters in an attempt to entrap David (1 Sam 18:17–28). Michal, David's wife and Jonathan's sister, is represented as inferior to Jonathan; after Jonathan's death and David's victory, she attempts to intervene in David's intimacy with Yahweh (expressed through his scantily clad dancing) and is punished with infertility (2 Sam 6:16–23). Bathsheba and Tamar are subjected to sexual harm, only to be silenced and elided from the narrative, as we have seen in this chapter and the previous one. Thus, throughout the text, masculinity is negotiated *between men*.[65] All of David's significant actions across the David story, meanwhile, are with other men: Yahweh first among them, though also Saul, Jonathan, Joab, Nathan, Uriah, Absalom, even Mephibosheth.

Sometimes, these readings of David go so far as to assimilate David to the contemporary categories of "homosexuality" or "bisexuality"; other readings caution against imposing modern sexuality on the ancient, while nevertheless holding open a space for alternate forms of eroticism and relationality between men. But whether we read David and Jonathan as queer lovers or warrior pals, whether we describe David as a "cock collector," a male "beloved," or a man with close male relationships (that need not be understood as erotic), all of these approaches suggest a privileging of masculine relations.[66] But this closeness comes at the expense of women. Sometimes, the women are simply absent, as when David and Saul achieve their moments of greatest intimacy: first in a cave, then in a military camp (1 Sam 24, 26). At the other extreme, women are treated with active harshness: Michal is punished with infertility for objecting to the intimate exposure of David's dancing before Yahweh (2 Sam 6:23). Still other women are set aside: Michal's older sister Merab enters the text as a possible wife for David, before disappearing from it; Abishag warms David's bed until his death, then becomes ensnared in royal intrigue as a potential marriage object for Adonijah, David's son and Solomon's rival.

In all of these instances, female characters are instrumentalized to advance the performance of masculinity. Relationships between men are privileged, while women are reduced to object status. Homosociality is intensified. Not only is Bathsheba "perempted by narrative," as discussed above, but her peremption also serves a larger narrative focus on complex representations of masculinity—representations that come, however, at the expense of women. David's negotiations with Uriah, in particular, reflect an intensity and an intimacy—Uriah will sleep nowhere but at David's house—that hints at a kind of s/m game, or at least a degree of obsession. The murder of Uriah brings this intimacy to an end, but it, too, is executed in a manner that cannot but highlight other entanglements and secrets passed between men, including Joab, David, and, until his death, Uriah himself.

What Does Bathsheba Want?

The text of 2 Samuel perempts Bathsheba in multiple ways. She is perempted by narrative, as the opportunity to narrate her own experience is denied to her, her experience pushed aside by Nathan's compulsory and divinely supported reading. And she is perempted by masculinity, as indeed are the other women of the David story. She is even possibly perempted by ethnicity: While Bathsheba's ethnic identity goes unmentioned, her husband Uriah is a Hittite, a fact the text mentions four times; it is possible that some sense of this ethnic otherness attaches to Bathsheba as well. After all, foreignness is sometimes a "sticky" category in the Hebrew Bible—thus the many prohibitions on sexual contact with foreigners, who, nevertheless, prove frequently irresistible to the Israelites.[67] Bathsheba is also associated with Tamar (Gen 38), Rahab, and Ruth in the gospel of Matthew, suggesting again a sense of her character as a foreign woman.[68] Insofar as there are strong narrative and affective norms surrounding foreignness, especially foreignness as it intersects with sexuality, Bathsheba threatens to be perempted by ethnicity as well.

Bathsheba is indeed perempted—but reading against her peremption, *What does Bathsheba want?* This is not a question that the text invites. As I have already drawn out, a curious opacity surrounds the textual representation of Bathsheba, striking even against the generally laconic style of biblical narrative. We know what David wants (first Bathsheba, then for Uriah to sleep with Bathsheba, then, finally, a resolution to the situation, even if it requires contract killing). We know what Yahweh wants: Nathan communicates this clearly enough. We can infer at least some of what Uriah wants, from his actions and his words. And even a relatively secondary figure such as Joab is fleshed out with a certain degree of indirect characterization.[69] In the Susanna story, clearly modeled on Bathsheba, we are given a stronger sense of the desires and anxieties that animate the bathing woman at the narrative's center. And artistic, cinematic, and literary representations of Bathsheba (and Susanna) consistently work to fill in this lacuna. But the biblical text gives us almost nothing. Perhaps it is unsurprising that Adele Berlin describes her as "a complete non-person . . . not even a minor character, but simply part of the plot."[70]

But look more closely. There are flickers of agency in the initial story in 2 Samuel 11:2–5. In narrating David's actions toward Bathsheba, a string of masculine verbs is interrupted by a single feminine one: David sent messengers and took her; *she came to him (wattābô' 'ēlāyw)*, and he lay with her (2 Sam 11:4, emphasis added). While I resist reading this as proof of Bathsheba's acquiescence or consent, for reasons I have already detailed earlier in this chapter, it is nevertheless equally important, for political and feminist reasons, to avoid glossing over this detail entirely. Perhaps what is signaled here is not consent but rather the need for a more robust and nuanced way of thinking about consent, coercion, forms of unfreedom, and ambiguity. After Bathsheba has come, and David has "lain with" (or, more likely, raped) her, two verses follow in which Bathsheba remains the actor: "She was purifying herself from her uncleanness. She returned to her house. The woman became pregnant. She sent and told David, 'I'm pregnant'" (2 Sam 11:2–5). Bathsheba's name disappears through this sequence of events; she is reduced to "the woman" or not referred to at all.[71] This can be taken to suggest the eclipse of Bathsheba as a person, and the erasure of her agency. But we might also consider, and counterbalance, the importance of her acting at all, even (or especially) in conditions of harm, violation, and vulnerability. Instead of viewing Bathsheba as *acceding to David's* predation or advances, what if we seek the hints of her acting to pursue what she might want, even in this situation of forced sex, coerced consent, instrumentalization, and objectification?

I have already described the tendency among some interpreters to suggest Bathsheba "wanted it"—that is, to read her as an empowered agent or even initiator; hence Nicol's "cunning woman" and Garroway's postfeminist "Bridget Jones." While I find these readings somewhat clumsy, too quick to gloss over the clear signs of exploitation and coercion in the text, they do undertake something important, insofar as they insist on the possibility of Bathsheba as a subject, a being with *wants*, and not simply an object. Thus, they ask the question I ask here—*What does Bathsheba want?*—though they answer it very differently. In seeking to represent this tricky balance of wanting and unwanted sex, of consent and rape and narrative peremption, I want to turn to Sara Maitland's short story "Siren Song," in which the Sirens recall the rape of Persephone and their own anger and sadness. At first, they are shocked to learn that Persephone, forcibly abducted by Hades, has willingly eaten the pomegranate seeds he offers:

> In our naïveté, we thought that to consent, to eat, to live rather than to die, meant that she had chosen. Now we know that sometimes, when there is no choice, when there is nothing that will change how the humiliation is then it is sometimes necessary to consent because that is the one, the only, thing that you can do; that you must do to be other than victim, to be yourself. That is a real thing and the worst thing.[72]

While Fischel's charting of peremption emphasizes a space of possibility, Maitland's Sirens hint at its flip side: a painful space, one that nevertheless also contains a space of possibility. Choice, however constrained or

epistemologically false, offers one way of imagining an alternative to predation. To choose peremption is also to name it, as well as to gesture beyond it.

Bathsheba and Abishag

Bathsheba's story does not end when she disappears from the text after the
birth of Solomon. Instead, she appears in two important scenes in 1 Kings,
both of which involve the future of Israel following the death of David.
In the first scene, Bathsheba appeals to David to appoint her son with
him, Solomon, as his successor, against efforts by another of David's sons,
Adonijah. Bathsheba's appeal is largely orchestrated by the prophet Nathan,
again positioned as an uneasy third in the relationship between Bathsheba
and David. The scheme is successful; David promises the throne to Solomon.
Bathsheba's second appearance comes a chapter later, when Solomon has
achieved the throne. This time she appears at the bequest of none other
than Adonijah, who asks her to petition Solomon on his behalf. His aim is
to marry Abishag the Shunammite, a young woman introduced previously
in the narrative as David's bed-warmer in his old age. Bathsheba complies.
As in the scene with David and Uriah in 2 Samuel 11, the scene is charged
with questions of who knows what and who believes what about whom. It is
not clear from the text whether Adonijah's is a sincere request, motivated by
desire or love, or whether he perceives marrying Abishag as staking a claim
to the throne. It is equally unclear what Bathsheba believes or intends: Does
she communicate the request in good faith with Adonijah, or with malice,
knowing that the request may well hasten his demise? Solomon's actions, in
any case, are unambiguous: Like his father confronted with the seemingly in-
tractable problem of Uriah, he has his rival killed.

The clear parallels between the scene involving Solomon, Bathsheba, and
Adonijah and the earlier scene with David and Uriah are compelling. They
show, in particular, the degree to which Bathsheba's character has shifted: no
longer a silent, sidelined object (a role now allocated to Abishag) but an actor
in her own right. David J. Zucker and Moshe Reiss write:

> The mature woman presented in Kings is very politically astute . . . The
> Bathsheba of the book of Kings is someone who knows how to make her
> way through the corridors of power. She clearly has friends, and knows how
> to influence events.[73]

This reading is not universally accepted: Exum, to take one strong counterexample, reads Bathsheba's actions here as a continuation of her exploitation by men. She goes so far as to suggest that

> Bathsheba is metaphorically raped again in these chapters . . . though she has a voice this time around, there is a real question whether or not she has a voice of her own. Nathan's words, then Adonijah's, are placed in her mouth.[74]

But while I follow Exum in finding gendered harm in this passage, I am not so convinced that Bathsheba remains innocent of it. Instead, it seems to me that Bathsheba the perempted has now become peremptor. And it is Abishag, instead, who occupies the space of peremption.

Pause and consider Abishag the Shunammite. She enters the narrative when David, an old man, is unable to warm himself:

> His servants said to him, Let a virgin girl be sought for my lord the king, and let her wait on him and be his attendant;[75] let her lie in your lap,[76] so that my lord the king might be warm. They searched for a beautiful girl through all the territory of Israel, and they found Abishag the Shunammite, and they brought her to the king. The girl was very beautiful. She became the king's attendant and she served him, but the king did not know her sexually. (1 Kgs 1:2–4)

While the text is careful to specify that David does not engage in sex with Abishag, she is perempted in the narrative all the same. The absence of rape or sexual exploitation—of *predation*—does not undo Abishag's *peremption* in being brought to warm the king's bed. Nor does it protect her from Adonijah's desire to marry her (whether genuine or otherwise) or the ways in which Bathsheba and Solomon weaponize this desire as a means of neutralizing the threat Adonijah poses as a rival and securing Solomon's political authority. There is clearly a threat to Abishag, whether of rape (or rape-by-marriage) with Adonijah, or of neglect, which seems to be her fate after her would-be husband is killed.[77] Here, Absalom's actions toward David's concubines in 2 Samuel 16:21–22 pose a chilling parallel. As part of his power struggle with his father over the throne, "They pitched a tent for Absalom on the roof. Absalom raped[78] his father's concubines in the eyes of all Israel" (2 Sam 16:22). This action is widely interpreted as a power play: By sexually dominating his father's women, Absalom asserts his dominance over his father as well. Of course, the women's consent is not sought, just as their welfare is not considered. And after Absalom's revolt fails and he dies, the concubines are imprisoned and guarded: "They were shut up until the day of their death, living as if in widowhood" (2 Sam 20:3). Though the fate of Abishag is not attended to by the book of Kings, this story of the concubines perhaps provides a hint. Thus while 1 Kings 2 still describes the sexual use of women to assert male power and adjudicate male relationships—a common feature of peremption by masculinity in the David story—Bathsheba is now on the other side. What lies at the heart of the story in 1 Kings 2 is the sexual use of women to assert male power and adjudicate male relationships. This final episode complicates a simple reading of Bathsheba as victim—a reading that, perhaps, was too simple all along.

It is tempting, at this juncture, to set Bathsheba aside and to turn instead to Abishag, who presents a clear example of peremption without the complications of sliding into the position of perpetrator (or, read more generously, unintended agent of harm). But to read in this way is to resist and refuse the complexity that the peremption model offers and the predation model does not. The problem is not that Bathsheba is not a "good victim" or a "good survivor," or even that she lacks an appropriate sense of solidarity. Nor does Bathsheba's apparent agency in 1 Kings 1 and 2 argue against her peremption in the earlier scenes. The problem lies, instead, with a too-narrow concept of victims/survivors that neglects *both* the lived experiences of sexual violence (what I have been calling throughout this book the fuzzy, messy, and icky) *and* the ways that sexual harm plays out, beyond binaries of predation/nonpredation. To have experienced sexual harm does not mean that you are unable to inflict harm upon others; furthermore, those who commit acts of sexual violence (and other forms of violence) are often victims of it themselves. Or even more simply: Victims are often also perpetrators; perpetrators are also victims.

Peremption holds space for this kind of complexity in reading sexual violence, just as it allows us to explore forms of harm without forcing the experiences of victims and survivors into a narrowly scripted box. It accommodates fuzziness, messiness, and ickiness without allowing them to disqualify forms of harm that do exceed, overflow, or fail to meet the thresholds and limits established by traditional models, which figure sexual harm as predation and "victims" and "perpetrators" as stable categories. Peremption may limit the future for the perempted individual, but it does not perempt further peremptions. I do not introduce these voices here to suggest that either Bathsheba or Abishag is somehow culpable in the events that ensnare them. Nor is this a call for sympathy for perpetrators. But what these insights summon us to is a movement beyond a simple logic of culpability, in favor of complexity. They urge us to trace the harms of peremption, over and beyond those of predation. And they ask us to confront the possibility of *desire* and of *wanting subjects*, even in the face of suffering and exploitation.

Peremption, unlike predation, does not depend upon the passivity, purity, or innocence of the victim/survivor in order to perceive harm. And harm is not limited to the narrowly described scene of exploitation or violation. Instead, peremption allows us to link the specific moment of sexual violence—or even a specific moment of consensual sex (or semi-consent or some other fuzziness/messiness/ickiness)—to other harms. Peremption describes the way specific experiences, including Bathsheba's in 2 Samuel 11:2–5, are forced into the compulsory shape of narratives, even as these shapes do not always fit what has happened. And peremption speaks, as well, to the question of futurity: Harm can also come through the precluding or preventing of possibility. Peremption further allows us to consider Bathsheba as a victim/survivor of sexual harm without either glossing over the stubborn ambiguity of the biblical narrative or neglecting Bathsheba's own turn against Abishag.

We do not need to apply a contemporary standard of consent to biblical stories to perceive the ways they limit freedom, inflict harm, perpetuate misogyny, mistreat female (and male) bodies, or foreclose possible futures. Instead, we need only the texts themselves, as well as flexible models for harm.

4

Rape and Other Ways of Reading

Hagar and Sarah in the Company of Women

In a now-classic essay entitled "Fighting Bodies, Fighting Words: A Theory and Politics of Rape Prevention," feminist theorist Sharon Marcus describes the gendered grammar of sexual violence. Rejecting the dominant practices of "rape prevention,"[1] Marcus begins by asserting that language is funda-mental both to understanding and to countering rape:

> A feminist politics which would fight rape cannot exist without developing a language about rape, nor, I will argue, without understanding rape as a language . . . I propose that we understand rape as a language and use this insight to imagine women as neither already raped nor inherently rapable. I will argue against the political efficacy of seeing rape as the fixed reality of women's lives, against an identity politics which defines women by our vio-lability, and for a shift of scene from rape and its aftermath to rape situations themselves and to rape prevention.[2]

A key part of this argument is understanding the "gendered grammar of vi-olence" that characterizes the "language of rape."[3] This grammar asserts that rape involves male subjects and female objects; it is something that the former does to the latter. As Marcus explains, the system functions by "assign[ing] people to positions within a script" and then associating those positions with specific gendered identities (regardless of the actual gender of perpetrator and/or victim). More precisely, "the gendered grammar of vio-lence predicates men as the objects of violence and the operators of its tools, and predicates women as the objects of violence and the subjects of fear."[4] Rape thus constitutes its victims, whatever their gender, as female; female-ness is further associated with fearfulness, woundedness, and vulnerability to sexual assault.

Importantly, the "gendered grammar of violence" is not limited to po-tential or actual sexual violence, but contaminates, as well, efforts either to

Texts after Terror. Rhiannon Graybill, Oxford University Press. © Oxford University Press 2021.
DOI: 10.1093/oso/9780190082314.003.0005

prevent rape or to respond to it after it has occurred. It is not only Marcus who has described this grammar or its effects. Rachel Hall, for example, has documented the ways that rape prevention efforts treat women as potential victims and always already rapable.[5] And Jennifer Doyle has explored the ways that responses to rape (whether administrative, disciplinary, legal, or ameliorative) take for granted the gendered grammar of rape. Writing in particular about the Title IX hearing process, used to adjudicate sexual violence in U.S. colleges and universities, Doyle observes,

> She, her—I repeat: she is, within this discourse, always female. Her own discourse is dangerous: her story about her own injury is a problem. Within the system the victim is a wound, but a bloodless one. The victim cannot know the truth of the situation . . . She should not speak it.[6]

Thus even ameliorative responses to sexual violence rely upon, and reinforce, the same gendered grammar as rape itself. This grammar positions the female victim ("she is, within this discourse, always female") as simultaneously injured and unable to speak of her injury. The woman/victim—these two identities are treated as interchangeable—cannot speak; she merely signals the existence of sexual violence.

There are many reasons to push back against the gendered grammar of rape. It is both sexist (in its representations of men and women) and heterosexist (in its presumption that sexual violence is something a man does to a woman).[7] It presents rape as inevitable and even natural (in this way, it functions similarly to the "predator" model of sexual violence critiqued in chapter 3). Marcus even suggests that this way of framing sexual violence actually encourages rape: "The language of rape solicits women to position ourselves as endangered, violable, and fearful and invites men to position themselves as legitimately violent and entitled to women's sexual services."[8] The gendered grammar of rape thus not only encourages sexual violence but also alters the ways that the very categories of "women" and "men" are socially constructed and experienced. I take seriously these critiques, and they inform my efforts to read rape stories differently. In this chapter, my focus is on resisting the claim that *rape is fundamentally about male subjects and female objects.* I resist this claim *from the perspective of the "female objects"*—that is, as they (we) relate to each other.[9] I will argue that relationships between women need not—and *should not*—be subordinated or treated as secondary when we read stories of sexual violence and rape. To the contrary: Female relationships are often an essential part of the larger narrative world of the rape story. These relationships may take multiple forms: friendship, sisterhood, or other forms of companionship or solidarity. Or they may be characterized by disgust, resentment, or even hatred. What matters is the entanglement of female lives and stories, shot through with intimacy and power.

The Hebrew Bible offers only a handful of stories from which an inquiry of this sort can be launched. There may be many rape stories in the biblical text, but only a few in which women interact with other women. The clearest examples are the stories describing the sexual and reproductive use of slaves. These biblical slaves or handmaids[10] include Hagar in Genesis 16 and Bilhah and Zilpah in Genesis 30. From one perspective, these narratives enact the familiar gendered grammar of rape: Abraham forcibly conceives a child with Hagar, Jacob does so twice with Bilhah and twice with Zilpah. But these are also stories of relationships between women. Interwoven in Jacob's narrative arc, we find multiple accounts of female relationships: between the sisters/rivals/reluctant collaborators Rachel and Leah, between various wives and their slaves, between Dinah and the "daughters of the land."[11]

In the case of Sarah and Hagar, the focus is narrower, involving just three human characters. The story is distributed over two chapters, Genesis 16 and 21. Chapter 16 describes Hagar's rape, pregnancy, abuse by Sarah (here still called Sarai), and flight from the household, followed by a theophany in the wilderness. Hagar encounters a messenger of Yahweh, who tells her to return to what she has fled; he also provides a name for her unborn child: Ishmael. In chapter 21, Hagar and Ishmael are banished from the household by Abraham, acting on Sarah's instructions; this time, they do not return, and instead make a home in the wilderness. Hagar's last act described by the text is to find a wife for her son—an Egyptian, someone from her people. It is Hagar and Sarah's shared story that is my focus, for it condenses in especially clear form the complicated questions of female relationality, interdependence, intimacy, and intimate violence that I take up here.

Hagar's rape is the starting point and not the ending point of this chapter. My focus is on the relationship between the story of heterosexual rape and the fraught representation of relationality between women. I will argue that a feminist theory of biblical sexual violence needs to account for the points of contact between rape stories and close relationships *between women*. The story of Hagar and Sarah is the most extensive biblical example of this pattern. While Hagar is raped, this experience of rape does not exhaust her story or her narrative importance. Similarly, the significance of Hagar and Sarah's re- lationship cannot be reduced to the scene of sexual exploitation. Nor should this act of rape be seen as the singular defining event of the story. Instead, the text presents a complex and entangled account of female relationality, one that can productively be read with attention to both intersectionality and in- timacy. Rape is a part of this story, but only one part.

In reading the story of Hagar and Sarah in this way, I also want to take on two larger, and often unspoken, interpretive assumptions, both of which reflect Marcus's "gendered grammar" of rape: first, that in a story of (heter- osexual) rape, the relationship between the (male) perpetrator and (female) victim is always the most important part of the story, and second, that other relationships, especially between women, are always secondary. The anal- ysis of Hagar and Sarah I offer here challenges and decenters the gendered grammar of rape, while also suggesting other ways of focalizing gender. This not only changes how we read Genesis 16 and 21 but also puts pressure on the gendered grammar of sexual violence more broadly. This is another way of exploring the fuzzy, the messy, and the icky in biblical rape stories—in this case, by directing attention to the points where the stories extend beyond a narrow framework of *men doing bad sexual things to women*. In addition, relationships *between women* offer their own fuzzy, messy, and icky terrain, which is too often left unexplored and even unthought.

As a way of accessing and activating these questions, this chapter reads Genesis 16 and 21 together with a selection of texts that offer alternatives to the gendered grammar of rape. Marcus's essay offers an overarching frame- work, which I flesh out with other literary and theoretical works. I begin with a sampling of recent novels that foreground complicated female relationships, focusing on two: Sally Rooney's *Conversations with Friends* (2017) and Lara Williams's *Supper Club* (2019). Both works also offer alternative perspectives into fuzzy, messy, and icky, both as these categories are expressed in scenes of heterosexual violence and as they play out between women more generally. I use these novels to construct an "alternate grammar" for thinking about entangled female relationships and heterosexual violence without subor- dinating the former to the latter. From here, I move to another text of fe- male entanglement, this one more directly linked to Sarah and Hagar: Sara Maitland's short story "Triptych," which reimagines the biblical account. Reading with and through Maitland's story, I argue that the biblical text of Genesis 16 and 21 presents a similar narrative of entanglement, desire, and exploitation, a pattern I also identify in the relationship between Ruth and Naomi in the book of Ruth. Finally, I turn to ethicist Lynne Huffer's reflections on "What if Hagar and Sarah Were Lovers?", found in her book *Are the Lips a Grave?: A Queer Feminist on the Ethics of Sex*. I draw on Huffer's reflections and speculation to bring together the questions of entanglement, intimacy, and violence between women, over and against the gendered grammar of rape. I end by considering Hagar and Sarah in the company of other biblical women, offering a contrapuntal reading of Ruth and Naomi as another female dyad bound in relations of exploitation, sexual violence, intimacy, and perhaps love.

Hagar and Sarah with and against the Gendered Grammar of Rape

The story of Hagar can be read with the gendered grammar of rape, sexual violence, and sexual exploitation that Marcus describes. Or it can read outside of this grammar, with a focus, instead, on female relationships, in all their complexity and ethical betrayal—the reading this chapter will explore. The story begins when Sarai, who is infertile, instructs Abram to have sexual intercourse with Hagar, hoping that she will become pregnant; the narrative unfolds quickly from there:

> Sarai said to Abram, "Look, Yahweh has prevented me from bearing children. Come to my slave; perhaps I will be built up through her." Abram listened to Sarai. Sarai, Abram's wife, took Hagar the Egyptian, her slave—after Abram had lived in the land of Canaan for ten years—and gave her to Abram her husband as a wife. He came to Hagar and she became pregnant. When she saw that she was pregnant, she looked on her mistress with contempt. Sarai said to Abram, "May my wrong be against you! I gave my slave to your embrace and when she saw that she was pregnant, she looked on me with contempt. May Yahweh judge between me and you!" Abram said to Sarai, "Look, your slave is in your hands. Do to her what is good in your eyes." Sarai abused her and she ran away. (Gen 16:2–6)

This passage seems to confirm the gendered grammar of sexual violence. Hagar is raped by Abram, on Sarai's instruction; Sarai herself assists in the process (not only is it her idea, but she gives her slave to her husband).[12] After the rape, Hagar is subjected to further violence, as Sarai's harsh treatment forces her to flee. But she does not find relief for long: In the wilderness, the pregnant Hagar meets a messenger of Yahweh, who tells her to return to slavery. Hagar's own interpretation of the situation she has fled is not viewed as acceptable: As Doyle writes of the victim in the Title IX process, "her story about her own injury is a problem."[13] It is for this reason that the angel's speech overwrites Hagar's, instructing her to return home while disallowing her to speak of her injury. Instead, a (male) future is promised to offset her present (female) suffering. The messenger promises her "a great multitude of descendants" through her son, who will be named Ishmael. The text adds a remarkable detail: "She named Yahweh who had spoken to her 'you are El Roi [God who sees],' for she said, 'Have I really seen and remained alive after seeing?'" (16:13). After this scene, she returns to Abram and Sarai.

Hagar and Ishmael reappear in Genesis 21, after Sarai, now called Sarah, has miraculously become pregnant and given birth to a child, Isaac. Sarah sees the two children playing and demands that Abram, now Abraham, send Ishmael and Hagar away: "She [Sarah] said to Abraham, 'Expel this one and her son, for the son of this slave will not inherit along with my son—with Isaac'" (21:10). Abraham is reluctant, but after reassurances from Yahweh, he agrees. Hagar and Ishmael are cast out with only some bread and a skin of water. When the water runs out, Hagar places her child under a bush so as not to be forced to watch his death; she weeps. They are near death when another messenger appears, along with a well. It is not her weeping, but rather "the voice of the boy" (21:16), that attracts Yahweh's attention and brings intercession. It is "the boy," too, who here receives the promise of a great nation—Hagar, though spared death, is now defined in relation to him. The subject positions charted in this chapter are all masculine ones: first Abraham, who expels Hagar, then Yahweh, and finally Ishmael. Thus "the gendered grammar of violence predicates men as the subjects of violence and the operators of its tools, and predicates women as the objects of violence and the subjects of fear."[14]

These larger subject–object relations—the fundamentals of the "gendered grammar"—are closely associated with the rape itself, which undergirds the larger narrative. Marcus writes, "The language of rape solicits women to position ourselves as endangered, violable, and fearful and invites men to position themselves as legitimately violent and entitled to women's sexual services."[15] This is precisely what happens in Genesis 16:4: Abraham is positioned as "legitimately [sexually] violent" and "entitled' to [Hagar's] sexual services." While the act of rape is confined to this verse, the logic extends to the text more broadly, across the two chapters. Furthermore, "Rape engenders a sexualized female body defined as a wound"[16]—to this we might add, in Genesis 16 (and the other handmaid stories), a wound is also a *womb*, available for the continuation of the male line.

But of course, this reading, which follows the contours of the gendered grammar of rape, is not the only way to approach the text. There is also fuzziness, messiness, and ickiness here. One complication comes from the figure of Sarai/Sarah. (For clarity, I will use "Sarah" and "Abraham" from this point onward, whether referring to Genesis 16, 21, or elsewhere in the text.) While Hagar can be read as mostly acted-upon object, Sarah is harder to frame in this way. She has power and agency, and she uses both in icky ways. Hagar is Sarah's slave, the text specifies not "Sarah and Abraham's," but Sarah's alone (Gen 16:8; 25:12). While Abraham assumes the role of rapist, the sexual exploitation in Genesis 16 is Sarah's idea, as the text repeatedly stresses: through Sarah's direct speech, through her actions, through Abraham's direct speech, and through Yahweh's reference to Hagar as "Sarai's slave" (Gen 16:8). Hagar's contempt is likewise directed not at Abraham, but at Sarah. In chapter 21, Sarah is again culpable: Although Abraham physically expels Hagar and Ishmael, it is Sarah who demands the violence (nonsexual this time—though also potentially deadly). One way of responding to these challenging details is to downplay Sarah's agency, perhaps by suggesting it represents an effort by the text to discredit her and/or shield Abraham. But I want to suggest, instead, that we take seriously Sarah's agency, however unfeminist its ends, as a point where the text refuses or moves outside of the gendered grammar of sexual violence. The text is messy on this point; we should not shy away from this.

As for Hagar: Though the narrative stresses the ways in which she is acted upon, she also acts—she flees from Sarah, she names Yahweh, she finds a way to make a life in the wilderness. And there is the detail of her contempt for Sarah: "she looked on her mistress with contempt" (Gen 16:4), or more literally, "her mistress was contemptible in her eyes." The statement principally addresses Hagar's perception of Sarah; it is, moreover, repeated by Sarah herself in 16:5, suggesting that we may be dealing, instead, with *Sarah's* perception of Hagar's perception of her. (Put another way: The detail is important; its significance, however, is fuzzy, and perhaps messy as well.) But instead of sheltering the character of Hagar by dismissing the description of her attitude as projection or malice, I want to take seriously contempt as a meaningful and affectively saturated act. In looking with contempt, Hagar acts against Sarah. Moreover, it is clear that her relationship with Sarah, which begins in chapter 16 and unfolds further in chapter 21, is the literary, ethical, and narrative focus of the text. Abraham may possess the most structural and familial power; he is, nevertheless, of only secondary importance in this text. Indeed, the narrative's efforts to downplay his agency (for example, attributing motive to Sarah's discontent, not his own) merely underscore this point. We are left with a fuzzy, messy, and icky relationship between two women, one that cannot be resolved by applying a neat paradigm of heterosexual rape and the complicity of powerful women in the exploitation of the powerless. Furthermore, the complexity and ongoing entanglement of Hagar and Sarah's relationship to each other suggest a different relational structure than the gendered grammar of rape I have been describing. To draw this out further, I turn to fiction.[17]

Alternative Grammars: Entangled Female Relationships in Literary Fiction

While my rejection of the gendered grammar of rape is grounded in feminist theory, it is also useful to consider what alternatives might already exist. In *A Room of One's Own*, Virginia Woolf begins to imagine the possibilities. Reflecting upon the simple statement "Chloe liked Olivia," a line that she has read in an (imaginary) novel by the (fictional) Mary Carmichael, Woolf's narrator is "struck" by "how immense a change was there":

> All these relationships between women, I thought, rapidly recalling the splendid gallery of fictitious women, are too simple. So much has been left out, unattempted. And I tried to remember any case in the course of my reading where two women are represented as friends. There is an attempt at it in *Diana of the Crossways*. They are confidantes, of course, in Racine and the Greek tragedies. They are now and then mothers and daughters. But almost without exception they are shown in their relation to men.[18]

Against this backdrop, Chloe, Olivia, and especially "Chloe liked Olivia," mark an alternate possibility for fiction, and for thinking relationships between women. Woolf was onto something. But it is in recent literary fiction, written from roughly 2010 on, that we find a particular bubbling up of work that centers complicated female relationships. ("Friendship" is too limited; the popular term "frenemy," while messy, captures some of the added range; there is also often, though not always, an erotic charge: *Chloe liked Olivia*.) For my purposes, I am especially interested in the subset of this literature that includes accounts of sexual violence or rape while also treating these events as secondary.

Perhaps the best-known recent example is Elena Ferrante's Neapolitan novels, beginning with *My Brilliant Friend*.[19] Narrated by Elena ("Lenù") Greco, the four novels trace her complicated friendship with her "brilliant friend" Lila, from childhood to late middle age. Set mostly in Naples and beginning in the 1950s, the novels include multiple episodes of sexual violence, from exposure to rape to marital abuse. Both Lenù and Lila suffer at the hands of multiple men, including sexual and physical abuse. But this is no rape novel, or series of rape novels. Instead, the focus throughout is on the relationship between the two friends: fascinating, difficult, troubled, intimate. Ferrante is not alone in tracing this pattern: A remarkable number of recent works of literary fiction, written mostly (though not entirely) by women, chart similarly fraught female relationships. A partial list of recent entries in the genre might include Rachel B. Glaser's *Paulina & Fran* (2016), Sally Rooney's *Conversations with Friends* (2017), Julie Buntin's *Marlena* (2017), Ottessa Moshfegh's *My Year of Rest and Relaxation* (2018), Tara Isabella Burton's *Social Creature* (2018), Lara Williams's *Supper Club* (2019), and Susan Choi's *Trust Exercise* (2019).[20] In television, Lena Dunham's *Girls* (2012–2017) and the first season of Phoebe Waller-Bridge's *Fleabag* (2016) traverse similar ground.

Repeatedly, these works present sexual encounters that lie in the murky terrain of bad sex, weird sex, or unwanted sex; they sometimes slip into rape, though the term itself is used only rarely. Instead, sexual encounters are consistently fuzzy, messy, and icky. But the key focus is on relationships between women. Like the heterosexual encounters that punctuate the narratives (even while remaining largely secondary), the relationships between women flirt with the fuzzy, messy, and icky, even as they toe the line of friendship, jealousy, resentment, and desire. Within the novels, events are typically narrated flatly, often balancing a minimalist style (for example, Rooney's avoidance of quotation marks) with explicit descriptions of body parts and sexual acts. These are "rape stories," in the broad sense that I have described in the Introduction—that is, *rape culture stories*, or stories that help illuminate what Nicola Gavey calls "the cultural scaffolding of rape."[21] But they offer a very different representation of both sexual violence and female relationships than we often find in biblical literature. It is precisely this difference—the *space between* biblical rape stories and contemporary fictions—that makes reading the former together with the latter illuminating. Furthermore, these narratives consistently offer descriptions of unwanted sex/rape that resist reducing the female protagonist and her range of relationships to a single traumatic experience.

I want to consider two examples in some detail before returning to Sarah and Hagar: Sally Rooney's *Conversations with Friends* and Lara Williams's *Supper Club*. Rooney's novel tells the story of best friends and ex-girlfriends Frances and Bobbi, both university students, and their relationship with a somewhat older couple, Melissa and Nick. Melissa is a journalist, while Nick is an actor. At the center of the plot is Frances's affair with Nick and its consequences for the four main characters—consequences mostly worked out through the "conversations" of the title, and without dramatic consequences. Narrated by Frances, the novel is both flatly told and darkly funny; Frances's relationship with Bobbi constitutes the emotional core of the novel. It is only at its edges that we find unwanted sex, sexual exploitation, and perhaps rape.

One such sexual encounter occurs between Frances and a man named Rossa she meets on "the dating thing," an app of some kind:

> Afterward he invited me back to his apartment and I let him unbutton my blouse. I thought: this is normal. This is a normal thing to do. He had a small, soft upper body, not at all like Nick, and he did none of the usual things that Nick did to me before we had sex, like touching me for a long time and talking in a low voice. It started right away, with no introduction really. Physically I felt almost nothing, just a mild discomfort. I let myself become rigid and silent, waiting for Rossa to notice my rigidity and stop what he was doing, but he didn't. I considered asking him to stop, but the idea that he might ignore me felt more serious than the situation needed to be. Don't get yourself into a big legal thing, I thought. I lay there and let him continue. He asked me if I liked it rough and I told him I didn't think so, but he pulled my hair anyway. I wanted to laugh, and after that I hated myself for feeling superior.[22]

Frances frames the encounter as nothing serious, but when she returns home, her first action is a small act of violence against herself:

I am normal, I thought. I have a body like anyone else. Then I scratched my arm open until it bled, just a faint spot of blood, widening into a droplet. I counted to three and afterward opened the bandage, placed it carefully over my arm, and disposed of the plastic wrap.[23]

The harm is contained—bandaged, the wrapper carefully disposed of. But there is messiness here, along with fuzziness and ickiness. The hurt of Frances's body, a pattern that continues across the novel, points to a larger economy of pain and suffering linked even to a seemingly banal encounter of bad sex. To call Frances a "survivor" feels incorrect, likewise a "victim." But there is also something clearly unsettling, in her sexual encounters and in her relationship to her body. Frances harms herself throughout the novel— pinching, cutting, chewing her cheek until it bleeds, cutting into her leg with a pair of nail scissors.[24]

The scene that I have quoted above is not among the most important or memorable in *Conversations with Friends*; Rossa never appears again, nor does Frances seem to reflect much on the incident. And the entire un- pleasant sexual encounter occurs as part of Frances's working through her relationships with Bobbi and with Nick (and with the former's resentment of the latter). But it is precisely the *insignificance* of this moment, along with Rooney's willingness to offer a glimpse of the space between sex and rape and how it is experienced, that makes it useful in (re)thinking the gen- dered grammar of rape. Even Frances's antagonism toward her own body, expressed most dramatically in her self-harming behaviors, is not reducible to the trauma of sexual encounter, and indeed only intersects orthogonally with it.

Extending a line of analysis that I have explored with respect to David and Bathsheba in the previous chapter, *Conversations with Friends* insists that sexual predation or rape is only one way of understanding harm, and that to focus exclusively on it is to neglect a broad range of other forms of pain, suffering, and harm irreducible to either heterosexuality or predation. This extends, moreover, to harm experienced in or in relation to sex or rape. The sexual encounters in *Conversations with Friends* are frequently fuzzy, messy, and/or icky. This is true not just of Frances and a minor character such as Rossa but also of Frances and Bobbi, Frances and Nick, even Nick's account of losing his virginity in a semi-coercive sexual encounter with an older teenage girl (like Frances, Nick refuses to categorize himself as a victim).[25] At the same time, it is not sex but relationships that lie at the heart of the book. Notably, the most important figure in Frances's life—and, aside from Frances, in the novel—is not Nick but Bobbi. It is Frances's relationship with Bobbi, her on-again, off-again girlfriend and best friend, that gives the novel its emotional heft. Indeed, in scripting the character of Bobbi, and refusing to position her *either* as romantic rival or as supportive friend, Rooney herself resists what we might call the "gendered grammar of adultery" (to this end, *The New Yorker* titled its review of Rooney's debut "A New Kind of Adultery Novel").[26] While the four-way dynamic of *Conversations with Friends* does not offer an easy parallel to Hagar, Sarah, and Abraham, it does challenge us to think about relationality and forms of harm—and flourishing—beyond a narrow focus on the heterosexual dyad and/or heterosexual rape. And it urges us to question, in particular, relations between women.

These themes also emerge in Williams's *Supper Club*, which interweaves friendship, jealousy, and female appetite. Like *Conversations with Friends*, the novel focuses on a complicated female friendship, this time between the un-comfortable and often unhappy Roberta and her best friend Stevie. Together, the two found a "supper club," where women eat excessively and generally rebel against the patriarchy. The supper club becomes increasingly charged, spiraling into illegal behavior, while Stevie grows jealous of Roberta's divided attentions, including her blossoming relationship with a former housemate, Adnan. The novel also includes flashbacks to Roberta's college years, one of which echoes, in more markedly negative form, Frances's icky and noncon-sensual sexual encounter with Rossa. Roberta has gone on a date with a fellow student, Michael, and then fallen asleep in his dorm room while watching a Woody Allen film. And then:

> I woke up scared, but I didn't know why. It was not a wild terror or panic, more a low-key fear, the sick knowledge that something bad was hap-pening. I registered the heft of a body on top of my own. The absence of my underwear. Something moving in and out of my vagina. *I am having sex,* I thought. *Oh God, I am having sex.*[27]

Roberta quickly realizes she wants the sexual encounter to stop—but what Roberta wants is not a concern for Michael. She considers screaming or making noise to make him stop but rejects the idea as "histrionic":

> I tried pushing him, not hard but enough . . . I started to wriggle. I wasn't strong, I couldn't overpower him, but I could wriggle. "Hold still," he said,

clasping his hand around my throat. The room was dark and smelled of the cigarettes I'd smoked earlier. His hand on my throat formed a line, my brain separate from my body. Below the hand was something I had no control over, but above the hand was still mine. Lack of oxygen started making me foggy. I coughed, feeling little specks of saliva land around my lips. "Stop it," he said. I coughed more, coughing deliberately. It was the smallest gesture of control, this last space of my own: my breath. I could cough and splutter. I could rip open my insides and spill out the terrible things inside me. I coughed myself hoarse. His penis inside my vagina. My phlegm on his neck. *This is the worst thing,* I thought. *This is the worst thing, and this is still happening.*[28]

Afterward, Michael walks her home.

Unlike Frances's experience with Rossa, what happens to Roberta is clearly legible as rape. But Roberta does not use this language, or frame the incident in this way, until the final scene of the novel, when the members of the Supper Club confess their fears to each other and then inscribe them in a book to be burned:

"I was raped." I spoke the words into the wind, directing them away from the flat, away from my friends. "It was at university. Years ago. I didn't know you then."[29]

But rather than offering further details, Roberta turns, instead, to how the rape has affected her, connecting a particular instance of suffering to a larger pattern of peremption (Fischel's term, discussed in the previous chapter) or being "weird about relationships" (as Roberta herself puts it).[30] The rape itself does not actually appear again in her description of its consequences for her; instead, Roberta describes a *different* troubling sexual relationship from her past, involving a much older university lecturer.[31] And the fears she confesses to her friends are less distinct, if no less terrifying: the dark, the stranger lurking under the bed, the rapist on the other side of the door. Thus while Roberta experiences rape, her pain and harm cannot be limited to, or even traced to, the specific incident. Instead, the rape is itself only one detail. The fuzziness, messiness, and ickiness here is not in the scene of the rape itself but rather in how this rape, and other scenes of sexual violence, relate to Roberta's larger story of loneliness, pain, and trauma.

The confession scene in *Supper Club* ends not with Roberta but with her friend Stevie:

> Stevie leaned with her back against the railing, staring at our reflection, superimposed with the shapes of our friends dancing inside. She shook her head, looking suddenly teary and defiant.
> "I'm afraid you're going to leave. I'm afraid you're going to realize I'm not good for you. That I'm not good for anyone. I'm afraid everyone is going to leave when they figure that out."[32]

As in *Conversations with Friends*, what is most significant to *Supper Club* is not rape but friendship. Notably, it is Stevie's confession, not Roberta's, that functions as the climactic revelation. It is not sexual violence but tension between friends—Roberta and Stevie's relationship is filled with resentment, jealousy, and semi-sabotage—that propels the novel forward. In the final pages, it is Stevie's unexpected confession that ushers in a new intimacy between the two friends. And it is here that the emotional weight of the novel hangs.

If *Conversations with Friends* suggests a way of reading rape that admits the presence of unwanted sex and bodily threat without reducing the narrative to either a rape or an adultery/jealousy plot, *Supper Club* allows us to take seriously unwanted sex as rape without collapsing a range of harms and suffering into a single narrative of victimization and predation. Read in this way, we can consider Hagar's experience as one of rape without reducing the complexity of her story into the contours of "Hagar was raped." And like *Conversations with Friends*, *Supper Club* also puts pressure, in particular, on the question of relationships between women—including the ways in which women harm or hurt each other.

Rooney's and Williams's novels are just two examples of a larger pattern, reflected across a significant swath of contemporary fiction. Sexual violence by men is present in the lives of nearly all the protagonists. But it is not the focus of the text: That remains the relationships between women. These stories thus index a very different relationship between gender, power, and sexual violence, one in which rape is simultaneously present and secondary. And they press us as readers to take complicated relationships between women seriously without insisting that those relationships are ultimately secondary to the trauma of rape. By carving out a space to think about female relationships, over and against defaulting to heterosexual sexual violence as the defining narrative, emotional, or affective event, these novels undertake an important kind of feminist work.

Hagar and Sarah, Entangled

While I have described the literary dyads of Frances and Bobbi, and of Roberta and Stevie, as "friendships," that term under-names the hostility, violence, and mutual pain that characterizes both pairs. Bobbi is deeply hurt when Frances, strapped for money, publishes a story that is clearly about her. She is also upset by Frances's relationship with Nick. Frances, too, has her own fraught feelings toward Bobbi—jealousy, vulnerability, heartbreak, rivalry. In *Supper Club*, Stevie and Roberta spend much of the novel trying to sabotage each other; romantic jealousy is only a small part of the complicated mess of emotions and petty acts of violence that characterize their ongoing reactions. If these details seem "smaller" or "pettier" than the plots of Genesis 16 and 21—rape, contempt, near-death theophany, and so on—this is indeed the point. I am interested in a reading that shifts the focus away from the moment of sexual violence and onto a larger context of entangled relationships. And this way of reading is in fact in alignment with the biblical text, which presents Hagar's rape as one facet of a larger story of violence, competition, and a relationship that can't seem to untangle itself.

When biblical scholarship takes up the issue of entanglement in Genesis 16 and 21, it is often from the perspective of intersectionality. Intersectional critique is an important part of feminist critique more broadly; *intersectionality* describes the ways that categories such as gender, race and ethnicity, class, sexuality, and disability interact with and on each other. A central claim of intersectional theory is that forms of oppression are not simply additive; neither are they separable. In the case of Hagar and Sarah, this means we cannot read the story only from the perspective of gender (Hagar and Sarah are both women), of ethnicity (Hagar is Egyptian, Sarah is a [proto]-Israelite), class (Hagar is a slave, Sarah is her owner), or disability (Sarah is infertile, Hagar is not). Instead, we need to consider these questions of identity, privilege, and oppression together. In the case of Genesis 16, this means that Sarah's class solidarity, or perhaps merely her own self-interest, overrides any gender solidarity she might feel toward Hagar as another woman in Abraham's household.[33] Similarly, Hagar's status as slave and foreigner intersects in complex ways with her able-bodiedness, represented as fertility. (Infertility is a form of disability in the biblical world.) While her fertility, in the context of Sarah's infertility, leads to her sexual abuse and reproductive exploitation, it also gives her a certain power over Sarah, framed as contempt.

This kind of intersectional reading does important work in directing our attention to the complexity of oppression. And it connects biblical texts to contemporary conversations in feminist theory and "women's studies" more broadly, where intersectionality has achieved overwhelming methodological dominance.[34] But while intersectionality focalizes the entanglement of categories, it struggles to capture both specificity and feeling. "Intersectionality" originated as a term in legal theory; it was first used to describe classes of people (specifically, Black women) rather than individuals and individual stories.[35] As a method, intersectionality is also ill-suited to capturing ambiguity, vulnerability, and other forms of interpersonal entanglement—or what I have called the fuzzy, messy, and icky. In *Black Feminism Reimagined: After Intersectionality*, Jennifer Nash has suggested *intimacy* and *surrender* as alternative models that speak more clearly to the ways we are "done and undone through relationality."[36] Nash is speaking, in particular, to a specific dispute within feminist theory: the way intersectionality is often pitted against transnational and postcolonial feminisms as a rival method. But the *intimacy* and *surrender* she imagines between feminist "analytics" or forms of feminist theory also offer a useful model for thinking about relations between subjects—or the ways in which, as Judith Butler explores in *Undoing Gender*, "we're undone by each other."[37]

Intimacy is not always positive, or even pleasant. It may even be repulsive. But it is surely present in the Sarah–Hagar story. One way of reading the intimacy of the narrative is through negative forms of intimacy, such as hatred and disgust.[38] Sarah's demand that Hagar be expelled grows from this disgust; from this perspective, it represents not so much an end to intimacy as its continuation: as Juliana Claassens writes, "The immediate effect of disgust is that it causes the subject to create distance between the self and the object or subject he or she finds disgusting."[39] The second scene of leaving Abraham's household, in Genesis 21, functions similarly.

We can also find, in this repetition and in the transfer of disgust between Sarah and Hagar, traces of Ahmed's notion of stickiness, which I introduced in chapter 1.[40] Disgust is sticky; it is transferred between bodies and subjects and narratives. There is even a certain disgust at the narrative, and at Sarah's cruel actions in particular, that may transfer beyond it, to stick to us as readers. This is a phenomenon explored by a number of feminist interpreters;[41] interestingly, the sticky transfer of disgust over *Abraham's* conduct is less common.[42] In the world of the story, Hagar's contempt is reconfigured as resistance and even courage, qualities that are stickily transferred to her son, Ishmael, a "wild ass of a man" (Gen 16:12) who will never be a slave.[43] Claassens traces another vector of stickiness in the narrative, noting that the hypersexualization of foreigners, including Egyptians, attaches to and amplifies the representation of Hagar. In the midrash, Hagar is even associated with the passage praising the size of Egyptian penises (Ezek 23:20), while also being described with the sexually charged language of smell. This sexual disgust—itself closely bound up with desire, ambivalence, and frequently violence as well, as many queer readings have drawn out—attaches to the figure of Hagar, while also connecting this story not simply to other narratives of slavery in the Hebrew Bible but also to a pattern of the hypersexualization of foreigners. Of course, this informs the rape narrative as well—but also the storyworld that extends beyond it.

In the various forms of disgust—contemptuous, sexual, racial, sticky—we begin to see what Nash calls "the permeability between concepts and their imagined 'origins,' and between bodies," and which she associates conceptually with the term "intimacy."[44] There is a certain narrative permeability between the idea of fertility and the lived experience of the bodies of Sarah and Hagar, even as these bodies are at once marked by, and distinct from, their "imagined 'origins'" (as Egyptian, African, Arab, from Ur, belonging to Abraham, etc.). There is a similar permeability, expressed as interchangeability, between Hagar's fertile body and Sarah's infertile body—the latter subsequently made fertile, either miraculously or through a nonconsensual act of divine intervention.[45] Another point of sticky contact is Sarah's threatened rape in Egypt in Genesis 12:10–20 and again in 20:1–18, suggesting another uneasy transference and blurring—a rendering fuzzy, messy, and icky—of the identity categories of "victim" and "perpetrator."

The intimacy and surrender that Nash describes is also a recurring theme in many of the novels that I have referred to earlier in the chapter. Throughout *Conversations with Friends*, Frances is concerned with the unraveling of her self. Her sexual encounters with Nick are presented as a series of threatened undoings; her relationship with Bobbi, though no longer sexual, continues to pull at her sense of self. Frances's health struggles—after intense bleeding and pain, she is diagnosed with endometriosis—are likewise framed as threats of undoing. In *Supper Club*, similarly, Roberta struggles with becoming undone. A period of intense and unhappy weight loss offers a physical manifestation of what is, throughout the novel, a pervasive personal threat. Roberta's final scene with Stevie offers a similar psychological undoing of both characters, which is then given literal form in the burning of the book in which they write their secrets. The novel ends with a recipe for "Hunter's Stew," a dish predicated on mixing and culinary/personal undoing: "It is made in a large pot, and the ingredients are anything you can find. The idea is that it is never finished, never emptied all the way—instead it is topped up perpetually. It is a stew with an unending cycle . . . It is said to improve with age."[46] This improvement occurs as the components blend into each other.

In Hagar and Sarah's story, too, we find the protagonists undone by each other. Undoing does not require love or even affection, as even a brief turn to other contemporary fiction reveals: Susan Choi's *Trust Exercise* ends with a violent shooting between former friends; the unnamed narrator of Ottessa Moshfegh's *My Year of Rest and Relaxation* is finally undone—and forced out of her year of pharmaceutically induced "rest and relaxation"—by the death of her best friend, Reva. But in all cases, this undoing does require intimacy. In Genesis 16 and 21, this intimacy takes many forms—rivalry, attempted murder, entangled lives, disgust—and, as a few interpreters have dared to suggest, perhaps eroticism and love as well. This, too, has parallels in the contemporary novels: *Conversations with Friends*'s Frances and Bobbi are ex-girlfriends; *Supper Club*'s Stevie is obsessed with Roberta, Tara Isabella Burton's *Social Creature* is shot through with sexual and other forms of desire (and, activating the old murderous bisexual trope, murder). And, of course, "Chloe liked Olivia." But Hagar and Sarah? Lovers? To pursue this line of inquiry further, I turn to another example from fiction.

Cracking Open the Text: Intimacy and Entanglement in "Triptych"

The entangled female relationships that have reached such prominence in contemporary fiction are not the only fictions to touch on these themes. It is of course possible to trace a history, or counterhistory, of women's relationships in fiction or folklore or fairy tales, as many scholars have already done. If the relatively recent texts I have discussed earlier have an advantage to this discussion, it is that they display the theme in an especially pronounced way, and they explicitly position female relationships against backdrops of (banal) male sexual violence against women—a present narrative feature, but not the story's focus. In this section and the following, I will broaden the analysis to include a story that deals explicitly with the Hagar and Sarah story, in order to advance my analysis further. While the work I discuss here predates the novels discussed in the previous section, reading it in light of the novels helps highlight certain themes or key details, pushing the analysis beyond a simple *How does Y retell X?*, where *X* is a biblical story and *Y* a contemporary midrash, short story, poem, or other literary retelling.

As the title suggests, Sara Maitland's "Triptych" unfolds in three parts: first Hagar, then Sarah, then the narrator, a version of Maitland herself. Abraham, for once, is not allowed to dominate the narrative or lay claim to sympathy; he has no voice here. Picking up on a point that is also made by various midrashim, Hagar is identified as a gift to Sarah following Sarah and Abraham's sojourn in Egypt; her entry into their household is a form of payment for Sarah's "immoral earnings" (the story's words) with Pharaoh.[47] Touching on many of the intersectional themes that feminist scholars also highlight in reading the biblical text, "Triptych" makes clear the age difference between the two women, as well as the question of power in their relationship—Sarah's ownership of Hagar, Hagar's youth and fertility, Abraham's obsessive pursuit of an heir, which ensnares both women. Maitland's Sarah is very much like a mother to Hagar, as well as a friend.

But Maitland's reimagining does not end here. Instead, Sarah is also a *lover*. Furthermore, and importantly, the maternal, the erotic, and the mistress/slave imagery are not separable in the text. This is especially clear in a passage where Hagar recalls giving birth:

> Memories of Sarah; Sarah's hands braiding gold threads and complex patterns into her hair. Sarah's arms around her, holding her in the night, in the women's tent, holding her against both their fears. Sarah's hands, strong and commanding, under her own armpits, Sarah's knees, steady and firm either side of her waist. Sarah's breast soft and warm against her head and shoulders, Sarah's voice gentle and determined . . . Sarah's hands untiring, loving, washing her with a soft cloth after the labor, washing tenderly and happily, all over, hands like cool honey all over her, mother, friend, lover. Sarah.[48]

As this passage suggests, the relationship between the two women is marked by complexity and contradiction. For much of the story, it is charged with resentment or even hate, but there is also love and a deep longing. The retelling of the relationship in multiple voices—first Hagar's, then Sarah's, then the narrator's own—has the effect of adjusting and readjusting our understanding and perception.

Throughout the story, Maitland invites us to experience both women's bodies. Both Sarah and Hagar are desired and desiring; they describe their own bodies, as well as each other's. More than words, touch is what brings the two women together and what grounds their relationship; in the wilderness, it is touch that Hagar longs for. Even her climactic seeing of God, an insistently visual moment in the biblical text, is also represented through touch—first with kisses and caresses, then with naked dancing. The body is also central to the relationship between two women: Hagar's memories of Sarah's hands; Sarah's memory of Hagar's wrist and stomach. But the body also facilitates moments of deceit and betrayal: When Abraham seizes Ishmael to circumcise him, Sarah distracts Hagar with caresses, "kiss[ing] her ears and eyes and mouth and genitals so she would not have to hear the screams." The body is also at the center of Sarah's plans for Hagar and Abraham:

> The two of them had lain together in the women's tent and Sarah had urged her, urged her, urged her to consent to him. She had said and said that it was Sarah she loved, Sarah that she served, that she whored for no married men, and Sarah in a sudden fury told her that she was the mistress, that Hagar was hers, hers to do as she willed with, and if she chose to use her to get children for her old age then that was just Hagar's bad luck. From the day she had received into her own hands Hagar's seal of ownership Sarah had never, ever, not once, mentioned the relationship between them until that night. Hagar had pushed Sarah away from her, stood up, stripped naked and in front of Sarah had oiled her body, flaunting the long curves of her buttocks and thighs, asked Sarah with impudence how her husband liked it best, how he would respond to virgin flesh, tight and sweet, after aged flesh, and with her mouth tasting of vomit she had gone out that night and did not return for six days; and when she returned it was with a haughty knowledge and a wide sneer.[49]

It is not simply that Sarah tries to persuade Hagar to consent and, when she refuses, forces her to yield anyway (thereby revealing the hollowness of consent all along). Instead, I want to direct attention to the ways the body—and in particular the desired body—figures here. Though Maitland does not shy away from representing Abraham as a bully, fanatic, and rapist, he is fundamentally secondary in the narrative. Even the violation of Hagar's sexual encounter is framed, fundamentally, as a violation of her relationship with *Sarah*. While one sort of reading might pick up on this tendency and follow the hints in the story to trafficking or exploitation—recasting Hagar as victim yet again—Maitland refuses this kind of simplicity.

The ending of "Triptych" is not an ending, at least in the conventional sense. Indeed, the entire third part—which is called "Abraham" despite refusing to address the perspective of Abraham—is something else, something unfamiliar. After rejecting the demand to "write Abraham's story," Maitland instructs her readers to sneak into a hotel and steal a Bible if the story is really so unfamiliar, then offers a jokey, acidic riff on traditional biblical criticism. In a section identified as "a few brief notes from the *S.L. Maitland Biblical Commentary*," Maitland recaps literary source criticism, criticizes Abraham ("frankly, a real bastard"), considers Sarah and Hagar as wife and mistress, directs our attention to the exceptional fact of Hagar seeing God, and suggests that the compilers of the biblical text, for all their misogyny, were unable to control the story they sought to tell: "in the face of their best efforts, they dismally fail to write out, or suppress, the abiding emotional reality of Sarah and Hagar. At their every appearance the text vibrates, leaping, shining, buoyant, alive."[50] And then the narrative breaks off: "You probably don't like the tone of this bit of the story. I don't blame you," the narrator confides, before returning to Sarah and Hagar, suggesting that a piece of her is in both of them. She ends with a refusal to forgive:

> I do wish I could. But it is too soon and too late. To understand all is to forgive all. And I do not want to forgive. I cannot forgive. I am Hagar who is driven into the desert. I am Sarah who betrays her friend. This nasty cynicism which destroys joy, hope, transformation, magic, truth, love, it is still necessary, still—as always—a useful mutation, an adaptation vital to the survival of the species. As we dance, dance on the hot sands and rejoice, as we laugh, laugh in the cool tents and weep, we must remember and give thanks for that too, alas.[51]

It is (Maitland's) Hagar who dances on the sands and rejoices, (Maitland's) Sarah who laughs and weeps in the tent, Maitland herself who refuses forgiveness, and with it, a "proper" ending. But it is this refusal to close the narrative or to insist on a happy ending that gives it its power.

In its open-endedness, Maitland's story drives home the open-endedness of the biblical account. While Sarah's desire for a child, Hagar's haughtiness, and Sarah's jealousy are all clear in the story, the ending is not. Of Sarah, Phyllis Trible writes, "The biblical story allows no opportunity, however small, for Sarah to be healed. It attributes to her no action or word that might temper her affliction. Instead, it leaves her a jealous and selfish woman."[52] But while Sarah is left a bitter and unhappy character—her next action in the narrative is to die (Gen 23:1–2)—Hagar casts even less of a shadow over the remaining text. She resurfaces a single additional time, in a genealogical list of Abraham's descendants (Gen 25:12).[53] In Genesis 25, she is again identified as a slave (šipḥah), a repetition that also functions to erase the narrative growth and transformation that has unfolded since Hagar's first appearance in 16:1, where she is likewise identified as šipḥah. But reading the biblical account together with Maitland's story exposes the omissions and elisions of this return to the language of slavery, as well as what remains hinted at but unsaid. Hagar is not simply a slave, šipḥah, but Sarah's slave, šipḥat śārāh. And this relationship of servitude and subjugation also names a relationship of complex entanglement—a relationship the text describes but then abandons, turning, instead, to the pursuits of male characters and the unfolding of male genealogies. "Triptych," in contrast, asks us to pause, to take seriously Hagar and Sarah as entangled bodies, lives, intimacies, loves.

In tracing out the irreducible complexities of the relationship, Maitland includes care, desire, and eroticism in her reimagining. In "Triptych," Sarah and Hagar are mistress and slave, mother and daughter, friends, mutual victims of Abraham—and lovers. Sex is not removed from power—both Sarah and Hagar use it to influence and control each other, as well as Abraham—but it is also, importantly, a part of the entangled relationship. "What if Hagar and Sarah were lovers?" philosopher Lynne Huffer asks; Maitland gives us one answer—and opens another possibility in the biblical text.[54] Instead of dismissing this reading as a sympathetic fantasy that covers over the structural violence of the text, I am interested in what it tells us about Sarah and Hagar, and how it might crack open our reading practices. I will turn to Huffer in exploring this question further below. First, however, I want to set the possibility of Hagar and Sarah as lovers against a different biblical text, one that also describes the intimacies and exploitations of a pair of women bound to each other: Ruth and Naomi in the book of Ruth.

From Hagar and Sarah to Ruth and Naomi

Hagar and Sarah are not the only pair of biblical women to display this complex intimacy. We find a similar pattern, I suggest, in the account of Ruth and Naomi, found in the book of Ruth. Like Hagar and Sarah, Ruth and Naomi's story is fraught with intersectional complexities, though in ways that reverse the dynamics of reading. Like Hagar, Ruth is a foreign woman, living and working outside her homeland. Like Hagar, she gives birth to a son who is the ancestor of a nation. And like Hagar, Ruth does not unambiguously consent to this sex, if consent is even a meaningful category to use here; it is, in any case, not her idea, but rather that of an older woman, to whom the young foreigner is bound. Hagar is Sarah's slave, while Ruth has pledged herself to Naomi—a woman old enough to be her mother, now childless and filled with bitterness. It is this woman who devises the plan to have the young woman bear a child; Sarah hopes to be "built up" (Gen 16:2), while the birth of Ruth's son Obed is celebrated with cries of "a child is born to Naomi!" (Ruth 4:17). These cries come from women; this is a story of women, much as Genesis 16 and 21 are stories of women: Both Boaz and Abraham, while ostensible patriarchs, are oddly passive in their respective stories.

Ruth's words pledging herself to Naomi are well known: "Wherever you go, I will go; wherever you lodge, I will lodge; your people will be my people, and your God will be my God; where you die, I will die, and there I will be buried" (Ruth 1:16–17). Indeed, on the strength of Ruth's devotion as expressed here, the story is often read through a lesbian, queer, or bisexual lens.[55] The book of Ruth has a long history in lesbian fiction.[56] Other readers find the story to be a narrative of female friendship and survival against the odds. Ruth and Naomi: a happy story at last?[57] But if Hagar and Sarah's story is a clear narrative of exploitation that nevertheless reveals hints of a more complicated relationship of friendship, eroticism, and care, then the story of Ruth and Naomi is the opposite: a seeming narrative of love and/or friendship that reveals itself to be a potential scene of exploitation, including sexual exploitation.[58] Readings celebrating Ruth's relationship with Naomi often dwell on her words, but less often do they consider Naomi's response: silence—"She saw that she was determined to go with her, and she said nothing to her" (1:18). Indeed, her first words following Ruth's occur in the following chapter, when Naomi declares herself bitter. Her subsequent actions, too, can be read in ways less favorable to both the relationship and the story: Naomi exploits Ruth, perhaps even pimps her out, to ensure her own safety. It is Naomi who devises the plan involving Boaz, but Ruth who must carry it out. From this perspective, Naomi is a pimp or sex trafficker, as much as a friend, mother, or lover.

This is a hard reading, especially for those who have found the story a space of solace or love in the text. It challenges what we would like to find in biblical narrative, how we would like to find ourselves or our interests reflected. Reading friendship, eroticism, or love in the Hagar and Sarah story has a similar effect. It is disorienting and unsettling. It challenges what we believe we already know about the text. It disrupts the "already-read text" (a notion I will explore further in the following chapter) and suggests, instead, that in reading, especially in reading with literature, we may find something wholly different.[59] To a lesser degree, the novels of friendship, enmity, and intimacy that I have used as intertexts engender similar effects—especially concentrated around their representations of sexual violence. They challenge our assumed sense of what "ought" to be the emphasis—rape or sexual violence committed by men and experienced by women, not the relationships of women that surround and exceed the scene of violence. But in offering a way of reading such as this, they challenge the gendered grammar of rape, urging us to seek alternatives.

Elsewhere, I have written about the affective and emotional pull between readings that celebrate Ruth and Naomi and those that insist on the story's hard truth as a narrative of oppression. Here, I want to consider Ruth and Naomi together with Hagar and Sarah as two examples of a pattern of narrative and ethical complexity, in which intimacy and betrayal are inseparable. As Huffer suggests of Hagar and Sarah, "Although love does not conquer all, neither does betrayal"—the same can be said, I would suggest, of the book of Ruth.[60] Naomi may act in bad faith toward Ruth or even betray her; this does not, however, exhaust the complexity of her character or of the book's central relationship—even if this relationship is compressed in the representation of the text. So too with Sarah and Hagar: There is bad faith, hostility, jealousy, even murderous intent here—but this does not mean there is not intimacy as well, even if that intimacy is primarily expressed as disgust and/or hatred. Reading the two stories together also helps draw out the possibilities of narratives, especially narratives of intimacy and injustice, beyond tracking their intersectional identity categories. Reflecting on Hagar and Sarah together with Maitland's short story, Huffer writes, "the process of retelling invites new ways of thinking about the narrative dimension of history and the ways in which ideas or events from the past sustain multiple stories."[61]

For Huffer, it is less the specific retelling than "the process of retelling itself" and "the dynamic interplay ... between *what is* and *what might be*" that opens this space of possibility.[62] I have found a similar effect, not just in retelling, but in reading texts together—here, in reading the Genesis 16 and 21 account together with the book of Ruth. I want now to consider the dynamics of betrayal, intimacy, and possibility in and beyond the text—all of which challenge the gendered grammar of rape.

"What if Hagar and Sarah Were Lovers?" And What about Ruth and Naomi and All the Others?

I have alluded several times to queer feminist ethicist Lynne Huffer's reading of Hagar and Sarah; I will bring this chapter to an end by turning to her directly. "What if Hagar and Sarah Were Lovers?" is the title that Huffer gives to the seventh chapter of her book *Are The Lips a Grave?*. The question posed by the title is both an inquiry into the biblical story and something beyond it; Huffer's larger concern is with a wide-ranging inquiry into queer feminist ethics, vulnerability, and care. Hagar and Sarah join Luce Irigaray, Michel Foucault, Colette, Valerie Solanas, and a host of other figures, real and imagined, that Huffer uses to mark the contours of her work. Her reading of the biblical story triangulates between Maitland's "Triptych," the classic womanist interpretation of the biblical text offered by Delores Williams's *Sisters in the Wilderness*,[63] and Huffer's own experiences of hostility, betrayal, and love in a queer interracial relationship. In reading all three of these sources, as well as the biblical text, she focuses on "the moment where love falters"[64]— and yet in doing so, Huffer also asks us to hold space for the possibility of love, prior to its faltering.

As Huffer argues, queer feminisms and queer feminist sexual ethics—and perhaps all sexual ethics—need to account for relations *between* women, including those moments when relations break down or turn to failure or betrayal. Equally, a feminist theorization of biblical sexual violence must consider not just what happens to vulnerable bodies in the text but also how sexual violence is facilitated, encouraged, or taken advantage of *between* bodies and subjects, including *between women*. This is another way of naming the intimacy, surrender, and becoming undone that Nash associates with a move beyond intersectional critique. Huffer finds such complexity in the rich textures of narrative detail, as well as in the act of storytelling and retelling.[65] If Nash offers intimacy and surrender as modes of moving beyond the stasis of intersectionality—a stasis that limits the ways we can imagine Sarah and Hagar, or Ruth and Naomi, or other intersectional entangled pairs and collectives—then Huffer, somewhat unexpectedly, offers storytelling.

It is not enough simply to map relations of domination and oppression. Instead, ethical practice requires telling and retelling stories, in order to uncover their complexities. The moments where the dominant narrative breaks down can allow alternative ways of reading to emerge:

> Like cracks in granite, these fissures expose alternative stories, new configurations of meaning that serve both to acknowledge and resignify injustice and victimization. Read differently, these chapters in *Genesis* where Hagar and Sarah reside might tell a story not only about domination, betrayal, and complicit silence, but also about love.[66]

Huffer thus ends where Maitland has already brought us—at the *both/and*. Sarah is *both* victim *and* perpetrator, suffering from Abraham and her own infertility, even as she oppresses Hagar. So too does Hagar occupy multiple categories, suffering at Sarah's hands but also maintaining a certain power over her. But the dynamics are not static. Instead, as "Triptych" draws out, the biblical text insinuates a complex and shifting relationship between its two protagonists, one that transgresses categories in ways both thrilling and uncomfortable. Slavery, friendship, eroticism, love, anger, care, betrayal all mingle across the short story. To Huffer's question *What if Hagar and Sarah were lovers?* Maitland's answer is at once affirming and complicating. "Triptych" gives us images of Hagar and Sarah's relationship that resist easy simplification while insisting on the complexity of emotion and the centrality of ambivalence. And "like cracks in granite," this retelling "expose[s] alternative stories, new configurations of meaning that serve both to acknowledge and resignify injustice and victimization"—Huffer's phrase, Maitland's story, my own reading of the biblical text.

Furthermore, the intimacy, betrayal, and ambivalence that Huffer and Maitland find in Hagar and Sarah also characterize the recent literary fiction that I have used to frame this chapter. The Hagar and Sarah story that emerges resembles not the stereotypes of biblical narrative (a world of men, women as objects) but rather the complicated intimacies, cutting across friendship, hatred, desire, and entanglement, that we find in other, nonbiblical literary texts. Hagar and Sarah are somewhere between Frances and

Bobbi (jealous friends and lovers), Roberta and Stevie (even more jealous friends, not quite lovers), and Choi's Karen and Sarah (friendship turned resentment, climaxing in murder), or perhaps closer still to Ferrante's Lenù and Lila ("brilliant friends," with all the ambiguity of that phrase).[67] The narrative we have in Genesis is still, of course, refracted through the patriarchal concerns of the narrator. But in reading the biblical text with and through other stories, we find something new.

But also something old. Even as Huffer explores the space of possibility her reading opens, she is also careful not to abandon violence or betrayal:

> Thus the old—Sarah and Hagar as mistress and slave—become the new— Sarah and Hagar as lovers. But the new identities hardly cancel out the old ones; rather; the two coexist uncomfortably, even agonistically. It is precisely in that space of uncomfortable coexistence—where competing stories and contradictory identities resist each other—that new (unknowable) possibilities emerge.[68]

And perhaps, confronted with the tyranny of old stories, the emergence of such multiple possibilities and competing stories is the best we can hope for.

Lovers and Grammars: Hagar and Sarah in the Company of Women

In an interesting way, Huffer's appeal to "competing stories" and narrative retelling recalls Marcus's rejection of the gendered grammar of rape. Huffer's argument operates on the level of the story; Marcus's prefers the more foundational metaphor of a "grammar," but both offer responses to violence that are, fundamentally, *new ways of telling*. The fiction I have sampled here functions similarly: While acknowledging the presence of heterosexual sexual violence, it refuses to cede dominance to these narratives, offering, instead, a different set of stories. These stories foreground female intimacy, female disgust, love and jealousy, hatred and ambivalence. Even in "Cat Person," the story ends not with the relationship between Margot (narrator, protagonist, possible victim) and Robert (bad date, harasser, "perpetrator"), but rather with Margo and her female friend, Tamara.[69] The fuzzy-messy-icky rape story is refracted and reshaped through conversations between women.

My reading of Hagar and Sarah outside the strictures of the gendered grammar of rape has encompassed a range of texts, theories, and ways of reading. But across the works considered here—a theory of rape and language, a handful of contemporary novels, a short story (part of a larger literary tradition of feminist "fractured fairy tales"), another biblical text, a philosophical work on queer sexual ethics—questions of love, guilt, and exploitation have recurred. So too have Hagar and Sarah. These characters from Genesis join Frances and Bobbi and the entangled dyads of literary fiction, Maitland's reimagined characters, Ruth and Naomi, and Huffer's queer feminist ethics of sex in finding ways to talk about female relationships and sexual and other forms of violence together, without subordinating the former to the latter. This is the work that Huffer, Maitland, and novelists such as Rooney and Williams all undertake. And, I have suggested, this kind of alternative is also present in the biblical story of Hagar and Sarah (as, indeed, it is in the story of Ruth and Naomi)—we only need to learn to look for it.

5

A Grittier Daughter Zion

Lamentations and the Archive of Rape Stories

Most biblical rape stories do not devote much attention to what happens *after* the rape. We know that Tamar laments her fate and lives, desolate, in the house of her brother Absalom. We know that Bathsheba becomes a part of David's household (though we don't know how she herself feels about this fact). Sometimes, the text gives a longitudinal view: The children of Lot and his daughters go on to become the Ammonites and Moabites; Hagar's son Ishmael is the ancestor of the Arabs. As explored in the previous chapter, Hagar herself has one of the more developed "after rape" stories: She flees from Abraham and Sarah's household, is persuaded to return by a divine messenger, and apparently remains for several years until her second, permanent departure (instigated by Sarah). The last the text tells of Hagar, she is living in the wilderness of Paran and has sought a wife for her son "from among her people."

The exceptions to this pattern come mostly in poetry. The prophets, especially Hosea and Ezekiel, offer us tangled accounts of sexual violence as punishment for female promiscuity and infidelity; these acts of violence are followed by re-seduction (in Hos 2) or further physical violence (as in Ezek 16 and 23). In these texts, however, both the sexual violence and its aftermath are focalized through the perspective of the perpetrator, Yahweh. Not so in the book of Lamentations, which offers the other major textual exploration of the *afters* of sexual violence. Rape and other forms of sexual violence are described across the book. In chapters 1 and 2, a female figure known as Daughter Zion speaks, describing her suffering and devastation. As such, Lamentations presents something otherwise unparalleled in biblical narrative: a female victim/survivor of sexual violence who is represented as describing her own experience, including its aftermath.

On this account, Lamentations and Daughter Zion have become objects of special interest for feminist interpreters and others concerned with

Texts after Terror. Rhiannon Graybill, Oxford University Press. © Oxford University Press 2021.
DOI: 10.1093/oso/9780190082314.003.0006

gender, trauma, and bodily suffering. Frequently, this body of scholarship elevates Daughter Zion to the status of exemplary victim, who represents a specific (and specifically commendable) theological and/or ethical position. In addition to praising Daughter Zion, this scholarship often describes readers as compelled to respond to the book in certain ways. In the first half of this chapter, I will track some representative examples of this scholarship, in order to trace its contours and to draw out, in particular, the ways it represents Daughter Zion as an ideal and praiseworthy victim/survivor. While I am sympathetic to the impulses that motivate these interpretations, I will argue that the readings they produce are patronizing, problematic, and bad readings, insofar as they do not capture either the literary complexity of the text or the experiential and ethical complexity of the *afters* of sexual violence.

In the second half of the chapter, I will offer an alternative mode of reading sexual violence in Lamentations, centered on the idea of the archive. The "archival turn" is a familiar move in feminist and queer theory, though it remains mostly absent in feminist biblical studies. My own framing of the archive is particularly influenced by Ann Cvetkovich, whose work explores the possibilities of the archive for reading sexual violence and trauma. In *An Archive of Feelings*, she curates an unconventional trauma archive that includes queer performance art, butch memoirs, lesbian responses to incest, and AIDS activism, among other materials. This productive eclecticism inspires my own. Following her lead, I have intentionally avoided the dominant voices in feminist and popular framings of sexual violence, especially biblical sexual violence—Susan Brownmiller's *Against Our Will* (on rape), Ellen Bass's *The Courage to Heal* (on child sexual abuse), and Judith Herman's *Trauma and Recovery* (on trauma), as well as the various works of Andrea Dworkin and Catharine MacKinnon (on pornography and heterosexual violence).[1] Instead, I have looked elsewhere for representations of sexual violence and its *afters*. The "survivor archive" collected here features Jennifer Patterson's *Queering Sexual Violence: Radical Voices from Within the Anti-Violence Movement*, Leah Lakshmi Piepzna-Samarasinha's *Care Work: Dreaming Disability Justice*, and Carmen Maria Machado's *In the Dream House*, along with Lamentations 1–2.[2] Though their details vary, all four texts challenge, sometimes stridently, the received conventions and clichés of *how to tell a rape story*. This includes, I will argue, the rape story we find in the poetry of Lamentations.

The non-biblical texts included in the archive each represent variations on the memoir or essay; they are, moreover, authored by survivors.[3] But I have not chosen these texts to anchor the archive because of any belief in the authenticity of experience. Like Cvetkovich curating her "archive of feelings"—and unlike many readers of Lamentations—I am specifically uninterested in discourses of testimony, witnessing, and experience as frames for reading the sexual violence in the text.[4] This is especially important given that Daughter Zion is not a "real" survivor but rather a complex literary representation, whose "voice" sounds in a larger poetic collection. The texts in the archive are valuable not because they offer "authentic" or unmediated access to sexual trauma but for the ways they challenge the assumptions of transparency in experience and suffering. Consistently, both Daughter Zion's speeches in Lamentations and the texts in the archive *do not give us what we want*—and this is precisely the point. Similarly, *Queering Sexual Violence* puts pressure on the convenient identity categories of "victim" and "survivor." *Care Work* challenges both compelled disclosure and cure. And *In the Dream House* shows us that writing about sexual violence, far from a *cri de coeur*, can be tricky and formally innovative . . . just as Lamentations itself is.

Unlike the scholarship that elevates Daughter Zion to an exemplary figure of pity, my alternative archive lingers with the fuzziness, messiness, and ickiness of sexual violence and its aftermaths. Holding space for the fuzzy, the assembled texts challenge received scripts about what it means to be a victim or survivor and how a survivor story ought to be told. Trafficking in the messy, they put pressure on the demand to represent the "good victim" or to be a "good survivor." Taking seriously the icky, they refuse the demand to share the worst parts of a story and to perform suffering for greedy observers. Traversing the full terrain of fuzzy, messy, and icky in an effort to narrate the space of the *after*, they challenge both the representation of rape as something that can be overcome (the cure model) and the idea that rape is impossible to recover from (the brokenness model). And they offer sharp lessons on how (not) to memorialize trauma, lingering, instead, with fuzzy, messy, and icky. The Daughter Zion that emerges from this chapter's reading looks rather different from other iterations of her character. She is no longer simply a tragic figure. She still speaks, and speaks angrily, but her words are no longer a summons to mourning or pity. Instead, the poetry of Lamentations 1 and 2, and the passages associated with Daughter Zion in particular, becomes a powerful variation on how a rape story can be told.

Lamentations as a Rape Story

The book of Lamentations is a work of poetry. Its five chapters present a series of laments over the fall of Jerusalem and the destruction of the temple
by the Babylonians. These poems contain multiple speakers, including *Bat
Zion*, or "Daughter Zion," who represents the devastated city, an unidenti-
fied poetic speaker in chapters 1 and 2, the suffering male voice of chapter 3,
and additional voices in chapters 4 and 5.[5] At times, Yahweh's voice breaks in,
though always quoted by others.

The "gender of sound" is always a difficult question, doubly so when
speakers are not clearly identified, as in Lamentations.[6] Voices and identities blur into each other; quotation and imitation abound. And gender,
never binary to begin with, becomes especially complicated when our only
access to it is through *voice*. Thus, while many critics treat Daughter Zion
as a character, one whose speech and actions are defined and delimited in
the text, she remains simply a voice. Peter J. Sabo has proposed reading
Lamentations as a "ghost town," filled with ghostly voices that haunt each
other; I will treat the text as a poetic assemblage of voices.[7] I am especially
interested in how sexual violence is represented in this poetic archive,
and in how these representations cross over with questions of gender and
sound. I will suggest that the portions of poetry associated with Daughter
Zion—herself represented as the *object* of sexual violence in other portions
of the text—complicate the questions of sexual violence more broadly.
Against the image of a female victim/survivor Finding Her Voice to
Speak Her Truth, they dwell with the fuzzy, the messy, and the icky. These
representations also resonate with other, non-biblical representations of
the aftermath, and *afters*, of sexual violence, as I explore in the second half
of the chapter.

Lamentations is also a rape story, in the sense that I have used this term
throughout this book. To be clear: This category includes poetry as well as
prose, and nonlinear and nonnarrative texts (such as Lamentations) as well
as linear and narrative ones. The "story" in "rape story" does not name a specific literary form or genre. Instead, I have proposed the term as an intentionally flexible and open category that names a wide range of representations
of sexual violence. Representation is crucial here: Rape stories are "stories"
insofar as they are ways we narrativize, organize, or otherwise *represent*
sexual violence, to others or to ourselves. And so while the nonlinear lyric
poetry of Lamentations represents rape differently than the biblical narrative

of Genesis or the Deuteronomistic History, it offers us "rape stories" all the same.

Because the descriptions of sexual violence are concentrated in Lamentations 1–2, my reading will concentrate on these texts. Historically, these chapters have bred a certain degree of anxiety among interpreters; more recently, they have attracted sustained attention from both feminist and trauma-oriented readers.[8] They also contain the greatest density of images of sexual violence and rape. One crux of the imagery comes in Lam 1:8–10:

> Jerusalem truly sinned; on this account she became bleeding and filthy.[9]
>> All who honored her despise her because they have seen her nakedness;
>> she herself groans and turns away.
> Her uncleanness was in her skirts, she did not remember her end,
>> she fell in an astonishing way, without anyone to comfort her—
>> Look, Yahweh, at my affliction, for the enemy has become strong!
> The enemy stretched out his hands over all of her precious things,
>> for she has seen the nations enter the sanctuary,
>> the ones you had forbidden to enter your congregation.

There are multiple indications of rape in these three verses. The reference to seeing Daughter Zion's "nakedness" ('erwāh) is clearly sexual, reinforced by the following verse's elaboration, "her uncleanness was in her skirts" (ṭumʾātāh běšûlêhā). The word I have translated "skirts," šûlîm, can refer to the hem of a garment, the garment itself, or the parts of the body covered by the garment. In Jeremiah 13:22 and 26, "skirts" (šûlîm) are lifted up to expose the genitals and humiliate the wearer; here too they are associated with shame and violation: thus, F. W. Dobbs-Allsopp and Tod Linafelt describe the forced exposure of the woman's body as "an institutionally sanctioned form of rape."[10] In the following verse, the grasping of "precious things" and forced entry into the "sanctuary" offer images of sexual assault. Zion's "precious things" (maḥămaddêhā) are, on one level, the treasures of the temple; they also represent her genitals.[11] The imagery of penetrating the inner sanctuary of the city (common in ancient Near Eastern siege/rape imagery), the verb "to enter" (bâʾ, also used of sexual entry) and the noun yad (hand, also penis, in 1:10), as well as parallels to other ancient Near Eastern texts, all point to sexual violence. If the city is a woman, then a siege is a rape.

Nor is the sexual violence limited to these verses. Deryn Guest adduces additional hints of rape in Lamentations 1:3, which includes the line "All of her pursuers have overtaken her in her distress."[12] The female figure is over-taken by those hunting her, an image implicitly if not explicitly (sexually) violent.[13] And in chapter 2, the female body is again threatened, here overlaid with the image of the city itself (cities being widely represented as feminine in the ancient Near East):

> Yahweh determined to destroy the wall of Daughter Zion,
>   he stretched out the line, he did not restrain his hand from destroying.
>   Rampart and wall lament; they languish together
> Her gates have sunk into the ground, he has ruined and broken her
>   bars. (2:8–9a)

Walls, doors, and gates are all used to figure the sexual openings of the female body in the Hebrew Bible; the womb, in particular, is imagined as having both doors and bars. The violation of the wall and the sinking of the city's gates are, in this context, sexualized images. And as in 1:10, "hand" is a common euphemism for "penis," just as the military penetration of a city's defenses is represented as its rape.[14]

The images of sexual violence are further entangled with another set of images, centered on the impurity of the female body. In a passage I have already considered, Lamentations 1:8–10, Daughter Zion is described as "bleeding and filthy" (*niddāh*) and as possessing "uncleanness" (*ṭum'āh*).[15] Lamentations 1:17 repeats the charge, describing Jerusalem as a "bleeding and filthy thing (*niddāh*) in their midst." The language here clearly refers to menstruation and menstrual impurity. Once again, the text invokes the over-lapping realms of signification between menstruation, female sexuality, and the female body, all of which are represented as messy and icky.

Reading Critics Reading Lamentations

Filled as they are with female suffering, these chapters have proven almost irresistible to feminist and trauma-oriented commentators. Daughter Zion presents a clear victim, thrust into a situation of almost unimaginable suf-fering, and stands at the center of these readings. In *Lamentations and the Tears of the World*, Kathleen O'Connor draws on Alan Mintz's study of the "representation of catastrophe" in Lamentations to offer a vivid picture of the horror:

> As a survivor of trauma, there is no aspect of [Daughter Zion's] body, spirit, or her environment unaffected by the catastrophe. *All that could be added is a slow, tortured death, and death would be a release.* As a survivor of assault and rape, she becomes a "living witness to a pain that knows no release."[16]

In O'Connor's reading, rape is imbricated in a larger network of suffering, part of a world of unbearable pain. Furthermore, in putting such pain on display, the text compels a response—of compassion and empathy—from its readers. In a more narrowly focused account of the rape scene in Lamentations 1, Dobbs-Allsopp and Linafelt offer a similar account of Daughter Zion's suffering and the response it compels from readers. After painstakingly tracing out what they term "a network of mutually reinforcing images of rape," they conclude:

> The poet's figuration of Zion as rape victim personalizes the city's destruction in a way that is not easily ignored. *We are compelled to compassion* by these images of victimization, and in so far as Yhwh is envisioned as the perpetrator of this crime (Thr 1,12b.13c.22b) we are led by the poet to question the ethics of Yhwh's actions. Is there anything that can justify such an abhorrent crime? *Our answer, and we believe the poet's answer as well, must be an emphatic No!*[17]

According to Dobbs-Allsopp and Linafelt, in putting such pain on display, the text requires a response—of compassion and empathy—from its readers. This same compassion and empathy should lead us to reject the text. O'Connor describes the same violence but offers a different response: "Lamentations urges us to do the difficult work of reclaiming our passion for life, for justice and empathy," part of "a theology of witnessing."[18] If for Dobbs-Allsopp and Linafelt, the text compels us to say "no!" to the violence it represents, then for O'Connor, we are summoned to say "yes" to an ethics of care.

These two interpretive responses—saying *No!* to the text on ethical grounds (Dobbs-Allsopp and Linafelt) or discerning in its horrors an ethical summons (O'Connor)—are two sides of the same coin. They both frame the violence of the text in terms of a specific moral response that it invites, or demands, from readers. They are also echoed in much of the other scholarship on sexual violence and Lamentations. Guest, for example, argues that the text demands a "recriminative response," which begins by resisting the text's representation of Daughter Zion. She goes on to suggest that "*an appropriate response* to the personification of Zion/Woman in Lamentations is one of resistance to the text and female solidarity with those ancient women."[19] And Carleen Mandolfo proposes that while the dominant representation of Daughter Zion (especially in the prophetic literature) is highly negative, Lamentations compels us to read otherwise: "The text of Lam 1–2 *leads us* in this direction naturally. *We are induced* to read *with* Daughter Zion and *toward* god/male as object."[20] Significantly, Mandolfo codes this reading as both "induced"—which is another way of saying "compelled"—and "natural." Like Guest's "appropriate response," this language used to describe the (correct) reading of Lamentations encodes its own set of ethical and hermeneutic assumptions.[21]

While they diverge in the details, I want to note two important features that these assorted readings share. First, they are, on a basic level, affectively and emotionally aligned. There is a strong, generally unstated, assumption that there are certain appropriate ways for readers, especially feminist readers and fellow travelers, to encounter texts such as Lamentations 1–2. The specific response prescribed may be different—whether to reject the text or to reclaim it—but the *feeling* that underlies it is assumed to be the same. The text creates an affective response (discomfort, sadness, even horror); we feel compelled to respond to the feeling by *doing something* (typically, applying a certain interpretive framework to the text). Furthermore, such feelings are not merely personal; they are, rather, the feelings that any "good" (or "good feminist") reader should have upon encountering this text. Second, the ethical suppositions that underlie these readings of rape in Lamentations transform it into what literary theorist Barbara Johnson calls an "already-read text": that is, a text whose contents and contours are (believed to be) known, even before they are read. As Johnson writes, "what we can see in a text the first time is already in us, not in it."[22] In the case of Lamentations 1–2, what is "already in" the text—or in us—is clear: gendered violence; intense suffering; a heroic, pitiable, and eminently feminine victim. Thus when Daughter Zion "speaks," we are induced to listen—and to respond, typically with pity, compassion, or a renewed ethical orientation toward the world. Furthermore, these readings are not simply offered up as possibilities—they are, instead, framed as compulsory, unavoidable, or ethically weighted conclusions: "We are compelled to compassion," in Dobbs-Allsopp and Linafelt's words.

But there are also ethical complications with sympathy, just as there are with interpreting or acting "on behalf of" someone else. In *No Future*, queer theorist Lee Edelman offers a scathing critique of "compassion's compulsion" and the violence that acting in sympathy for the other can engender.[23] Postcolonial and decolonial feminist and queer critics such as Partha Chatterjee, Jasbir Puar, and Lena Salaymeh have likewise challenged well intentioned but damaging liberal feminist interventions *on behalf of* women in the global south or two-thirds world.[24] And in the next chapter, I will take up the question of "telling sad stories," a particularly sticky and pernicious part of a hermeneutics of sympathy, in greater detail. For now, I want to remain with a more basic point: Interpreting *in sympathy with* or *on behalf of* can also mean speaking *in place of*. This can lead to silencing, or to the placing of words in the mouths of others. Or it can produce other forms of erasure and violence.

In addition, to approach Lamentations 1–2 as an "already-read" text is to ignore its complexity as well as its inherent fuzziness, messiness, and ickiness. Seeking to shape Daughter Zion into the ideal victim/survivor, readers downplay or neglect certain more difficult pieces of her story—beginning with the ways that she herself describes her experience of trauma. This elevation of the idealized or "already-read" victim story over and against the actual victim is something that victims and survivors have often observed; as Samantha Barrick writes, "Our experiences will never match up to these stories of perfect victims that rarely exist. Our survival stories are almost always a lot grittier."[25] As is Daughter Zion's: She is a survivor, but she is an imperfect, contradictory survivor—as perhaps almost all survivors are, when we listen to their stories beyond what we already expect to hear.

"Grit" has gained some currency in recent popular discourse as a kind of catch-all shorthand for perseverance, hard work, and stick-to-it-ness. But the grittiness that Barrick describes, and that characterizes many victim and survivor narratives, is something else. This is grit that interrupts the smooth working of the system, grit that contaminates, grit that gets in the way. What Barrick describes as grittiness is another way of naming what I have called the fuzzy, messy, and icky. Grit disturbs us; it discomforts us; it nags at us. It interrupts smooth processes and complicates them. A gritty story is also a fuzzy story, a messy story, an icky story. Like the stories of many survivors, these stories are more complicated and troubling—"grittier"—than we might expect, or might have wished for.

The Grit in Daughter Zion's Story

I want to turn now to this question of grit as it figures in Lamentations 1–2, focusing on the passages where Daughter Zion "speaks." Daughter Zion is, of course, a metaphorical figure and not either a real survivor or a fully human character; furthermore, the points at which she is the speaker are only indirectly signaled in the text (that is, there are no signals such as "Daughter Zion raised her voice and said . . ."). But in spite of these difficulties, it is useful to consider the words that seem to be hers as a body of text—and one that provides a rather different representation than the other passages from Lamentations. If the book represents a series of experiments in how to tell a rape story, then the specific rape story Daughter Zion tells, or does not tell, is important.

Daughter Zion is generally identified as having two significant speeches: in Lamentations 1:12–22 (with a brief interruption in 1:17c) and again in 2:20–22.[26] The first begins:

> Is it nothing to you, all who pass by the way? Look and see,
>   if there is a pain which is like my pain, which was inflicted on me,
>   which Yahweh inflicted on the day of his burning anger.
> From on high he set a fire and it went deep in my bones,
>   he spread out a net for my feet, he turned me back,
>   he left me all alone, I was bleeding[27] all day. (Lam 1:12–13)

From her first words, Daughter Zion demands that witnesses observe her sorrow. Previously in Lamentations 1, as in other places in the Hebrew Bible (e.g., Ezek 16, 23; Num 5), the presence of observers is part of the punishment of the transgressing woman; thus Yahweh summons Israel's lovers to witness her torture and punishment in Ezekiel 16:37. Here, however, it is Daughter Zion who invokes witnesses, to observe the intensity of her suffering—for which Yahweh is clearly named as responsible.

The specifics of this suffering, however, are less clearly expressed; they remain somewhat fuzzy. The passage offers a sequence of images—fire in the bones, a net that entraps, desolation, sickness—that are common across the biblical corpus. But while elsewhere the poetry speaks relatively clearly of rape and other forms of sexual abuse, the language here is more elliptical. There are hints: Daughter Zion complains, for example, that Yahweh has "set a fire" in her bones, an expression that is also used in Jeremiah 20:9 with a sense of sexual aggression. But rather than pursue this line of accusation further, the text then turns to her own transgressions:

> My offenses were yoked by his hand, they were braided together,
>> they weighed upon my neck, they caused my strength to falter.
>> My Lord gave me into the hands of the ones I cannot withstand,
> My Lord has thrown away all of the powerful ones in my midst,
>> he has announced a time against me, to crush my men;
>> My Lord has trodden the virgin daughter Judah like a winepress. (1:14–15)

The two themes here—Daughter Zion's guilt and Yahweh's culpability in her suffering—recur throughout the speech in chapter 1. Beyond listing the causes of her pain, Zion describes her suffering somatically: "I weep, my eyes pour out tears" (1:16); "my guts churn, my heart flutters inside me" (1:20). She also locates her pain interpersonally, expressing fear for her children (1:16), as well as the people located inside the city. Zion also speaks repeatedly about her enemies, who surround her, celebrate her punishment (1:21), and participate in it (1:14).

Zion's speech in chapter 2 is much shorter, just three verses:

> Look, Yahweh, and consider—to whom have you done this?
>> Should women eat their offspring, the children they have borne,
>> Should priest and prophet be killed in the sanctuary of my Lord?
> The young and the old are lying on the ground in the streets,
>> my young women and young men have fallen by the sword,
>> You have killed them in the day of your anger, slaughtering without mercy.
> You summoned the ones I fear around me, as for a festival;
>> on the day of the anger of Yahweh, no one escaped or survived,
>> My enemy destroyed those whom I bore and reared. (2:20–22)

Surveying chapters 1 and 2, we can observe a few key tendencies in these passages. There is a notable focus on Daughter Zion's role as *mother*, including through references to her children and her own maternal instinct.[28] There is a consistent blaming of Yahweh for causing the suffering. And there is an emphasis on the broad swath of destruction, which ensnares both young and old (1:18–19; 2:21). It is also worth observing what is missing or understated in Zion's speeches: acceptance of suffering or punishment as right or just, explicit discussion of rape or other sexual violence, and any mention of the body as unclean, contaminated, or contaminating.[29]

For some critics, what matters most in these passages in that Daughter Zion speaks at all. Dorothea Erbele-Küster, for example, writes, "This is the empowering strength of Lamentations in the midst of all its fragility: the trauma is not silenced. For me, this is the first step from inhumanity to grace. The woman is empowered (by the text) to cry out in public for the inhumanity she had suffered."[30] I want to suggest, however, that the fact that Zion is "empowered . . . to cry out" is not enough. Instead, the specific content of her speech matters, and we find in this content fuzziness, messiness, and ickiness. This is particularly the case when it comes to the features of Daughter Zion's speech that mark it as a "gritty" survivor story—grittier than readers, especially sympathetic readers, are often willing to admit. I will now turn to three of these gritty features, which can be summed up as a complication, an omission, and a neglected detail.

A Complication: Daughter Zion's Guilt

In reading rape stories, there is a strong desire for a certain sort of victim/ survivor protagonist. While she may take several forms—the "very young girl," the victim shattered by trauma, the brave survivor who has overcome and "'moved beyond' the act of violence"—her innocence is always desired.[31] Daughter Zion, too, is frequently treated as an innocent victim by commentators. Given this background, it is striking to note that Lamentations 1–2 includes multiple statements by Daughter Zion expressing her responsibility or even guilt. This guilt takes several forms. More than once, she speaks of her "offenses" (1:14, 22), which seem to justify her punishment.[32] She further describes herself as "very rebellious" (1:20), which she positions in contrast to Yahweh:

Yahweh is righteous, for I have rebelled against him.
   Listen, all peoples, and see my pain,
   my young women and young men have gone into captivity. (1:18)

Here, Daughter Zion associates her rebellion with her pain; she does not, however, insist upon her innocence. This stands in contrast to many other biblical texts of lament and protest (most dramatically, Job's speeches).

Instead, we have something messier here: She emphasizes her *suffering*, without inserting it into an economy of right and wrong punishment.

Furthermore, there are other points in the poetry where Daughter Zion seems to link her guilt to specific improper acts. In 1:19, she refers to her "lovers" and their failure to provide help: "I called out to my lovers; they betrayed me." Though the lovers here appear in a sequence of others who have failed to help (priests and elders appear in the second half of the verse), their presence has also attracted some suspicion, especially given the influence of the "marriage metaphor"—Yahweh as husband, Israel/Jerusalem/Zion as wife, the worship of other gods as adultery—in the Hebrew Prophets. Thus this brief mention is sometimes read as a double confession: In describing her lovers' failure to help her, Zion admits their existence and thus her transgression (against Yahweh) in having lovers at all. Nor are her lovers Zion's only transgression. Other unpleasant and icky things linger around the edges of her speech. Chief among these is cannibalism—more specifically, maternal cannibalism. In Lamentations 2:20, Zion asks, "Should women eat their offspring, the children they have borne?"[33] While she leaves her own question unanswered, it lingers uneasily, especially given Zion's frequent and insistent representation of herself as a mother in her speeches. Neither does Daughter Zion insist on her innocence; if anything, in raising the question, she implicates herself. But importantly, it is precisely from this position of complicity and even active participation in horror that Zion calls on Yahweh to acknowledge the extremity of her position. Thus Daughter Zion's expressions of guilt are part of a practice of ethical location and self-positioning in the very fuzzy, messy, icky space of the non-innocent victim/survivor.

And yet to many critics, taking seriously Zion's expressions of culpability and responsibility sounds uncomfortably close to victim blaming. Against Daughter Zion's claims of guilt, they have sought, instead, to demonstrate that the case is not so straightforward. Carleen Mandolfo, for example, suggests that there is no reason for Zion to insist on her innocence, even if it is the truth, "if a declaration of innocence serves no better purpose than getting her raped and her children slaughtered."[34] Or there may be a subtler literary device at work: Daughter Zion's "guilt" may not reflect actual guilt so much as the influence of literary and generic convention, perhaps used hollowly or even ironically.[35]

While these readings rightly draw attention to the literary sophistication of the text, they also suggest a certain desire to shape Daughter Zion into a "better" survivor. By removing rebelliousness, guilt, or even complicity, they produce something closer to a model victim. But while well intentioned, these sorts of readings flatten the complex and prickly account the text provides. They neglect the fuzzy, messy, and icky features of the text. And by suggesting that a good survivor story is a "pure" survivor story, they risk perpetuating the very rape myths and rape scripts that feminist critiques of rape culture seek to dismantle.

An Omission: Daughter Zion's Refusal to Describe Her Rape

A second source of "grittiness" (or fuzziness, messiness, and ickiness) in Daughter Zion's story comes in what she does *not* say: While she speaks openly about her rebellion and "offenses," she never describes her rape. Thus the sexual violence that appears elsewhere in the poetry is never validated by Daughter Zion's own report. Indeed, with the possible exception of an allusion via the description of sorrow as "inflicted on me" (1:12) and of "fire in my bones" (1:13), there is no reference to sexual violence at all. This is especially notable given Daughter Zion's open acknowledgment of other forms of sex and sexual transgression in the text. She also speaks frequently and graphically about her physical suffering, as well as the suffering of her children. And yet around her rape or other forms of sexual humiliation, she remains notably taciturn.

Daughter Zion is often described as a rape victim/survivor;[36] I have assumed this description in including Lamentations 1–2 in this book. And yet it is important to acknowledge that *in the portions of the text where Daughter Zion speaks, the speaker does not actively identify herself in this way.* This does not mean that she is not a victim or survivor, or that she is not raped, but it does point to an important difference in the economies of representation between Daughter Zion's speeches and those of the lamenter, as well as the question of whose version of events is accepted by readers.

Here again, Johnson's "already-read text" comes into play: We already know that Lamentations is a text filled with unthinkable horrors—Hugh Pyper calls it "monstrous"; Sabo calls the text "a revelation of darkness."[37] We would of course imagine that these horrors extend to rape. Rape is, after all, commonly described as "unthinkable," "terrible," "the worst thing imaginable," or even "worse than death."[38] Of course we expect such a fate for Daughter Zion, that "living witness to a pain that knows no release."[39] This assumption is reinforced by other biblical texts, such as the prophetic marriage metaphor texts, as well as other portions of Lamentations, which describe sexual violence relatively clearly. But equally importantly, the detail that Daughter Zion never describes her own rape is a detail that matters. This silence matters. The portions of the poem associated with a female speaker do not repeat the equation *ultimate horror* = *rape*: This matters. And the easy critical move to fill Daughter Zion's silence with details borrowed from elsewhere demands a critical investigation of its own. Notably, feminist theorists of sexual violence are among the harshest critics of equating *rape* with *unspeakable horror* (unspeakable in both scope and horribleness).[40] Their critiques add further weight to Daughter Zion's specific silence and should give us pause before we seek to fill it in.

A Neglected Detail: Form and Formalism in Lamentations

Much of the discussion in this chapter, including my previous two points, has focused on the content of Lamentations (as, indeed, does much of the feminist and trauma-oriented scholarship on the book). But I want to turn, now, to the flipside of content: poetic form. Lamentations is not just a text saturated with pain and suffering; it is also a rigorously formal text. Structurally, the first four chapters of the book are alphabetic acrostic poems: chapters 1, 2, and 4 are each twenty-two verses, following the sequence of the alphabet, while chapter 3 consists of sixty-six very short verses, three per letter. Chapter 5 abandons the alphabetic scheme but maintains an identical length to chapters 1, 2, and 4.[41] Together, the five chapters are better described as a collection or assemblage of poems on a theme rather than a single unified work; the relationship between chapters is not strictly causal or sequential. Instead, themes and voices resonate from one poem to another—or, to use language I have introduced earlier, the poems in Lamentations are sticky, rubbing up against, clinging to, and contaminating each other, in ways that often "stick" to their readers as well.

The tension between Lamentations' highly crafted form and its seemingly primal outpouring of grief and suffering is a matter of interest. Does form tame pain, or sharpen it? Could it do both? For O'Connor, structure is a device for containing pain: "the alphabetic devices embody struggles of survivors to contain and control the chaos of unstructured pain."[42] Elizabeth Boase suggests that the "fragmented voices" of Lamentations have a community-constituting function, "gather[ing] a fragmented community around a shared narrative in order to facilitate collective unity and identity."[43] In these readings and other similar ones, form functions as a (partial) counterweight to suffering. By organizing pain into a story (again, I use the term loosely to suggest meaning and coherence, not a specific literary genre), the text creates order and begins the work of "remaking the world," in response to its "unmaking" through pain (an argument associated most closely with Elaine Scarry and *The Body in Pain*; Scarry also argues that pain shatters language itself).[44] By transfiguring pain into a text and making this text available for community use, poetic form thus performs world-building work.

A second formal concern involves the question of closure—both of chapters and of verses. The acrostic form (and, in the case of chapter 5, the twenty-two-letter pseudo-acrostic) imposes strict limits on the text. And yet there is also a persistent, pervasive refusal of resolution. The complaints that are raised across the poems are *not* resolved; pain and suffering do not come to an end when the poetry does. In this vein, some critics direct attention to the open or unfinished ending: Thus, both Linafelt and Scott Ellington suggest that the book's failure to end, or to end properly, is an intentional lack of closure, one that either expresses theological ambiguity (Ellington) or serves as an indictment (Linafelt).[45]

I will return to these arguments about form later in the chapter. For now, I want merely to note the uneasy fit between the text's highly crafted form and any reading that takes Daughter Zion's speeches as authentic outpourings of pain and trauma. Her words are often praised for speaking to the heart of suffering: Thus, "Despite her broken, violated core, Woman Zion's direct and straightforward recitation suggests she has found the courage to confront her aggressor with the brutal consequences of his deeds" (Hens-Piazza's assessment) or even "Literature such as the book of Lamentations gives voice to the silenced" (Erbele-Küster).[46] The adversarial or dialogic relationship between Daughter Zion's speeches and the other portions of Lamentations are likewise praised—in Mandolfo's influential reading, Daughter Zion does not simply talk but "talks *back*."[47] And yet the voices of Lamentations, including Daughter Zion's voice, are all situated within the larger frame of the acrostic form. Thus, while the content and tone of Daughter Zion's speeches may push back against the other voices in the text, on the level of form, what she says flows seamlessly from what precedes it. Indeed, the formal and poetic unity that each chapter displays is one reason that Daughter Zion is not always recognized or acknowledged by readers as a distinct character in her own right. I am not suggesting that formal ingenuity or rigor negates the emotional or affective power of a text such as Zion's lament. I am, however, emphasizing that we must take form seriously, not just when reading the text as a whole but also Zion's words in particular. This is not simply a spontaneous out-pouring of anguish. Instead, it is a rigorously formal text.

The question of closure and endings is also germane to this point. Daughter Zion's voice speaks in chapters 1 and 2, only to remain silent for the remainder of the book. If this is a story about a woman/victim/survivor finding her voice, then what do we make of her silence? Is it a *silencing*, or simply an absence? One solution, of course, is an appeal to textual history— the five chapters represent originally separate poems and should not be read together, or in any particular order.[48] But this does not solve the problem so much as displace it. As much as her speech, Daughter Zion's extended silences are formally as well as meaningfully significant.

Cvetkovich and the Archive as a Response to Trauma

The grit in Daughter Zion's survivor story requires a new way of reading these texts. Such a reading attends to literary form rather than treating it as either decorative or secondary. It acknowledges the statements of culpability that are placed in Daughter Zion's own voice. And it takes seriously the reluc-tance in her portions of the poem to speak openly about sexual trauma, even as she expresses guilt; engages in other painful, icky, and compromising ac-tivities; and fails to bring her story to a fitting end. In seeking a way of reading that fits this model of unspeaking/unspoken sexual trauma, I find myself less interested in compelling Daughter Zion to speak (or in filling in her silences for her) than in lingering with the silence and its echoes. I am also drawn to the points where Daughter Zion's specific survivor story resonates with other survivor stories, especially those that resist or challenge the "already-read" rape story. One way of responding to Daughter Zion's story differently involves the archive.

In theorizing and curating a survivor archive for framing and under-standing Daughter Zion, I have drawn on Cvetkovich and especially her work *An Archive of Feelings*. As the title suggests, the work itself is a kind of archive, though an unconventional one, gathering together queer per-formance art, butch subcultures, musical performances by Tribe 8 and Le Tigre, lesbian art about incest, and interviews and artifacts documenting early lesbian AIDS activism. The goal of the archive is to explore and doc-ument how "public cultures" form in response to trauma, especially sexual trauma. Cvetkovich resists, however, following the established contours of trauma studies, including discourses of witnessing, the use of the Holocaust as a point of reference, the special privileging of survivor narratives, and "the feminist recommendation to tell my story" of sexual abuse.[49] Instead, she insists on approaching trauma with an emphasis on queer and lesbian cultures and subcultures, and on perspectives that are often occluded or omitted from trauma studies as such. The result is "an archive of feelings," which Cvetkovich describes as "an exploration of cultural texts as repositories of feelings and emotions, which are encoded not only in the content of the texts themselves but in the practices that surround their production and reception."[50] While trauma is the archive's starting point, it is not its end: It becomes, instead, "a point of entry into a vast archive of feelings, the many forms of love, rage, intimacy, grief, shame, and more that are part of the vibrancy of queer cultures."[51]

Cvetkovich is not the only recent thinker to consider the archive; other thinkers engaged in queer theory have also explored archival turns.[52] But her specific mode of engaging the archive offers a useful framing for this chapter's project for two reasons. First, Cvetkovich's complicated attitude toward trauma, especially sexual trauma, resonates with my own critique of the "already-read" survivor story and the fetishization of a narrow sort of survivor narrative. Of *An Archive of Feelings'* unconventional assemblages and approach, she writes,

> Although I was interested in feminist approaches to trauma, the solemnity of so much feminist work on incest did not speak to me. I wanted something more than self-righteous anger or hushed tones of sympathy or respectful silence. I found what I was looking for in lesbian subcultures that cut through narratives of innocent victims and therapeutic healing to present something that was raw, confrontational, and even sexy . . . Their writings have also been points of reference when theoretical concepts fail me.[53]

This passage stresses that theoretical concepts can, and often do, fail to capture the felt experience of sexual trauma, and nondominant approaches—elsewhere Cvetkovich calls them "unabashedly minoritarian"—offer a different vocabulary for, and framing of, trauma.[54] Importantly, this framing does not cleanse narratives of their grit, just as it refuses to maintain a safe distance between sex and violence, abuse and agency, pleasure and love. In bringing these features together, and in insisting on their intermingling, the archive instead takes seriously the fuzzy, messy, and icky as they figure in sexual trauma. Cvetkovich's archive touches on a number of icky things (beginning with incest). It insists on messy ways of telling stories. And it holds space for fuzzy, whether fuzzy stories, fuzzy feelings, or a fuzzily ambivalent relationship to dominant cultural narratives.

Second, Cvetkovich's description aligns with the contours of the archive I sketch in what follows. Her archive is filled with experimental works and minor genres, though it also includes more conventional texts, such as feature films and novels. Still other archival entries are more ephemeral: a performance piece, an interview, a feeling. Indeed, it is feeling that unites the materials in the archive, as well as the relationship between feeling and "public cultures," especially the public cultures that form around trauma. My own archive is narrower than Cvetkovich's—all of its entries are essays or memoirs, published by independent presses, though with varying degrees of readership and mainstream recognition.[55] Furthermore, while all three texts are "queer," each is also in conversation with different public cultures or countercultures, though there are also significant points of overlap. And the archive this chapter offers is only a beginning—it reaches out, as well, to the literary and theoretical texts in the other chapters of *Texts after Terror*, as well as to many texts and objects that lie beyond this work.

My archive is not as ambitious or wide-ranging as Cvetkovich's "archive of feelings." And yet it shares in its orientation, all the same. Rather than purify the category of the victim or insist on drawing meaning from suffering, Cvetkovich's archive holds space for the fuzzy, messy, and icky. Furthermore, it puts them to use: "[T]rauma can be a foundation for creating counterpublic spheres rather than evacuating them."[56] In what follows, I seek to create a "counterpublic sphere" of my own for reading and relating to Daughter Zion and her trauma. Reading Lamentations 1 and 2 together with other, contemporary texts of sexual violence and sexual trauma—particularly queer, minoritized, and formally experimental texts—offers new ways of reading Daughter Zion.

Queering Sexual Violence: Against the "Good Victim" and "Good Survivor"

The first text for the archive is the anthology *Queering Sexual Violence: Radical Voices from Within the Anti-Violence Movement*, edited by Jennifer

Patterson. The collection is among the first book-length works to address the intersections of sexuality, sexual violence, and queer communities. Divided into four sections—Redefining, Resisting, Reclaiming, Reimagining—this is very much a book by and for activists, filled with contributions by authors with deep experience in social justice work and activism against sexual violence. The perspectives are consistently queer and insistently intersectional, rejecting the "violence against women" framework in favor of a critical analysis of sexuality, gender, race, and class. While most of the contributions are essays, there are also poems and drawings scattered among them. Many of the pieces are short; nearly all are charged through with urgency: This is praxis, not theory, and the time to act is *now*. In *An Archive of Feelings*, Cvetkovich suggests that "anthologies with a mixture of voices and genres render visible counterpublics that haven't produced major novels or films"—or, we might add, dominant intellectual frameworks for understanding sexual and gender-based violence.[57] This is certainly true of *Queering Sexual Violence*.

On one level, *Queering Sexual Violence* is significant simply because it exists. In this way, it resembles Daughter Zion's speech and a certain line of argument that has emerged in response to it: *What matters is not what she says, so much as the fact that Daughter Zion has a voice at all.* The same could be said of *Queering Sexual Violence*: What matters is that these voices can speak at all—indeed, a version of this argument occurs in both the foreword and the introduction to the book.[58] But with respect to both *Queering Sexual Violence* and Lamentations, this response downplays and devalues the significance of the intervention each text is making. Daughter Zion has specific pains and specific complaints. Listening to Daughter Zion means holding a space for this specificity. It also means refusing to collapse specific traumas into a larger category of trauma as such. Here Cvetkovich's comments on sexual trauma are instructive:

> Sometimes the impact of sexual trauma doesn't seem to measure up to that of collectively experienced historical events, such as war and genocide. Sometimes it seems invisible because it is confined to the domestic or private sphere. Sometimes it doesn't appear sufficiently catastrophic because it doesn't produce dead bodies or even, necessarily, damaged ones.[59]

Lamentations, of course, is filled with dead and damaged bodies, even as the "collectively experienced historical events" of the Exile are an all-too-present trauma everywhere in the book. But historical trauma does not negate or override all other trauma: Multiple forms of pain and suffering can exist simultaneously. This is a point that Lamentations scholarship, in its rush to comprehend the immensity of trauma, sometimes misses. O'Connor, for example, writes, "Lamentations is about the collapse of a physical, emotional, and spiritual universe of an entire people, not about individual sorrows except in a metaphoric and symbolic manner."[60] I disagree: Although the book includes much collective sorrow, it also lingers with individual suffering, beginning with Daughter Zion's own description. She insists on the specificity of her suffering, not its representative status. More importantly, the larger point, also articulated in various ways in *Queering Sexual Violence*, stands: Taking trauma seriously does not mean being compelled to frame it or narrativize it in certain ways. And the contributors in *Queering Sexual Violence* offer many specific and concrete suggestions for how we might respond to sexual violence differently. While many of these are specific to contemporary contexts, there are also resonances with the biblical text. I single out in particular the repeated pressure the essays put on the category of the victim/survivor—who counts as a victim, what it means to be a "good" victim or survivor, how certain forms of survival are criticized or punished.[61]

Adding a diverse company of queer voices to the survivor archive, *Queering Sexual Violence* questions who is given access to the categories of "victim" or "survivor" at all, or what this access means. Multiple contributors criticize the figure of the victim and the way she[62] is represented. In her introduction, Patterson singles out the "mainstream understanding of violence in which the 'victim' is (assumed) to be a white, cisgender, heterosexual, virginal woman—the perfect survivor," a set of assumptions that limits our ways of understanding and responding to sexual violence.[63] But the problem is not simply one of broadening the category of "victim." Instead, the category itself, like the category of "survivor," is a source of difficulty. Many victims and survivors find that the language and concept of "survivor" implies a specific *sort* of survivor. This is especially apparent in communities that are or perceive themselves to be outside the traditional domain of survivorship. Upon hearing the term "survivor" used at a "Take Back the Night" rally against sexual violence, Rousse Arielle reflects,

> And standing there, I asked myself: am I a Survivor? I had survived my battles—I was alive, after all—but she made it sound like this Survivor was someone in particular, someone unabashed, sweet, optimistic . . . someone

with an obligation. And I knew I could never be that Survivor. In the midst of all the words of "empowerment," I burned with jealousy and humiliation at my failure and incapacity to feel all those things I was supposed to feel. I felt like an outsider, like I was all wrong in my actions and reactions to the trauma I had experienced.[64]

Arielle proceeds to offer a scathing indictment of the way the Survivor overwhelms and forecloses the experiences of actual survivors and victims (the category "Victim" fares little better).[65]

Other essays echo these critiques. Barrick criticizes "haunting ill-fitting narratives of saintly victims."[66] Sassafras Lowrey's piece is titled "Not a Good Survivor."[67] Katherine Schott Nelson offers a searing account of surviving an abusive relationship while also insisting on her abuser's past history of abuse as a tragedy of its own, insisting that "My justice is her justice."[68] And Patterson writes, "I have also been a survivor who perpetrates harm on others."[69] A central problem shared by "victim" and "survivor" is the way in which terms intended as descriptions come to imply narratives. As Arielle, Lowrey, Barrick, and others chart out, these terms come to contain within their meanings both a description of character (a victim or a survivor is supposed to be a certain sort of person) and a trajectory of action (the victim/survivor is supposed to act in a certain way following the sexual violence itself). Furthermore, the victim or survivor is supposed to be oriented in a certain way, both toward what has happened to her and especially toward the future. Like the rape stories in which they figure, the terms "victim" and "survivor" become "already-read texts" in miniature.

All this speaks to the difficulty surrounding the category of "victim" in Daughter Zion's speech, especially in chapter 1. There are the repeated suggestions, both in her own speech and that of others, that she is neither a "good victim" nor a "good survivor."[70] She has lovers (Lam 1:2,19); worse, her lovers are *bad* lovers—they abandon her in time of need. This is a tacit reflection on her judgment or perhaps her desirability. It is also a common biblical rhetorical strategy: At multiple points in the "marriage metaphor" texts, Israel is accused of being a whore who works for free, an identity apparently much worse than an ordinary whore. She is likewise rebellious—a charge she does not deny but rather repeats several times. While these and other related confessions are sometimes interpreted as survivor guilt or even a form of trauma-induced false consciousness, I propose we take them seriously. Rather than trying to sanitize Daughter Zion into an idealized victim, the radical response is to reject the demand that she be remade in this image.

Taking this portion of the archive seriously also means rejecting the demand that Daughter Zion act as a "good survivor" in favor of allowing her a fuzzier, messier, and ickier way of representing sexual trauma. This "good survivor" can take multiple forms. She may grieve properly and appropriately; she may fight back to protect herself from assault; she does not, however, struggle to share her story.[71] And yet: Daughter Zion alternates between lamenting her pain and blaming herself, even as she refuses to narrate her sexual assault. She does not describe herself as "fighting back"; indeed, it seems that she socialized with "the wrong people" (that is, her lovers). Her pain has not ended. These are hard truths, but they are also truths that reflect the ways survivors narrate their own experiences, against the "already-read" survivor stories that are pressed upon them.

Care Work: On Refusing to "Prove It" and Resisting Cure

The second text for the archive is Leah Lakshmi Piepzna-Samarasinha's *Care Work: Dreaming Disability Justice*. Piepzna-Samarasinha's volume is a collection of essays, organized around "disability justice"—not simply justice *for* disabled communities, but also what other activist communities can learn from critical work in disability and crip activism. A significant part of this analysis involves sexual violence and sexual trauma, as well as the complex identities of survivors of many sorts (sexual violence, abuse, disability, trauma). Like *Queering Sexual Violence*, *Care Work* crosses genres—mostly essays, though also conversations, lists, manifestos, imaginary letters, and bits of memoir and metamemoir; several of the pieces were first published online or in activist-oriented anthologies. Sexual violence and sexual trauma are braided into the larger tapestry of concerns, including disability justice, activism, art, and trauma.

Like the contributors of *Queering Sexual Violence*, Piepzna-Samarasinha calls out the narrow constraints placed upon survivor stories, which ignore and silence actual survivors. She is especially critical of what she terms "traditional abuse survivor narratives," as well as the limited inventory of accepted and acceptable "ideas of what a survivor narrative is."[72] Insofar as they treat sexual violence as exceptional and unthinkable, they ignore the way that it is woven into everyday life. Piepzna-Samarasinha writes,

> For so many QTBIPOC [Queer Trans Black Indigenous People of Color],
> surviving violence is just life. We survive so many forms of violence and
> are resilient, and not. We make it, and we don't, and we make it side-
> ways . . . Survivorhood is not just what would be in the police file. Far from
> it. It is all our stories of every moment we survive.[73]

Against the exceptionality of violence, Piepzna-Samarasinha insists on its
everydayness. And in this reality, survival is contingent, partial, ongoing,
complicated.

The omnipresence of violence, including sexual violence, produces an attitude of suspicion toward the demand to "prove" the existence of violence
by exposing it to public view. As I have already described in chapter 1, Eve
Kosofsky Sedgwick describes "faith in exposure" as part of a paranoid hermeneutics: The idea that exposing (sexual) violence will lead to its cessation
is an essentially paranoid attitude.[74] All of Sedgwick's critiques of this hermeneutic strategy apply here as well, of course. But Piepzna-Samarasinha's critique goes further, putting pressure on the specific "the dynamic of 'prove it' "
that is pressed upon survivors. She refers to the demand that survivors narrativize and display "the most overt, gruesome moments of abuse."[75] This is
part of a discourse of truth. Without such suffering—and the *display* of such
suffering—the experience of sexual violence is not accepted as "real." In this
way, survivor narratives are asked to function much like torture: They expose
truth through pain. Words may lie, but the purity of suffering does not.[76]

The demand to show pain is frequently applied to contemporary rape
stories; the "Victim Impact Statement" is one legal instantiation of the imperative. But it also appears in the context of biblical rape stories, and nowhere
more than in Lamentations. The exhibition of Daughter Zion's suffering
body, as well as the desire of critics (feminist and otherwise) to linger with
her pain, is a form of amplification that also doubles as sadism. The reader/
viewer's desire for the suffering of the body is privileged over that body itself. Importantly, I am not saying (nor is Piepzna-Samarasinha) that stories
of pain should not be told, or that to describe pain is always to exploit a survivor. I am merely following Piepzna-Samarasinha in her highly salient point
that the demand for truth-through-suffering both constrains and disciplines
survivors, even as they are compelled to share their stories. In the case of
Daughter Zion, this suggests that we should pause before either criticizing
the text for withholding details of her sexual abuse (in her own speeches) or
moving to fill in these details (based on other texts, whether in Lamentations

or beyond). It also means resisting the desire to find resolution in the text, either by answering Daughter Zion's lament with words of comfort from other texts or by framing her cries as a clarion call for justice. Piepzna-Samarasinha observes: "We want the pain, the trauma of surviving sexual abuse or assault to be over."[77] But it is not always over, not always healed.

Like many survivors, Piepzna-Samarasinha is skeptical of the compulsion to cure and the demands for wholeness and healing that are placed upon survivors. But she also goes further, calling for an "anti-ableist vision of survivorhood."[78] A key part of this work is refusing to frame survival in terms of cure. Drawing on disability justice, she critiques a fixation with cure, imagining, instead, a model of living with trauma that is not limited to either "fixed" or "broken" subjects. Survival is not something to overcome but rather an ongoing process of learning, living, and remembering. Piepzna-Samarasinha asks us to hold open a space for grief and pain, while considering the possibility of survival outside of repair:

> And even more dangerous, I want to venture: What if some things aren't fixable? What if some things really never will be the same—and that might not be great, but it might be okay? . . . What if some trauma wounds really never will go away—and we still might have great lives?[79]

Piepzna-Samarasinha's larger concern is with survivors of trauma of a wide variety, not merely sexual violence. But her vision of survival without repair offers a powerful alternative to the obsession with repair that dominates narratives of survival, and the way those narratives are received. Elsewhere, I have written about how the sexual violence survivor becomes an "unhappy object" (Sara Ahmed's term) when she fails to tell the "right" story or to display the proper mode of cure.[80] By drawing on disability justice and centering crip and disabled perspectives, Piepzna-Samarasinha offers a powerful alternative model, one that does not ignore fuzziness, messiness, or ickiness, and one in which we are "able to imagine survivor futures where we are *thriving* but not *cured.*"[81]

Piepzna-Samarasinha is not alone in her refusal of the fantasy of cure. Instead, her intervention connects survivor stories to already ongoing conversations in disability and crip studies. Eli Clare, for example, has put pressure on "cure" as a category that limits and precludes disabled futures.[82] Taking up the figure of the cancer survivor, M. Cooper Minister has argued strenuously against survivor discourses as harmful, sacrificing actual cancer patients and survivors for the sake of the Survivor as an ideal and an ideological figure. Minister's alternative is a model of "survival without optimism," which they argue allows the possibility of flourishing without repair.[83] And Brandy Daniels has argued for the theological and ethical importance of holding space for the self shattered by sexual violence, rather than insisting on fitting the pieces back together again.[84] Considered together, these voices raise the possibility of an alternative future of "*thriving* but not *cured*" (Piepzna-Samarasinha's phrase). What these futures look like is different for each thinker—what connects them, instead, is the move outside of cure.

All of this is highly relevant to Daughter Zion and to biblical rape texts, which are no less vulnerable to the demands for resolution—whether effected through repair or through mourning—than are contemporary survivor stories. It is not, strictly speaking, possible to *heal* Daughter Zion— though some intertextual readings, such as those that pair her laments and the marriage metaphor passages with the more "hopeful" texts in Second Isaiah and elsewhere attempt this.[85] But I suggest that readings of the text are still overwhelmingly framed around the reparative/curative model. Just as "cure infects survivor dialogues" (Piepzna-Samarasinha), so too does it affect the reading of Daughter Zion. If she cannot be cured—Salters describes her as "beyond repair"[86]—then she must be mourned. But this is precisely what Piepzna-Samarasinha warns against: "the binary of fixed or broken . . . [that] stops us from being able to imagine survivor futures where we are *thriving* but not *cured*."[87] The text may not describe Daughter Zion as thriving; indeed, she may never thrive. She may remain shattered, like the survivor selves that Daniels describes. Or she may choose "survival without optimism," as Minister imagines the future of the cancer survivor. Yet drawing on Piepzna-Samarasinha's analysis in *Care Work*, I suggest that there is something deeply damaging, and deeply limiting, in insisting on framing Daughter Zion and other biblical stories of survival through a dichotomy of brokenness and repair, or redemption and unredeemable grief. Instead, we need to hold space for the ambivalence, and the fuzziness, messiness, and ickiness, that Daughter Zion and Lamentations more broadly describe.

In the Dream House: Form and Experiment

The third text for the archive is Carmen Maria Machado's *In the Dream House*, a haunting, formally experimental account of queer domestic violence and abuse. Machado traverses much of the same ground as *Care Work* and *Queering Sexual Violence*: trauma, memory, sexual violence and abuse in queer communities, the invisibility of certain stories.[88] Beyond adding to a still small body of literature about queer trauma and abuse, Machado's memoir is notable especially for its formal features. The "dream house" of the title is both a literal physical location—the home where much of the abuse chronicled by the memoir takes place—and a framing device that structures the memoir, which is itself another kind of "dream house." To this end, every chapter is entitled "*Dream House as* _____," with the blank filled by a noun or descriptive phrase.[89] After "*Dream House as* Overture" and "*Dream House as* Prologue," the first chapter is "*Dream House as* Not a Metaphor," followed by "*Dream House as* Picaresque," ". . . Perpetual Motion Machine," and ". . . an Exercise in Point of View."[90] The dream house/*Dream House* also takes on various literary genres: Thus we find "*Dream House* as Lesbian Cult Classic" and "Lesbian Pulp Novel," "*Dream House* as American Gothic," "*Dream House* as Noir," and "*Dream House* as Romance Novel." A lengthy sequence entitled "*Dream House as* Choose Your Own Adventure®" repurposes the young adult novels of the 1970s and 1980s as an unnerving trap of domestic violence.[91] Still other forms are piercingly specific: an anechoic chamber, Adam's naming of the animals, a mystical pregnancy.[92] The titles hint at what each chapter contains; most are only a few pages, many even less.

On one level, *In the Dream House* becomes an exploration of genre, a question of how to tell a story that is not already familiar, or that feels impossible. Is her narrative of abuse and trauma a *Bildungsroman*? A cautionary tale? An epiphany? Something else?[93] More broadly, this is a question of whether form can help us narrate what is otherwise unspeakable. Genres, like houses, provide homes for stories; *In the Dream House* is an exploration of what shape this might take. An archive is also a home, as Machado tells us in "*Dream House as* Prologue": The word derives from *arkheion*, "the house of the ruler."[94] Archives are dream houses, even as *Dream House* is an unusual sort of archive.

Another formal feature that structures the memoir is the use of folk and fairy tales. Machado compares her abuser to Bluebeard and herself to Lot's wife, unable to let go or leave Sodom behind.[95] The fairy tale heroine who cannot speak—the Little Mermaid, Eliza in the "The Wild Swans," the Goose Girl—becomes a figure of Machado's own struggle to name her abuse. In a chapter entitled "*Dream House as* Folktale Taxonomy," discussing these figures, Machado writes,

Sometimes your tongue is removed, sometimes you still it of your own accord. Sometimes you live, sometimes you die. Sometimes you have a name, sometimes you are named for what—not who—you are. The story always looks a little different, depending upon who is telling it.[96]

These borrowed figures from folklore are frequently accompanied by references to Stith Thompson's *Motif-Index of Folk-Literature* (later incorporated into the Aarne–Thompson–Uther Index), a classic reference work dedicated to chronicling and organizing motifs in folk⋅literature. The textual apparatus of Machado's memoir—another example of her play with form—thus presents an additional level of argument. It is fitting, then, that the book's final chapter, "*Dream House as* Epilogue," which describes the writing of the book, ends with a footnote to Thompson's motif D2161.3.6.1, "Magic restoration of cut-out tongue."[97] Machado has regained her tongue at last.

Machado's memoir touches on many of the themes I have described in reference to both *Queering Sexual Violence* and *Care Work*. She returns, repeatedly but elliptically, to the difficulty of claiming the identity of "victim," which seems to fit uneasily with her own experience. Nowhere is this point made more clearly than in "*Dream House as* Epiphany," which consists of a single sentence: "Most types of domestic abuse are completely legal."[98] And she resists both cure and closure, nowhere more than in "*Dream House as* Ending," which begins, "That there's a real ending to anything is, I'm pretty sure, the lie of all autobiographical writing."[99] Instead of a single story, Machado leaves us with a dizzying assemblage of fragments—the Dream House as a series of Dream Houses, the story told many ways as a way of telling it at all. Taken as a whole, *In the Dream House* reinforces the arguments of the contributors to *Queering Sexual Violence* and of Piepzna-Samarasinha, offering a vision of a future beyond good victims, fixed survivors, on-demand performances of pain, and the language of cure. It charts a fuzzy, messy, and icky terrain, a different way of describing sexual trauma and what comes after.

But this is not Machado's greatest contribution to the archive—that is, instead, the form and structure of her text. As I have already described, Lamentations is a rigorously structured text, one whose form challenges any attempt to read Daughter Zion's speeches as pure unfiltered outpouring or *cri de coeur*. While the form of the biblical book is often analyzed in relation to other ancient laments, *In the Dream House* makes a compelling case for reading the biblical text with and through a contemporary survivor story. Machado's memoir seamlessly integrates folklore, scholarly forms (such as the citations to the tale type index), and an overarching formal device—the naming of chapters—that *ought* to suffocate the text but instead function, against all odds, to create its most powerful literary effects. In this way, it functions analogously to the alphabetic acrostic form of Lamentations 1–4 (and the modified continuation of that form in chapter 5).

Machado also provides an illuminating parallel to Lamentations' refusal of closure. If *In the Dream House* produces a greater sense of closure than Daughter Zion's speeches (or the book of Lamentations as a whole), it is only through literary sleight of hand, as Machado herself admits (in both "*Dream House as* Ending" and "*Dream House as* Epilogue").[100] One form such sleight of hand takes is the repetition of the ending of a Panamanian folktale, which itself forecloses the possibility of an ending: "My tale only goes to here, it ends, and the wind carries it off."[101] The truer ending comes in the "Choose Your Own Adventure" sequence, in which no ending or escape is possible, without imagination or cheating. ("That's not how it happened, but okay. We can pretend. I'll give it to you, just this once.")[102] Daughter Zion is less generous: There is no ending, only destruction:

> You summoned the ones I fear around me, as for a festival,
> on the day of the anger of Yahweh, no one escaped or survived.
> My enemy destroyed those whom I bore and reared. (Lam 2:22)

There is no choosing a different adventure; no escaping this story.

Crossing Texts, Crossing Over

Queering Sexual Violence, Care Work, In the Dream House: three different ways of telling a survivor story, three perspectives on abuse, three experiments in queering (or cripping, or dreaming, all of which are ways of *retelling*) sexual violence. While I have treated them separately, drawing out different themes in each—the trap of the "good victim" or "good survivor" in *Queering Sexual Violence*, the demand for the icky details and the refusal to fetishize cure in *Care Work*, the use of form and structure in *In the Dream House*—these themes cross over and travel between texts. Piepzna-Samarasinha has little patience for the "good survivor"; Machado does not see herself reflected in this figure. *In the Dream House* is not a narrative of overcoming or curing trauma so much as an exploration of how we might live with it, with the haunted houses and haunted archives that persist in dreams and memory. Several authors in *Queering Sexual Violence* suggest the importance of holding space for survivor stories without putting pressure on them to resolve as stories of healing or cure: River Willow Fagan imagines a "genderqueer community of survivors," whose stories come together in "a map to liberation and healing" that is nevertheless "messily bordered" and "constantly evolving"; Avory Faucette turns to "play," including sexual play, as an alternative to a sterile resolution that silences trauma.[103] And all of the texts experiment with form and nontraditional modes of writing about sexual violence (though *In the Dream House* is clearly much more deeply positioned in a tradition of literary experiment).

Read apart and together, these texts—the founding entries in an archive of survivor stories—suggest new and different ways of reading Daughter Zion in Lamentations. When we look at the opening chapters of Lamentations as more than an "already-read text," we are confronted with a text in which Daughter Zion's survivor story comes with "grit"—her complicity, guilt, and rebelliousness; her refusal to describe her rape; the ickiness that clings to her story; her failure to find resolution. While feminist and trauma readings often skip over or seek to "cleanse" the narrative of this grit, I approach it through the archive, which suggests it is not contamination to remove but rather an essential part of the survivor story as Daughter Zion, and others, tell it. Drawing on the archive, I have further suggested several important points for reading biblical and other survivor texts: resisting the demand for "good victims" and "good survivors," and the demand that survivors share the worst parts of their stories, insisting on alternatives to recovery and cure, and treating form as integral, not secondary, to the narrating of trauma.

The Daughter Zion who emerges from this reading looks rather different from other iterations of her character. She is no longer simply a tragic figure. She still speaks, and speaks angrily, but her summons is not to mourning or pity. Daughter Zion demands a witness, as is often observed of Lamentations. My reading has suggested that while the act of witnessing is important, so too is the question of what is witnessed. And what we find here is not what we have "already read" into the text. Rather, the account is filled with formal complexity, uncomfortable silence, discomfiting guilt, poetic art and artifice. And, of course, the fuzzy, messy, and icky. These features are not secondary;

they are, instead, central to Daughter Zion's speech and to Lamentations' vision—as, indeed, they are to other texts in the trauma archive. As Julietta Singh describes in *No Archive Will Restore You*, another text that fits well with the beginnings of an archive that this chapter has assembled, the body itself is an "impossible, deteriorating archive," "messy, embodied [and] illegitimate."[104] But it is in this archive that we find new truths, new ways of reading. So too with the bodies and archives here—and first among these archives, Daughter Zion herself.

6

Sad Stories and Unhappy Reading

The introduction of Phyllis Trible's *Texts of Terror* is titled "On Telling Sad Stories." This is not simply a literary flourish: For Trible, one practice of feminist criticism—perhaps its most important duty—is "telling sad stories," especially "tales of terror with women as victims." In this book, I have followed other paths, exploring a different kind of reading practice for biblical rape stories. Instead of announcing the sadness and sufferings that fill these texts, I have sought to burrow into them, to find other ways of reading, understanding, and living with their stories. Some of the texts I have considered are often described as "texts of terror," a phrase still closely associated with Trible; two of my key examples, Hagar and Tamar, receive chapter-length treatments in *Texts of Terror* as well. Other stories I have canvassed do not appear in that work, but they present additional and troubling permutations of biblical sexual violence: Dinah and Shechem, Lot and his daughters, the sexual exploitation of Bathsheba and Abishag by David, Daughter Zion and her enemies, Nineveh sexually exposed and humiliated by Yahweh.

While I value the work that the category of "texts of terror" has done, and continues to do, I have sought other ways of describing biblical rape stories such as these, beginning by drawing out the frequent fuzziness, messiness, and ickiness of stories of sexual violence. I have also offered a series of tactics for reading that emphasize the fuzzy, messy, and icky. These include resisting claims of innocence, refusing paranoid reading positions, following the traces of sticky affect, and reading with and through literature. This chapter offers a final weaving together of the threads of interpretation that *Texts after Terror* has pursued. I also want to articulate more clearly how the feminist approach described and practiced here represents a movement beyond the feminist hermeneutics of "telling sad stories" into a broader and more flexible interpretive practice that I will describe as "unhappy reading." Drawing together the arguments of the previous chapters, I will argue that telling sad stories is not enough, particularly when the sad stories are biblical rape stories. Telling sad stories fails to capture what is fuzzy, messy, and icky about sexual violence. In contrast, unhappy reading offers an essential

Texts after Terror. Rhiannon Graybill, Oxford University Press. © Oxford University Press 2021.
DOI: 10.1093/oso/9780190082314.003.0007

alternative to readings of "sad stories" that either fetishize trauma or privilege catharsis over holding space for complexity and unhappiness, including the complexity and unhappiness of both sexual violence and narrative. To tell a sad story is to pronounce a judgment on it—whether a judgment about what the story contains (that is, *something sad*), what the story should make us feel (*sadness*), or the fixity of the story's meaning (*stable enough to "tell"*). Telling sad stories forecloses possible meanings and lines of interpretation. Unhappy reading, in contrast, emphasizes possibility and openness.

My call for practices of reading that take seriously both textual difficulties and painful plots without trying to resolve them builds on Sara Ahmed's work on unhappiness and the "freedom to be unhappy."[1] In *The Promise of Happiness*, Ahmed argues for the importance, possibility, and even world-building potential of unhappiness, even as happiness can be a coercive or oppressive category. I take up the possibilities of unhappiness here, advocating for readings that, in place of the catharsis and comfort of sadness, keep us in a suspended state of unhappiness and discomfort toward the text—what Donna Haraway calls "staying with the trouble." Instead of passing over the difficulties of biblical rape stories—including, as I will take up, the difficulty of framing them as (just) fuzzy, messy, and icky—unhappy reading concentrates on the difficulties in our reading processes, and in the stories themselves.

To demonstrate how unhappy reading works, and works differently from telling sad stories, I turn to a final biblical story: the gang rape and murder of the Levite's concubine in Judges 19. Widely recognized as a "text of terror," including by Trible, the story has attracted a density of feminist commentary and critique.[2] These feminist responses overwhelmingly follow the telling sad stories model. For this reason, examining them carefully illuminates the limits of that approach. I emphasize three issues: failing to differentiate rape from murder (thereby unwittingly replicating the assertion that *rape = death*), fetishizing the voice of the female victim, and ignoring the problems with readings that are focused on saving women. After drawing out these difficulties, I sketch out how an unhappy reading proceeds differently. My goal in this chapter is not to offer a comprehensive reading of the story but rather to show how the interpretive tactics offered here, and across *Texts after Terror*, operate differently, opening texts and readers to new questions, new feelings, and new ways of relating to the text and the world.

In *Texts of Terror*, Trible describes feminist interpretation as a journey into "a land of terror from whose bourn no traveler returns unscarred."[3] In this chapter, even more than those that have preceded it, I venture into this land. But rather than follow Trible's footsteps, I consider other itineraries; I sketch other maps. I also envisage other encounters, with both the stories and the vulnerable women that the texts of terror at once conceal and reveal. The reading offered here is not a practice of memory and grief, any more than it reflects an effort to save women. But neither am I suggesting that we as interpreters will emerge unscarred—rather, the scars, or some of them, were already with us, even before the journey began. There is no innocent place from which to begin the journey into the text, or from which to begin telling a story: Unhappy reading takes this seriously. What might we find when we stop looking for happiness, even the satisfaction of a sad story well told?

On Telling Sad Stories

As I have suggested in the Introduction, the concept and category of "texts of terror" remains Trible's most influential contribution to feminist biblical studies.[4] But Trible herself often uses different language to describe the work of feminist criticism, especially when confronted with difficult, painful, or horrifying texts. In her own words, feminist criticism "recounts tales of terror *in memoriam* to offer sympathetic readings of abused women."[5]

It does this by "telling sad stories."[6] This phrase is quoted much less frequently than "texts of terror," perhaps because it lacks the alliteration and the always-pleasing appeal to "terror." But "telling sad stories" offers a fuller description of Trible's method, as well as a better representation of the forms of influence it still exerts over feminist approaches to sexual violence. Let's pause, then, with "telling sad stories," and unpack some of its meanings. At first pass, describing the work of criticism as "telling" or "recounting" may seem to be a humble act, or even a strategy for downplaying the role of the interpreter. But look more closely: "Telling sad stories," like any act of "telling," is a process of narration and narrative-production, as much as it is of interpretation.[7] In telling a story, I also shape it, or fit it to the shape I have presumed is proper all along. There are always other ways to tell stories, and the ways chosen are never neutral.[8] The point is not which story is *right*, but rather what else the grammar of the story communicates and conceals.

For Trible, the practice of telling is grounded in lived and observed experience in the world—more specifically, in experiences of misogyny and gendered violence. She explains:

Choice and chance inspire my telling these particular tales: hearing a black woman describe herself as a daughter of Hagar outside the covenant; seeing an abused woman on the streets of New York with a sign, "My name is Tamar"; reading news reports of the dismembered body of a woman found in a trash can; attending worship services in memory of nameless women; and wrestling with the silence, absence, and opposition of God. All these experiences and others have led me to a land of terror from whose bourn no traveler returns unscarred.[9]

Texts of Terror is written from this place of woundedness and witnessing; according to Trible, feminist criticism occurs, or should occur, from this same place. Equally importantly, although the passage begins by dwelling on the pain of female victims, it ends with the (sympathetic) suffering of the interpreter, scarred by her journey to "a land of terror."[10] This way of telling rape stories—as *sad stories*—telegraphs that rape and sexual violence are terrible and even perhaps unbearable; close contact with them forever alters the reader. As for the victim/survivor, she is changed forever, if she survives at all.

The target of this intervention is not simply the text, nor the past, but also the present: "In telling sad stories, a feminist hermeneutic seeks to redeem the time."[11] "Redeem[ing] the time," a phrase borrowed from Ephesians 5:16, suggests a project of deliverance, rescuing female victims from texts that ensnare them and thereby solving misogyny along the way. It implies that feminist criticism can *save us* from something—misogyny, perhaps, or a misogynistic Bible, or a world where sexual violence is simultaneously unacknowledged and pervasive. But there are also problems with dreams of salvation history, serious ones.[12] Across *Texts after Terror*, I have insisted that our starting points and motives are never innocent when we interpret texts. In the case of Trible's *Texts of Terror* it is worth noting that the "journey" her book undertakes is framed in explicitly Christian theological terms.[13] And as I have already described in the previous chapter, there are also serious hermeneutic and ethical concerns with sympathetic readings and interpretations offered on behalf of others. To repeat an important point: Interpreting *in sympathy with* or *on behalf of* can also mean speaking *in place of*. Feminist interpretation often criticizes the tendency of patriarchal orders to "think with" women; that is, to use the stories of women, as well as their bodies and experiences, to work through masculine anxieties or intellectual problems.[14] To this,

I wish to add a critique of using women, particularly victims and survivors of sexual violence, to "grieve with." "Grieving with" instrumentalizes women, stories, and suffering. And it assumes that the lives and bodies of victims and survivors are broken—or if not broken, breakable, the better to fit the paradigm of grief.

In the previous chapter, I explored extensively the tension between the stories we want to hear from victims and survivors and the stories that victims and survivors themselves tell. Multiple authors in *Queering Sexual Violence* push back against the way their stories seem scripted for them, even before they begin to speak. Leah Lakshmi Piepzna-Samarasinha names and refuses the demand that survivors bare the worst moments of their lives to eager listeners, exposing their pain in the service of someone else's ideological project. Piepzna-Samarasinha, M. Cooper Minister, and Brandy Daniels likewise critique the demand for cure, that survivors can be fully healed. And the "Choose Your Own Adventure" sequence in Carmen Maria Machado's *In the Dream House* captures, with disturbing accuracy, the sense of being trapped in a story that cannot come to a happy ending.[15]

Building on these critiques, I insist that telling sad stories is not enough. And sometimes, our desire to tell sad stories—or the demand of listeners and readers that the stories we tell must be sad—leads to omissions, misrepresentations, even bad tellings. Perhaps this is inevitable: telling sad stories is fundamentally an act of euologizing, bound up with both memory and death. Partway through Shakespeare's *Richard II*, King Richard tells the Duke of Aumerle, "For God's sake, let us sit upon the ground / And tell sad stories of the death of kings."[16] To tell sad stories is to invoke the dead—even when death is not the outcome for the stories themselves.

But what if we set aside this preoccupation with death? It is notable that *Texts of Terror* ends with a page labeled "*in memoriam*" listing four women: "The Daughter of Jephthah / An Unnamed Woman / Tamar / Hagar."[17] This is a powerful gesture of elegy. But at the same time, it is also a misleading one: unlike the kings that Richard speaks of, *not all of these women are dead.*[18] What if terror or sadness is not the end of the story? Of the four women whom Trible memorializes, two do survive: Tamar and Hagar. Surely the differences between these "sad stories"—their forms of sadness, their very different endings—matter as much as their similarities, even if they disrupt the neat elegiac form of a list of victims. But beyond telling sad stories, how should we respond to such difficult texts? I propose, as an alternative, *unhappy reading.*

From Telling Sad Stories to Unhappy Reading

Unhappy reading, as I describe it here, is not a rigid method; instead, it is better described as an orientation toward both stories and ways of reading them. As I have suggested throughout *Texts after Terror*, biblical rape stories are at risk of becoming what Barbara Johnson terms "already-read texts"— that is, we know their contents even without reading them. The telling sad stories approach reflects this tendency: It relies on a predetermined form (the "sad story") while solidifying the position of the interpreter as "teller," recounting a stable and predetermined meaning. In telling a story, the narrator (or interpreter) knows what is to come, even if the readers do not. Reading, in contrast, describes something more open, more flexible, and local to the story itself.[19] Reading is open to surprise, including what Johnson names, in another memorable phrase, "the surprise of otherness": Thus, "the impossible but necessary task of the reader is to set herself up to be surprised."[20] Focusing on *reading*, rather than *telling*, is one way of opening ourselves to this sort of possibility for surprise.

In crafting an alternative to telling sad stories, I have suggested not just *reading*, but *unhappy reading*. Why the unhappiness? My aim is certainly not to suggest that all surprises are unhappy surprises (a belief that Sedgwick associates with the paranoid position). Instead, I want to hold on to what I find most valuable about the telling sad stories framework— chiefly, the space it carves out for sadness. Describing stories as *sad*, and not simply "misogynistic" or "patriarchal" (though they are that as well), also carves out a space for the way these stories make us feel, and the pull they exert upon us. This is especially true for feminist readers, a dynamic I have touched upon at several points in this book and will return to again subsequently. *Unhappy* also points to this dynamic, but at the same time, it names a more expansive terrain than sadness. Of course, sad stories make us unhappy, but "unhappy" also describes what is infelicitous, resistant, or frustrating to our interpretive desires. Unhappy reading can refer simply to reading unhappy stories. It can describe practices of reading that make us unhappy (for example, when applying a familiar feminist method does not produce a desired feminist result). It can identify interpretations that are unhappy in other ways (for example, by failing to produce closure or a stable meaning—an unhappy outcome from the perspective of narrative theory). Or an unhappy reading may refer to an act of reading that leaves the reader unhappy—I have read this story, and now I am unhappy about it (and perhaps even surprised by my own unhappiness). I may be unhappy because the story made me sad, or because it did not make me sad enough. I may feel confused or dissatisfied; my feelings may not be what I think they should be. I may feel compelled to share the story with others, or to withhold it from them. What unites this range of feelings and responses is that they are all, in some way, unhappy. In using the phrase unhappy reading, I intend all of these meanings, as well as the spaces where they cross over and inform—or stickily touch—each other.

If reading as a way of being "surprised by otherness" evokes Barbara Johnson, then the turn to unhappiness I offer here follows Sara Ahmed. In *The Promise of Happiness*, Ahmed makes a number of important points about the categories *happy* and *unhappy*. She argues that happiness is not an inherent quality of objects but rather an affect that becomes associated with them—it's not that good things make us happy, but rather that we treat happy objects as good.[21] Happiness functions as an orienting device, by teaching us to orient ourselves in certain ways. And happiness can be coercive. Throughout *The Promise of Happiness*, Ahmed traces the entanglement of *happy* with *good*, revealing that appeals to happiness are often used to manipulate or oppress or, whether explicitly or through more subtle forms of coercion (consider "I just want you to be happy," a statement and sentiment that Ahmed analyzes extensively).[22]

All of this opens a space for reconsidering unhappiness—in fact, in unhappiness, Ahmed finds the possibility of freedom and even alternative ways of flourishing. She describes "the freedom to be unhappy" as

> the freedom to be affected by what is unhappy, and to live a life that might affect others unhappily. The freedom to be unhappy would be the freedom to live a life that deviates from the paths of happiness, wherever that deviation takes us . . . if we no longer presume happiness is our telos, unhappiness would register as more than what gets in the way.[23]

This description of unhappiness does not preclude sadness, but neither is it limited to it. And like the "surprise of otherness" that reading can reveal, it opens onto other spaces of possibility.

For Ahmed, one such example is the character of the Savage in Aldous Huxley's *Brave New World*. The Savage lives in the inland of America; he refuses to be a part of the organized society—organized, we might note, around happiness—that constitutes the "brave new world." The encounters between the Savage and other characters in the novel are unhappy ones. And yet the Savage and the position he represents are essential. Ahmed writes,

> The Savage is the one who articulates the wisdom of the book. "All right then," said the Savage defiantly, "I'm claiming the right to be unhappy." Unhappiness becomes a right in a world that makes happiness compulsory.[24]

Employing a tactic much like what I have called reading through literature, Ahmed uncovers in Huxley's novel a compelling alternative to happiness. The Savage is unhappy; it is not the case that his happiness is simply different from those around him; this is not a counter-happiness. But it is his unhappiness that makes imagining a different way of being possible. Equally importantly, his unhappiness is sticky; it sticks with the reader, more than the many technofuturist innovations of the novel.

So too, I suggest, might we be unhappy readers when confronted with difficult biblical texts, especially my focus here, biblical rape texts. As a practice of interpretation, *unhappy reading* takes seriously "the freedom to be affected by what is unhappy"—including sad or terrible things in biblical texts.[25] But it also holds the possibility of reading, including reading sad stories or texts of terror, in ways "that might affect others unhappily"—beginning with other feminist interpreters. Unhappy reading permits us to deviate from the familiar paths of feminist criticism, which still follow, strongly, the itinerary charted by Trible. It likewise rejects the imperative to find happiness, if only the satisfaction of sad stories well told or the relief granted by catharsis. Instead, we can demand the freedom to linger with unhappiness, without demanding resolution or injecting fixed meaning into ambiguity, ambivalence, and discomfort.

From Unhappy Reading to the Levite's Concubine

Finding space for ambivalence and ambiguity offers a way of opening up biblical rape stories that have become too rigid and predictable in their retellings. An openness toward unhappiness—whether unhappiness in the events of the story, unhappiness with where the reading process leads us, or even unhappiness as a way of describing narrative and interpretive non-closure (a "happy" ending is a plot that ends; an unhappy ending is a failure to end)[26]—opens new possibilities in reading old stories. The preceding chapters have explored some of these possibilities: I have argued for considering Dinah, Tamar, and Lot and his daughters outside the too-rigid framework of consent; for reevaluating the forms of harm that Bathsheba experiences (and perpetrates); for centering relationships between *women*, rather than heterosexual rape, in the account of Hagar and Sarah; for relocating Daughter Zion to a company of queer survivors who subvert the dominant victim/survivor paradigm. In multiple ways, these readings open onto the unhappy. It is unhappy, for example, to loosen our hold on the concept of "consent," which has become a cornerstone of contemporary anti-rape advocacy. It is unhappy to be unable to establish with certainty whether or not Dinah is raped, and whether Lot rapes his daughters or is raped by them (or whether this sexual encounter should be understood in different terms). The representation of Bathsheba as David's victim is destabilized by considering her as a figure who perpetrates sexual harm on other women, beginning with Abishag the Shunammite.

In the relationship of Hagar and Sarah, there are multiple forms of unhappiness: the sexual violence and violation Hagar experiences, Sarah's complicity in this violence, the question of whether Abraham deserves greater critical attention (*Isn't he a perpetrator?*) or whether we should set him aside (*Don't male perpetrators already dominate too much of the text, and too much of the discourse about sexual violence?*), the lack of closure following Hagar's second departure. The history of interpretation offers up other forms of unhappiness: One interpretive tradition summons us to observe that Hagar is an African slave, and that her rape and exploitation echo a long and unhappy tradition of White women facilitating the abuse of Black women; a counter-approach points out that the Blackness of Hagar is largely a contemporary invention—but this, too, is an unhappy interpretive twist, insofar as it undercuts the theological and identity-based readings of "Black Hagar."[27] And the reading of Daughter Zion offered in the previous chapter is unhappy in multiple ways, beginning with the way the texts in the "survivor archive"—including Daughter Zion's—challenge our expectations of how a survivor story ought to be told. Daughter Zion's speeches are angrier, guiltier, and more formally intricate than the clichés (or "already-read text") of a rape story dictate; she refuses pity and resolution alike. It is a difficult task to make ourselves listen to what the text *says*, and not simply what we believe it to say. Difficult, but also essential.

Unhappy reading serves as a kind of umbrella that provides shelter for all of these readings, and for others. It does not insist that we apply the same interpretive tactics to every story, or assume the same outcome. Resisting paranoid reading goes both ways: I am not interested in offering a single master narrative of biblical rape stories that explains and exhausts every detail of sexual violence in the biblical narrative. Such a theory would be both too strong and too weak—in trying to speak to everything, it would end up flattening difference, and the very attention to nuance that I have attempted to name with the language of fuzzy, messy, and icky. But these stories all share at least one important feature, beyond their representation of sexual violence in some form: They do not end with death; their rapes are not fatal. But this is not always the case in the Hebrew Bible. The story of the Levite's concubine, in particular, is among the Bible's most infamous rape stories, as well as its most brutal—it involves the gang rape of a nameless woman, followed by her murder and dismemberment. What happens when we introduce a story such as this—inarguably a "sad story"—to the interpretive orientation and assembly of tactics that I have called "unhappy reading"? Is "unhappy reading" sufficient to the task, or does this very categorization undersell the tragedy and trauma of the story, and of other accounts of extreme (sexual) violence?

The story of the Levite's concubine appears in Judges 19; its consequences spill over into chapters 20 and 21, bringing the book to a close.[28] The woman at its center is nameless, described only as a *pilegeš*, a word often translated "concubine" but also "secondary wife."[29] The narrative begins when she leaves her husband, the also-nameless Levite, and returns to her father's home; he follows to retrieve her. After several days of feasting with his father-in-law, they depart to return home but must stop overnight in Gibeah, located in Benjamin. As they are about to sleep in the town square, an old man offers them shelter. But this offer does not bring safety. Instead, the men of the city, "a wicked bunch," surround the house and demand, "Bring out the man who came to your house so that we may rape him" (Judg 19:22).[30] The old man objects and proposes two female substitutes: his virgin daughter and the Levite's concubine. The men of the city reject this offer. "The man"—it is unclear whether this refers to the old man (the host) or the Levite (the guest)— then seizes the concubine and pushes her out to the mob:

> They raped her[31] and abused her all night until morning. As dawn broke, they let her go. As morning appeared, the woman came and collapsed at the opening of the man's house where her master was, until it was light. In the morning, her master got up, opened the doors of the house, and went out to go on his way. There was the woman, his concubine, fallen at the opening of

the house. Her hands were on the threshold. He said to her, "Get up, we're going," but there was no answer. He put her on the donkey. The man went on his way home. When he came to his house, he took a knife and, grasping his concubine, cut her body[32] into twelve pieces and sent her through all the territory of Israel. (Judg 19:25–29)

After death, the woman's body is transformed into a message that rallies the tribes of Israel to war against Benjamin, in response to the "outrage" that the Levite has experienced.

In the aftermath of the war, additional rape and violence follows. The eleven tribes who have gone to war with Benjamin have also sworn not to intermarry with their enemy (Judg 21:1, 8), leaving the Benjaminite men without wives. Instead of intermarriage, the Benjaminites undertake the mass kidnapping and forced marriage (read: rape) of many women: first four hundred from Jabesh-Gilead, which failed to join the war effort (21:9–14) and then, when these abductees are insufficient, additional young women snatched from a festival in Shiloh (21:19–23). These actions are not critiqued by the other tribes, who are more interested in the survival of Benjamin than in the fate of non-Benjaminite women. In addition, the married women and all the men of Jabesh-Gilead are killed, because of their failure to join the war against Benjamin. With this, the book of Judges ends.

Fuzzy, Messy, Icky—and Terribly Sad

I have suggested that biblical rape stories are fuzzy, messy, and icky; these terms speak, as well, to Judges 19. I will focus my discussion primarily on the events directly involving the Levite's concubine and not the war and mass rapes that follow in chapters 20 and 21. The fuzziness begins with ambiguity and elision: All of the characters in this narrative are nameless and almost without descriptive qualities (though the husband is identified as a Levite and the men of the city are described as a "wicked bunch"). The story includes multiple characters who appear briefly and then disappear, including the servant accompanying the Levite and his concubine and the old man's daughter. The term *pilegeš*, often translated "concubine," is fuzzy: It is not clear what, precisely, it means or what sort of marital relationship it describes. There are also several important points of plot ambiguity (that is, fuzziness): The Hebrew text does not specify whether the old man (who offers his daughter and the concubine to the mob) also pushes the concubine out, or whether it is the Levite who does so. Equally obscure in the Hebrew text is at what point the woman dies—on the threshold, on the return journey, or only when her husband dismembers her. The Septuagint (Greek translation) avoids this ambiguity by specifying "she did not answer, because she was dead" in 19:28, after the Levite speaks to her.[33] And in rallying the tribes to war, the Levite brings up the "outrage" he has experienced but makes no mention of the rape threat against himself, focusing instead on the danger to his life and the violation of his property, who happens to be a human woman. His representation of the events points to the entanglement of homophobia, misogynistic violence, and masculinity that haunts the text, as well as its intertext in Genesis 19 (the threat to rape the male messengers at Sodom and Gomorrah). In Sodom, the nameless daughters are offered for mob rape but miraculously saved by the divine messengers; the nameless woman in Judges 19 receives no such kindness.

The story of the Levite's concubine is also messy, beginning with the bloody violence inflicted on the body of the woman. This is not just killing but the transmutation of the female body into an animal body, appropriate for sacrifice or dismemberment (cf. 1 Sam 11:7).[34] The subsequent narrative transfigures her messy death into messiness on a much larger scale: war, mass kidnapping, and genocide all follow; in lieu of resolution, the text only offers a terse comment that "every man did what was right in his own eyes." The messiness of the woman's death and dismemberment stands, metonymically, for the violence and abuse of women throughout the book of Judges, ending with the events at Jabesh-Gilead and Shiloh.

Then there is icky—there is so much ickiness here. The gang rape and the dismemberment of the woman's body are deeply icky, as are the events that follow: mass abduction, rape, and genocide at Jabesh-Gilead and mass kidnapping and rape at Shiloh. The text's lack of censure or judgment for all these events is a second source of ickiness. The transformation of body parts into a messaging device is another icky touch, as is the use of the individual woman's fragmented body to symbolize the broken collective body of Israel. That a woman needs to be raped and murdered for this point to be made is both misogynistic and icky. Ickiness is also sticky, as I have explored at several points. The misogyny of this story sticks to and cross-contaminates other stories about women in Judges; the account of Jephthah's daughter is especially closely linked.[35] There is also a sticky transfer between the story of the Levite and his concubine in Gibeah and the story of Sodom in Genesis 19. There, too, the men of the city seek to rape male visitors; Lot, like the old man in Gibeah, offers as a substitute his virgin daughters. The accounts in Judges, in which violence is not just threatened but actualized, haunt their Genesis parallels, threatening to contaminate them with their ickiness.

And yet, to describe the story of the Levite's concubine as fuzzy, messy, and icky feels, itself, rather icky. This is a text of extreme, fatal violence; it verges on the sadistic. While it is true that the story contains fuzzy details, messy bloodshed, and all manner of ickiness, this language also feels inadequate to the task of describing either the stories or their effects on us as readers.[36] That I feel icky after reading Judges 19 (or Judg 20–21) reflects my own position as an interpreter, my distance from the text as much as my sympathy. Perhaps I should feel icky about feeling (just) icky. But this is also the point: The language of fuzzy, messy, and icky was never intended as a comprehensive description of all sexual violence, still less all sexualized or misogynistic violence. My goal has never been the wholesale replacement of one set of words for speaking and writing about sexual violence with another. Instead, I have advocated for the terms fuzzy, messy, and icky as a supplement, albeit an important one, to other existing ways of speaking. In particular, I have introduced this language as an everyday way of talking about the everyday ambiguities and ambivalences of sexual violence.

One of Sedgwick's critiques of paranoid reading is that paranoia is a "strong theory"—that is, it seeks to explain everything through a single master narrative.[37] Against such strong theories, she advocates for multiple weak theories, locally positioned, flexible, and specific. "Reparative reading" (Sedgwick's term) is one way of describing this alternative to strong para- noid reading. "Unhappy reading" is another. Similarly, fuzzy, messy, and icky are not strong terms but rather weak ones. And they do not apply equally to every rape story, just as they do not exhaust the meaning of every rape story. In fact, I suggest that the narrative of Judges 19 shows the *limits* of this language as a way of describing sexual violence as much as its possibilities. But equally importantly, observing the limits of fuzzy, messy, and icky does not mean that there is no space for unhappy reading here. Or put another way: There is more to unhappy reading than tracing fuzziness, messiness, and ickiness. Just as fuzzy, messy, and icky are not technical terms, but rather alternative ways of naming and describing sexual violence and rape culture, unhappy reading is an orientation toward interpretation rather than a tightly crafted procedure.

Furthermore, descriptive terms such as fuzzy, messy, and icky, like the larger framing of unhappy reading, force us to stay with the story and its difficulties in a way that a "telling sad stories" approach does not. To tell the sad story of the Levite's concubine is to stabilize its meaning, as well as its place in the hierarchy of biblical rape stories—as the most terrible story of all, the limit that cannot be crossed, the terrible truth that must be reckoned with. I am not persuaded that a theory of biblical rape stories should focus on this story over and against all the other rape stories, any more than I think that a theory of rape as such should focus on gang rape and/or fatal sexual assault over and against all other forms of rape. The desire to rank and compare rape stories ("your rape is worse than mine") is both pervasive and largely unproductive, as Sohaila Abdulali points out in *What We Talk About When We Talk About Rape*.[38] And yet I also admit that an account of biblical rape stories, such as this book, needs to speak to the worst stories, too—even if to admit that they strain the framework I have sketched in prior chapters.

In what follows, I will consider some of the most influential and persistent ways that the sad story of the Levite's concubine has been told. My goal is not to provide a comprehensive overview of the existing scholarship on this topic—such overviews already exist[39]—but rather to show how the "telling sad stories" approach of *Texts of Terror* continues to shape the way this story is read. Furthermore, this shaping does not actually provide a feminist reading of the story, as I will draw out with reference to three areas of difficulty: the collapsing of the categories of "rape" and "murder," the problem of the "speaking body," and the difficulty with ventriloquizing victims. Against this limited "sad stories" perspective, I unveil the alternative horizon of possibilities that "unhappy reading" makes possible.

"No Friends to Aid Her in Life or Mourn Her in Death": Feminist Responses to the Levite's Concubine

In many ways, Trible's analysis of Judges 19 in *Texts of Terror* continues to set the standard for how feminists read the story.[40] Her reading is an extended reflection on the unnamed woman's suffering:

Of all the characters in scripture, she is the least. Appearing at the beginning and close of a story that rapes her, she is alone in a world of men. Neither the other characters nor the narrator recognizes her humanity.

She is property, object, tool, and literary device. Without name, speech, or power, she has no friends to aid her in life or mourn her in death. Passing her back and forth among themselves, the men of Israel have obliterated her totally. Captured, betrayed, raped, tortured, murdered, dismembered, and scattered—this woman is the most sinned against. In the end, she is no more than the oxen that Saul will later cut (*nṯḥ*) in pieces and send (*šlḥ*) throughout all the territory of Israel as a call to war (1 Sam 11:7). Her body has been broken and given to many. Lesser power has no woman than this, that her life is laid down by a man.[41]

But as powerless as the woman is, her story exerts a powerful pull on feminist readers and interpreters. Furthermore, the themes that Trible inventories here—the woman's dehumanization and isolation, her conversion from human being to object, her silence, the dismemberment of her body, her abuse after death and transformation into a message-object between men—remain important themes in feminist readings of the text. But more than anything, it is the *feeling* and tone that animate Trible's reading that continue to shape the way we read the story. Channeling John 15:13,[42] Trible replaces the "man"—Jesus—with the nameless woman, and a sacrifice born of love with sadistic misogyny.

Trible is not the only feminist commentator to take up the Levite's concubine and her story. Judges 19 casts a long shadow over the field. In addition to *Texts of Terror*, the story plays an important role in J. Cheryl Exum's *Fragmented Women* and Mieke Bal's *Death and Dissymmetry in the Book of Judges*, among other foundational works. And for subsequent generations of feminist scholars, it has become almost a rite of passage to wrestle with the story, to seek what new feminist truth might be extracted from its bloody and dismembered pieces. These feminist readings often seek to elaborate on the frustratingly sparse details the narrative provides us. Like Jephthah's nameless daughter before her, the nameless concubine is given a name by commentators, as part of a practice of transforming her from killable object to grievable life. These names vary among interpreters—Bal calls her "Beth"; Exum, "Bath-Sheber"; and Helen Paynter, "Beli-Fachad" or "Fearless One."[43] The ambiguities I have discussed in relation to fuzzy, messy, and icky earlier are likewise brought to the forefront: the uncertain meaning of the term *pilegeš*, the problem of who pushes the woman out of the door, the question of when she dies. And the specific details the text does provide are given careful attention: the duration of the woman's rape ordeal, her hands on the doorstep in the morning, the body divided into twelve parts. In this way the treatment of the Levite's concubine resembles that of Daughter Zion, discussed in the previous chapter: Observing becomes an act of critical witnessing, just as the female character is presented as a witness to the violence that surrounds her. Related to this focus on witnessing is the emphasis on duration, which draws out the text's horror. This is especially central to Bal's reading of the story, which emphasizes the ongoing unfolding of pain and terror in the text. Feminist reading becomes a practice of accompaniment, slowing the pace of the telling so that we may share in the woman's horror and pain.[44]

These strategies—naming, bearing witness, forcing readers to engage with the duration of suffering as well as its intensity—are all highly effective ways of telling a sad story, but they are not without difficulty. I offer three examples.

Rape Is Not Murder; Murder Is Not Rape

Judges 19 is the story of a rape. It is also the story of a murder. Too often, readings of the text—*especially* feminist readings—collapse the difference between these two acts, recounting the unnamed woman's story in such a way that her rape flows inevitably into her murder. Violent death is implicitly positioned as the inevitable, if tragic, outcome of extreme sexual violence. The discrete acts that constitute the woman's suffering—her being pushed out of the house, her rape, her collapse on the threshold, her dismemberment— are treated as a kind of horrific *Gesamtkunstwerk* of RAPEMURDER. This reading is articulated most strongly by Bal in *Death and Dissymmetry*, where she argues that the specifics of the death of the concubine (whom she calls "Beth") *do not actually matter*:

> Beth's death is described in its successive stages in so much detail that it is almost not represented in itself. The gift of her, the rape and torture, and the dragging of her (body) on the donkey, and the slaughtering are the four major phases of what we can refer to only as Beth's murder. All four *are* the murder; therefore, the question of the exact moment of her death is irrelevant.[45]

This is a remarkable, and—to me, at least—remarkably troubling claim. Bal suggests that rape and murder are undifferentiated in the text and, furthermore, should remain indistinguishable. On the question of when the woman dies—a question that I would suggest is a crucial one, even if the text occludes the answer—Bal's response is dismissive, even blasé: thus, "Is Beth dead when the morning comes, and when she is, ironically, 'released'? It does not matter, and of course she is."[46] It does not matter? Of course?

While Bal is perhaps most extreme in staking this position, she is hardly alone. Indeed, even readings that emphasize the woman's courage or suffering often do so by contrasting her experience to the total suffering she has experienced. The collapse of rape into murder, or the sublimation of both acts into the category of torture, is extremely effective at raising sympathy for the woman, as well as rendering her the focus of the text—its center, not simply the object of its various violences. But this reading also has troubling consequences. One consequence is letting the murderer off the hook.[47] The question of who killed the concubine—the men of Gibeah or her own husband with his knife—is too often dismissed as either unsolvable or as mere grammatical curiosity. But even as the text refuses to resolve the question, the question *Who killed her?* matters—unless we accept the deeply troubling and misogynistic logic of *rape = death*, the logical outcome of *rape = (a fate worse than) death*. This equation treats death as the natural (or even inevitable) response to sexual violence, especially horrific or terrible sexual violence, such as gang rape by ethnic others. *After a tragedy such as this, what other outcome could be possible?*

The narrative and critical elision of rape and murder into RAPEMURDER also erases, or deprioritizes, another ambiguity: Who pushed the woman out, the old man or the Levite? Ignoring this question suggests that the specific identity of the perpetrators matters less than the structure or ideology itself. From the perspective of structural critique, this may be true—and yet surely, it also matters who pushes the woman out of the door, just as surely as it matters that the text refuses to tell us who. This is an unhappy sticking point in reading the text. It would be satisfying either to resolve it, or to pronounce the question itself irrelevant. Many approaches to telling sad stories follow one or both of these strategies. An unhappy reading, in contrast, stays with the trouble, troubling as it may be, just as it stays with the trouble of *who or what killed the woman*—her rapists, her injuries, her husband, or some combination of all three. But what is *not* enough is to conclude, as Bal does, that she was already dead when the door closed on her, or if she was still alive, it doesn't matter, because she was about to die anyway. This is narrative play at the expense of careful attention to the particulars of suffering.[48]

Beyond dodging the question *Who did it?*, readings of Judges 19 that collapse rape into murder are troubling for an additional reason as well: They
imply that survival after rape, or after certain, especially heinous forms of rape
(such as violent gang rape) is impossible or worthless. And yet, *people survive
rapes, even gang rapes*. Not everyone does—this is essential to remember—
but also, and equally importantly, some people do. Death is not the inevitable
consequence of gang rape, any more than rape is the inevitable consequence
of wearing a short skirt or going out alone at night or any number of other
pernicious rape myths. But too frequently, feminist responses to the story of
the Levite's concubine do not acknowledge this possibility. Treating a raped
woman as already murdered turns rape into a fate equal to, or worse than,
death. *A rape, even a violent gang rape, is not a death sentence.*

A Corpse That "Speaks" Is Still Dead

One significant feature of Judges 19 is the woman's voicelessness. Across
the narrative, she never speaks—to her father, her husband, her host, or
her rapists. Even the Levite's servant is afforded a line of dialogue in the text
(19:11), but the woman is not. Her persistent silence echoes loudly. Therefore,
it is not surprising that in seeking to salvage *something* from the ruins of the
unnamed woman's story, feminist readers often turn to a critical examination of silence. Alice Bach, for example, suggests that seeking "the woman's
story muffled in the gaps and silences of the male narrative" and "listening
to the silence" offer feminist strategies for responding to Judges 19.[49] Other
readers, unwilling to let silence alone speak, seek a voice for the woman in
other ways. Two strategies are especially common: either imagining a voice
for the woman, to fill the space of her silence (an interpretive tendency I will
consider later) or arguing that the woman's *body* functions as a voice.

The body as a "voice" or something that "speaks" is an idea with a well-
established history. The literature of folk and fairy tales, for example, is
filled with talking bones and severed heads that speak and all manner of
related marvels. In the fairy tale "The Juniper Tree," a mother kills her son
and buries his body; a tree grows from his bones. A bird then sits in the tree
and announces the identity of his murderer (his mother). In "The Goose
Girl," the heroine's beloved horse is killed; fortunately, his head continues
to be able to speak and advise her. Other body parts speak in less fantas-
tical but equally persuasive ways: Consider the preponderance of body

parts (fingers, toes, horse heads) sent as messages in mob and crime fiction. Nor is this device limited to fiction: The desecration of the bodies of enemies to send a message is a well-known practice in the ancient world; (dead) bodies are transformed into messages to the living. Psychoanalysis, too, has made much of the way that the body can "speak," such as through the process Freud terms "somatic compliance," when the patient develops symptoms that communicate what she herself will not say aloud.[50] And for feminist theory influenced by psychoanalysis, the speaking female body offers at least a partial alternative to the masculine economy of language and discourse.

The body-as-voice argument suggests that the woman's silence in the text does not mean that she does not communicate. Instead, she "speaks" nonverbally, with her body. Moreover, this happens at multiple moments in the text. By fleeing the Levite and returning to the house of her father in the story's opening scene, she signals something important about the conditions of her relationship.[51] By collapsing with her hands on the threshold, she sends a message to the Levite and the old man safely ensconced in the house, and to the reader as well. Her silent body on the Levite's donkey sends another message: perhaps communicating her death, certainly telegraphing the scene's outrage. And finally, her dismembered body parts, sent to the tribes of Israel, are a message of their own: *An outrage has been committed against a woman, look and see!*

To read the unnamed woman's body as speaking, particularly after her death, is to read in accordance with the intentions of the text. In dismembering his wife and distributing her body, the Levite intends to send a message—this is clear from his instructions to the messengers he sends with the body parts (Judg 19:30). Furthermore, his actions do indeed lead to a war between Benjamin and the other eleven tribes, indicating that the message has been effectively communicated. Thus, the text itself suggests that bodies, or body parts, can "speak." Many feminist readings accept this basic principle, while reversing the meaning that the body-as-speech-act communicates. Exum tracks the disparities between what the narrator *says* and what the text itself *shows*, observing "a situation in which the narrator *tells* us that the tribes go to war to avenge what are certainly crimes against a man and his property. But he *shows* us horrible crimes against the woman, both the gang rape and the dismemberment."[52] Helen Paynter draws out this difference between narration and the true speech (communicated) by the female body even more strongly.[53] In her reading, the woman's dismembered body testifies to the misogyny of the narrative. Furthermore, it speaks more clearly than the patriarchal forces that seek to silence it (beginning with the Levite himself). Exum and Paynter do not agree fully in their reading of the story: While both describe the body as speaking, Exum argues that the woman's body's speech is eclipsed by the Levite's, while Paynter's reading is more optimistic. But both readings agree on the basic principle that the female body *speaks* in Judges 19, whether or not it is *heard*.

However: The woman who supposedly speaks through her body is dead. No matter how effective the communicative act, it is a serious error to treat the woman as the message's sender. Even if her corpse "speaks" the same message she herself would say if she were living—an assumption I will challenge in the next section—she herself is not. Because however much her body might "speak," she is still dead.

Presented with the suggestion that the Levite's concubine's body speaks, I am reminded of Alice Bolin's illuminating analysis of "Dead Girls" in popular culture, particularly as represented in what she terms the "Dead Girl Show." Of the conventions of the genre, Bolin writes,

> All Dead Girl Shows begin with the discovery of the murdered body of a young woman. The lead characters of the series are attempting to solve the (often impossibly complicated) mystery of who killed her. As such, the Dead Girl is not a "character" in the show, but rather, the memory of her is.[54]

Twin Peaks, with its tagline "Who killed Laura Palmer?", is a founding example of the "Dead Girl Show" genre; *Veronica Mars*, *Pretty Little Liars*, *True Detective*, and *How to Get Away with Murder* are among its best-known recent examples.[55] The Dead Girl is simultaneously at the center of the Dead Girl Show and strangely absent from it. She is an object of intense interest, even obsession, for those around her (typically though not always men.)[56] Her body and appearance are central: Thus, *Twin Peaks'* camera lingers repeatedly on images of Laura Palmer, both her smiling high school photo and the face of her corpse. The pull the Dead Girl exerts on the narrative is at least partly sexual; she is consistently represented as both sexually threatening and sexually threatened (often, she is a rape victim as well as a murder victim).[57] But despite the energy she—or better, her dead body—exerts over the narrative, *the story is not hers*. Instead, "the victim's body is a neutral arena on which to work out male problems"—and, I would add, to communicate messages that are not the Dead Girl's own.[58]

In analyzing the Dead Girl trope, Bolin twice quotes Gillian Flynn's 2012 novel *Gone Girl*: "Everyone loves the Dead Girl."[59] This is certainly true of *Twin Peaks'* Laura Palmer: Everyone seems to have loved her, or to have been at least a little in love with her (including the detective assigned to the case). But this story is not Laura's story, any more than Judges 19 is the concubine's story. This is not the Dead Girl's story. Even a brief peek at *Gone Girl* makes this point even more strongly. The character who utters these words is Amy Dunne—the murdered/missing "Gone Girl" of the title. But Amy is, in fact, very much alive, and hard at work to frame her cheating husband for her murder. As *Gone Girl* draws out, in detail, the distance between the meanings imposed on the Dead Girl's death and corpse and what she herself might say is significant indeed. This is true even if we read against the grain and suggest, for example, that the real "truth" of Laura's murder, and of *Twin Peaks*, is misogyny: We are still reading meaning in and through the dead body, and allowing the dead woman to speak.[60] *The woman is still dead.* This holds, as well, for the Levite's concubine. *A dead body, even a speaking body, is not a living woman.*

A Victim Is Not a Ventriloquist's Dummy: Against Speaking "On Behalf Of"

Feminist readings that treat the woman's corpse as a speaking body often assume that if the woman could speak, we know what she would say. Of course, she would protest her murder; of course, she would demand justice. And yet both feminist theory (from outside biblical studies) and other "sad stories" from the book of Judges suggest that this is not necessarily the case. As I have considered extensively in the previous chapter, victims and survivors of sexual violence do not always recount their experiences using the terms, scripts, or narrative patterns of modern readers. They have also put forward extensive and compelling critiques of the demands placed upon rape stories, which represent their own forms of subtle (or not-so-subtle) coercion. Daughter Zion's speeches in Lamentations 1 and 2 represent one such resistant discourse in the biblical text.

Daughter Zion is not alone. There are other biblical narratives that demonstrate, even more strongly, the refusal to be compelled to speak about "sad stories" in a particular way. An especially striking example is the story of Jephthah's daughter—not incidentally, the fourth and final story Trible includes in *Texts of Terror*. Like the Levite's concubine, the daughter is name-less; like the concubine, she dies a terrible death at the hands of men. The account, found in Judges 11:30–40, is brief but brutal: Jephthah, an Israelite judge, vows that if he is victorious in battle against the Ammonites, he will sacrifice the first thing he sees upon returning home.[61] He wins the battle—and is greeted upon his return by his daughter. After scolding her for her actions, he sacrifices her in fulfillment of his vow (though not before allowing her two weeks to "bewail [her] virginity" with her friends.

It is not surprising that feminist critics have struggled with how to read this story. As with the story of the Levite's concubine, there is often a sug-gestion that the narrative is unstable or somehow exceeds itself, thereby challenging its own representation of patriarchy and misogyny. In addition, many critics seek to salvage some kind of positive feminist meaning or possi-bility from within the seemingly straightforward narrative of violence. Both of these forms of feminist response conform to the basic parameters artic-ulated by *Texts of Terror*, seeking to remember and mourn for the daughter unjustly killed. Trible writes, "In her death we are all diminished; by our memory she is forever hallowed. Though not a 'survivor,' she becomes an un-mistakable symbol for all the courageous daughters of faithless fathers. Her story, brief as it is, evokes the imagination, calling forth a reader's response."[62] The responses that the story calls forth overwhelmingly involve celebrating or elevating the daughter, whether by praising her bravery, identifying her as the founder of a women's religious ritual or queer community, imagining her as a feisty character with a poetic voice, or even just bestowing upon her a name.[63] These readings may differ in their details, but they all represent forms of "telling sad stories."

One difficulty that these readings often face, however, is that the daughter is not actually silent. Instead, she speaks twice (11:36, 37)—including to en-courage her father to sacrifice her.[64] However, what she says does not satisfy many contemporary readers. Her refusal to resist her sacrifice is alternately troubling and infuriating to many interpreters, some of whom are compelled to give her a (different) voice in order to imagine her speaking back against her father.[65] But in giving the daughter a voice, these interpreters ignore what she actually says. They desire so much to save the daughter that they cannot hear when she states that she does not want to be saved.

I am not suggesting that the Levite's concubine wishes to die, or that she somehow accepts her fate. What I *am* suggesting is that we should show caution before assuming we can establish what she would say, if she were to speak. In the previous chapter, I have traced multiple examples of the difficulty of predicting how survivors will narrate their experiences. Notably, Trible's attempts to "take to heart this ancient story"—that is, Judges 19—and "to confess its present reality" offer up another example.[66] This "present reality" is elaborated in a footnote, which references a *New York Times* article entitled "Barroom Rape Shames Town of Proud Heritage," along with a brief summary of the facts of the case: "The woman was hoisted to a pool table, tormented and repeatedly raped by a group of men who held her there for more than two hours while the other men in the tavern stood watching, sometimes taunting her and cheering. No one aided her or called the police."[67] This is a reference to the infamous "Big Dan's" rape case from New Bedford, Massachusetts, in which a twenty-one-year-old woman was gang-raped in a bar; her four assailants were subsequently convicted in a highly publicized trial. At the time, the case attracted widespread attention and outrage, including an outpouring of feminist and general support for the victim. These events became the basis of the 1988 Academy Award–winning film *The Accused*, starring Jodie Foster and Kelly McGillis.[68]

But there are also important differences between the New Bedford rape case and the events of Gibeah, which Trible moves too quickly to gloss over. To begin: Cheryl Araujo, the New Bedford rape victim, was not murdered; she survived her rape and participated in a highly public trial against her rapists. She had a voice, in a way that the Levite's concubine did not. Second: Trible's appeal to the contemporary story, like much of the scholarship that seeks to give silenced women their voices, implies that were the concubine to speak, she would speak out for feminism and justice. (Paynter makes this argument even more strongly, writing that the concubine "urges us to notice the many points of comparison between her story and those of millions of women today. Her voice is loud and pressing and urges transformation.")[69] But this is also not true in Araujo's case—indeed, her experience presents an argument *against* the faith in the voice of witness that Trible and Paynter presume. In the flurry of press before the trial, Araujo refused to speak with even the sympathetic press or to update her statement, even as her credibility was challenged in the larger media coverage.[70] This refusal to speak was held against her. During the trial itself, Araujo was on the witness stand for several days. But this public opportunity to speak did her few favors—she was battered by defense attorneys, accused of promiscuity, blamed for her own rape, and traumatized by the legal process—such that the case has become a major point of reference in the mistreatment of rape victims in the courts and the press.[71]

Sometimes when victims and survivors speak, they do not say what we wish them to say. In other cases, the cost of speaking is too high. Cheryl Araujo is hardly the only survivor to be traumatized by the process of speaking about sexual violence; indeed, many survivors describe the process as worse than the rape itself.[72] All this should give us pause before we as critics boldly step in to speak for or as the Levite's concubine, or to assume that speaking would be her wish. *Speaking as or speaking on behalf of can be acts of violence. And we should not demand that the Levite's concubine speak.*

From Telling Sad Stories to Unhappy Reading

The reading of the Levite's concubine that I have offered is not comprehensive. Still, I hope that it has shown how telling sad stories can also mean circumventing or foreclosing important feminist concerns about the text. Rather than collapse the concubine's rape into her murder and produce a single story of RAPEMURDER (and, in the case of Judg 21, ABDUCTIONRAPEMURDER), I have sought to tug on the strands that weave these acts of violence together, and to pull them apart. I have likewise insisted that while the "speaking body" is a compelling narrative device, body parts are not the same as living bodies, and there is something perverse and troubling in filling in the woman's silences with messages attributed to her dismembered body. Finally, I have put pressure on the assumption that the Levite's concubine, or any victim, must want to speak, and that we can know what she would say. The words of Jephthah's daughter, and the testimony of many victims who do survive and do speak, sharply call this assumption into question.

My focus has been largely granular; I have emphasized the intimate over the structural. To be sure, we need structural critiques of misogyny, of rape culture, and of hegemonic masculinity, all of which are very much operating in this story. But we also need, as I have emphasized here, a space for feeling, beginning with *feeling unhappy*. Indeed, if I cannot fully shake off the appeal of the telling sad stories approach, it is because of the pull of the *sadness*, not the *telling*. In its irresolvable, irreducible fuzziness, messiness, and ickiness, Judges 19–21 exemplifies unhappy reading. Reading Judges 19, I find myself unhappy. I am unhappy about the story, unhappy about the limits of feminist and queer possibility when presented with a text like this, unhappy that feminist criticism is once again a practice of commemoration and sorrow, not of joy or play. I am unhappy that I cannot force this story to fit the neat contours of my fuzzy, messy, icky paradigm, unhappy that I cannot save the Levite's concubine from her fate. In perverse moments, I find myself happy about just how unhappy the story is—whipping out the sad story of the Levite's concubine is always a good trick for convincing uninterested students or well-intentioned interlocutors that the Bible is not all goodness and light. There is a kind of power in exposing the unhappiness of texts. But mostly, I find the experience of reading Judges 19–21 frustrating: I am frustrated that the story ends as it does, frustrated that there is nothing I can do to change it. The story itself ends with the textual equivalent of a shrug: "In those days there was no king in Israel; every man did what was right in his own eyes" (21:25).[73] Importantly, the text denies us the experience of closure and catharsis. We should stay with this trouble.

Unhappy reading resembles "telling sad stories" in two important ways: It acknowledges the pain and sadness in these stories and their effects on us as readers. But it does not insist on rewriting unhappy stories with happy endings, as certain forms of feminist criticism do (such as readings that insist that misogyny is merely textual, or suggest that behind every biblical rape story is a God who loves mercy, feminism, and gender justice, or even that meaning can be found in every needless misogynistic death). Unhappy reading allows us to linger with the unhappiness of stories, without, however, committing to a certain interpretive outcome. Instead, it holds space. It holds space for Bathsheba as victim, survivor, and perpetrator of sexual violence. It holds space for Hagar in her relationship to Sarah, and in her two flights into the wilderness and the possible (if also narratively elided) future she builds with Ishmael in the wilderness of Paran. It likewise holds a space for Tamar's *afters*, even though the text does not permit us access beyond the immediate aftermath of the rape. And, importantly, unhappy reading also names and holds space for our own unhappiness as readers with these endings— we would like to know more, would like to linger with these stories, would like closure, even the sad closure of catharsis. Sometimes "staying with the trouble" means staying in trouble, particularly when reading rape stories.[74]

Paynter suggests that a reparative reading of the story can begin to heal its pain and trauma, especially by amplifying the ways that the murdered woman's voice speaks today. I am not so persuaded that repair is possible; furthermore, following lines of argument from Piepzna-Samarsinha,

Minister, and Daniels introduced in the previous chapter, I want to acknowledge sexual trauma and violence without insisting on the need for repair or cure. I also am not convinced that rescue work is possible. Here, the problem is a similar one to what Heather Love describes in reflecting on Orpheus and Eurydice and the problem of queer history:

> Such is the relation of the queer historian to the past: we cannot help wanting to save the figures from the past, but this passion is doomed to fail. In part, this is because the dead are gone for good; in part, because the queer past is even more remote, more deeply marked by power's claw; and in part because this rescue is an emotional rescue, and in that sense, we are sure to botch it.[75]

Readings that seek to rescue or repair the Levite's concubine are precisely such emotional rescues, doomed to fail. So are readings that seek to rescue Jephthah's daughter, Daughter Zion, Hagar, Bathsheba, Lot's daughters, Tamar, Dinah, the metaphorical women of the prophetic books, or any of the other stories that I have surveyed here. Salvation, even or especially feminist salvation, is not the answer. And perhaps the most unparanoid way of reading this story is to read without insisting that redemption or repair lurks within it.[76]

And so we are left with our feelings—unhappy feelings. But these unhappy feelings also clear a space for unhappy reading.[77] An unhappy reading of Judges 19 listens for the concubine, while also acknowledging that we cannot hear her, and that to invent words for her is to risk new forms of violence. It is a reading that refuses the consolations of a clear meaning, by establishing, definitively, either what the story means (in the context of the book of Judges, in the world of feminist biblical criticism) or how it relates to the present moment. It is a reading that refuses salvation, staying, instead, with the trouble. And staying, as well, with the unhappiness this reading makes us feel. In this way, it continues the affective work of sad stories, while freeing us from the constraints of telling these stories in a certain way.[78] Unhappy reading also holds a place for unhappy *endings*—including the ending of the Levite's concubine's story, the ending of the book of Judges, perhaps even the ending of a search for a single feminist theory of biblical rape.

Unhappy reading is not always satisfying reading, as even a brief journey down its paths and into both biblical and non-biblical rape stories shows; it often denies us both closure and catharsis. And yet unhappy reading might also be the best we can hope for. Holding space for unhappiness, including unhappy readings, offers an essential alternative to readings of sad stories that either fetishize trauma or privilege catharsis over holding space for complexity and unhappiness, including the complexity and unhappiness of both sexual violence and narrative. Unhappiness also helps open the space of the *after*, bringing us full circle to my own commitment to staking a claim for a feminist practice of interpretation *after terror*. It is with this *after* that the book will end.

Conclusion

After Terror

A quarter century after *The Handmaid's Tale*, Margaret Atwood returned to Gilead, the coercive and violent theocracy that the first novel imagined so vividly. Her sequel, *The Testaments*, offers both a more detailed exploration of the world of Gilead and a vision of its ending. By its conclusion, Gilead is no more; furthermore, its collapse is the result of the heroic actions of several women, working together to bring down patriarchal theocracy. Compared to its predecessor (and even the majority of Atwood's works), this is a hopeful ending indeed. It is not simply that an individual woman such as Offred escapes (a possibility that the ending of *The Handmaid's Tale* teases but never resolves); instead, *Gilead itself falls*. There is, it seems, the possibility of an *after*.[1]

In returning to Gilead, if only to destroy it, Atwood offers a triumphant vision. But the second novel does not linger with the fuzzy, messy, and icky the way that *The Handmaid's Tale* does. And the collapse that *The Testaments* imagines for Gilead feels correspondingly too simple, even one-note. And so in imagining the possibilities of an *after* to biblical sexual violence, I have found myself turning to another work of alternative futures and feminist possibilities: Joanna Russ's 1975 novel *The Female Man*.[2] Russ's novel is not a rape story, though it contains incidents of sexual violence, sexual coercion, and fuzzy, messy, and icky sex. Neither is it a parable of reproductive coercion and control or even, strictly speaking, a novel about misogyny. But it is a novel organized around multiple possible futures, other ways of living in and being toward the world than the rape culture logic that dominates our own present.

The Female Man tells the story of four connected women named Janet, Jeannine, Joanna, and Jael. Each woman lives in a different possible iteration of the earth, in a different time and timeline; they are nevertheless forms of the same person. Janet is a peace officer from Whileaway, a future earth that has been without men for thirty generations. Jeannine lives in a world

Texts after Terror. Rhiannon Graybill, Oxford University Press. © Oxford University Press 2021.
DOI: 10.1093/oso/9780190082314.003.0008

where the Great Depression never ended. Joanna is a version of Russ herself. And Jael is an assassin from another earth's future, where men and women are engaged in brutal ongoing war. It is Jael, with her claws and metal teeth, who convenes the meeting of the women—first in Joanna's world, then in her own. All four of the women represent different possible accounts of an *after*, though to different traumas and disasters. Janet's world, it is revealed in the novel's climax, is the world of post-apocalypse, after a womanmade plague has killed off the men. Jeannine's world is a kind of anti-after, a world much like ours, only worse. Jael's world represents the possibility of a wholly other social organization, with violence (and sex) foregrounded but everyday rape culture removed. And Joanna's world is an exploration of what happens when these worlds touch on her (and our) own.

With her four heroines, Russ deconstructs what we expect of a novel, a narrator, and a feminist intervention. The novel is alternately angry, funny, perplexing, gleeful, and ambivalent, all at once. There is plenty of violence and misogyny, as well as more everyday scenes of hostility, including a painfully accurate description of tweed-wearing misogynists at an academic cocktail party. But there is also pleasure and possibility, which unfold without denying the pain that both precede it and persist into the present moment. Instead of a polite retelling or a modest reimagining, Russ appropriates the figure of Jael, and the biblical story of her deadly strike against Sisera (Judg 4–5), and uses her to imagine a different sort of story entirely. It is this spirit that has animated the readings that fill this book, as I have convened my own encounters that span women and worlds. And in the spirit of Russ's novel, I have suggested that feminist readings of biblical stories, even rape stories, should be angry, funny, perplexing, queer, and ambivalent, all at once. This is doubly true, I submit, when the stories are rape stories, or stories that involve sexual exploitation, sexual violence, or sexualized misogyny. We can do more than simply feel sadness about rape stories, whether biblical or contemporary. Russ's novel opens onto questions of the *what else* and the *what after*: *what else* we might do with biblical rape stories, and *what comes after*—after rape, after misogyny, after great pain.

This *after*, like the rape stories that precede and create it, is often fuzzy, messy, or icky, or some mixture of all three. Some biblical rape stories have endings that are erased entirely, or left too fuzzy in the text for us to read: Dinah's silence, Nineveh's destruction. Others are messy—the rape stories of Bathsheba and Tamar that leave their mark on the house of David, the entangled legacies of Sarah and Hagar. Or icky—incest, violence, exposure, devastation; Lot's daughters and Daughter Zion forced to go on, in spite of their suffering. But we can also notice other details, other ways of reading. In this spirit, *Texts after Terror* has sketched out tactics for reading that help open up rape stories (and stories of all kinds) in new ways: refusing to claim a position of innocence, resisting paranoia and paranoid reading, following the traces of sticky affect, and reading with and through literature. In pursuit of the final tactic, I have staged encounters between biblical rape texts and contemporary literary texts from a range of genres: novels, short stories, memoirs, essays, films, fragments of popular culture. Some of the sampled works are widely recognized as part of the contemporary literature of rape; others have a more elliptical or orthogonal relationship to sexual violence. My interest has not been in works that describe or retell the Bible (though Russ's novel and Sara Maitland's short story "Triptych" offer exceptions to this rule) so much as in work that changes how we perceive biblical rape stories.

In using these literary texts (and the occasional film or television reference), my aim has not been to suggest that they offer a "better" or "more authentic" perspective on (biblical) sexual violence. My goal, instead, has been to expand the range of ways we think about and understand sexual violence, including biblical rape stories. In this way, reading with literature complements and augments the hermeneutic insights that the other three tactics—refusing innocence, resisting paranoia, and following sticky affect—all instigate. Refusing innocence means rejecting both the conviction that rape stories must have "innocent" protagonist-victims (consider "Cat Person," or Daughter Zion) and the belief that we ever encounter a rape story from a fully innocent position ourselves—that is, untouched by other stories we have read or learned. Resisting paranoia means moving beyond "faith in exposure" with respect to sexual violence. It is not enough simply to expose the texts as sexually violent; we all already know this. Resisting paranoia also means rejecting a single "strong theory" that explains all aspects of biblical narrative; thus, the many literary intertexts I have explored here do not always agree with each other in how they represent sexual violence, nor should they. Nor should we. In *The Handmaid's Tale*, Offred insists she is not raped; in *Supper Club*, Roberta realizes the opposite. The survivor-essayists of *Queering Sexual Violence* refuse the mantle of the "good survivor," just as Leah Lakshmi Piepzna-Samarasinha refuses the command to be healed. In *Know My Name*, survivor Chanel Miller touches on these difficulties but also stubbornly insists on hope. Daughter Zion, meanwhile, refuses such hope.

We do not know what Sarah and Hagar hope for, though Maitland offers one set of answers in "Triptych." Even this brief revisit to the terrain of the previous chapters also shows the working of sticky affect: Stories touch each other, stories contaminate each other. Bathsheba looks different after *Doubt*. Roberta's "supper club" for women casts new light on Vashti's all-female feasts in Esther 1. Dinah may not speak, but these stories do.

Pausing for a final survey of the terrain of these chapters, several points emerge again and again. First, there is no single story or script for "rape stories." This includes many of the explanatory or affective frames we apply to rape stories, including "rape is the worst thing possible," "rape is exceptional," and "there is no *after* to rape." For some rape stories, one or more of these statements is true. But not always, and not for all rape stories. And we should not insist on fitting all rape stories into such a single narrow frame. The same is true for "survivor stories" or for identity categories such as "victim" and "survivor." A too-narrow model is bad reading and bad feminism. The variety of readings offered in the previous six chapters represent my attempt to capture the diversity of rape stories in and beyond the Hebrew Bible. The reading of Hagar and Sarah's relationship, over and against a focus on Hagar's rape (or, for that matter, Sarah's sexual exploitation), offers perhaps the clearest example of resistance to the pressure to tell a rape story a certain way—in this case, by refusing the demands of the "gendered grammar" of rape (Sharon Marcus's phrase). The archive of *after* stories gathered in chapter 5 and brought together with Daughter Zion's speeches in Lamentations offers another example of such alternative ways of reading. But this is present in all the chapters, from renarrating the stories of Dinah, Tamar, and Lot's daughters so they are not reducible to consent/nonconsent, to retelling Bathsheba's story along with Abishag's, to the unhappy reading of the "sad story" of the Levite's concubine.

Second, just as there is no one way to tell a rape story, there is no one way of framing harm. I have engaged this issue most thoroughly in chapter 3, where I consider harm in the Bathsheba story. Drawing on Joseph J. Fischel's *Sex and Harm in the Age of Consent*, I have argued that "predation," while a common model of sexual harm (and, in the case of Bathsheba, one offered by the text itself, in the form of Nathan's parable), is inadequate. In its place, I offer "peremption"—the irreversible limiting of possibility. We see peremption in the Bathsheba story, but also in the other rape stories explored here. Dinah's silence speaks her peremption, as does Tamar's dressing herself in widow's clothes and sequestering herself in her brother's house. Hagar is not only raped but also expelled into the wilderness—even as her peremption touches upon Sarah's peremption as well. Daughter Zion cries out in anger and pain, and yet many interpreters insist on imposing an external script on her words, rendering them an "already-read text." Peremption extends to the interpretive realm as well, such as when the sadness of a story such as Judges 19 perempts critical efforts to read it differently.

Third, what I have been calling "the *after*" of rape stories takes multiple forms. The *after* names both the immediate aftermath—what happens next in the narrative, for example—and the larger space in and around the story. How we respond to rape stories is part of their *after*. In the case of Chanel Miller and *Know My Name*, her (or "Emily Doe"'s) victim impact statement, and the huge outpouring of response it engendered, is part of this *after*.[3] But so too is Miller's anger, her outrage, and her struggle with the university officials who wanted to reduce her story to platitudes on a memorial plaque.[4] In other rape stories I have explored, the significance of the *after* is a refusal of healing or cure, an insistence that, in fact, victims and survivors do not always need or want to be "made whole." Or they may want this and be unable to realize it. Another, related part of the *after* is being willing to acknowledge that not all rape stories have an *after*. In the Hebrew Bible, sometimes what follows is silence, as with Dinah and with Lot's daughters. And sometimes it is death, as with the Levite's concubine. This story challenges the limits of the project I have sketched here; Judges 19 is better understood as a story of fatal misogynistic violence than as a rape story (though, of course, it includes rape). But it is also important, if a hard truth, to remember that not all rape stories can be redeemed, and not all biblical texts or characters can be "saved."

This leads to my fourth and final point: The work of feminist criticism is about finding ways to read and live with biblical rape stories. It is not about "telling sad stories," however much pleasure we may take from such a sad telling (here, the story of the Levite's concubine is a clear culprit). Neither is feminist criticism, including feminist reading of rape stories, about "saving women"—whether by insisting on positive readings, leveraging archaeology and material culture against textual representations, excavating countertraditions, or simply taking a feminist pair of scissors to the canon. In another of Margaret Atwood's novels, *The Blind Assassin*, the character Laura does just this, neatly snipping out the chapters and verses of the Bible she finds displeasing.[5] It is tempting to take scissors to the Bible and remove its most troubling stories, beginning with its texts of terror. It is equally tempting to relish the terror, to draw out every ounce of horror as a performance of voyeurism and catharsis. Lingering with terror can be a source of great pleasure, as the genre of horror teaches us. But I have sought a different kind of reading here. To do feminist work is, instead, to stay with the fuzzy, messy, and icky, even or especially when such readings seem difficult. Difficulty, after all, is part of the project. And if texts compel us in any way, if they place any demands upon us, it is this.

Partway through *The Female Man*, Russ writes about the book she is writing:

> This book is written in blood.
> Is it written entirely in blood?
> No, some of it is written in tears.
> Are the blood and tears all mine?
> Yes, they have been in the past. But the future is a different matter.[6]

So too this book; so too this future. After the rape stories, after the texts of terror, after the fuzzy, the messy, and the icky, after Dinah and Tamar and Lot's daughters and Bathsheba and Abishag and Hagar and Sarah and Daughter Zion and the Levite's concubine and all the others. These ways of reading offer the possibility of imagining an *after* to sexual violence, biblical and contemporary. The future is, I hope along with Russ, a different matter entirely.

Notes

Introduction

1. In this respect, my usage of the term "story" follows feminist theorist Clare Hemmings. See Hemmings, *Why Stories Matter: The Political Grammar of Feminist Theory* (Durham, NC: Duke University Press, 2011), 158.
2. Nicola Gavey, *Just Sex? The Cultural Scaffolding of Rape*, Women and Psychology (New York: Routledge, 2005).
3. Phyllis Trible, *Texts of Terror: Literary-Feminist Readings of Biblical Narratives*, Overtures to Biblical Theology (Minneapolis: Fortress Press, 1984).
4. E.g., Robert Goss, *Jesus Acted Up: A Gay and Lesbian Manifesto* (San Francisco: HarperSanFrancisco, 1994), 88–89; Caroline Blyth and Emily Colgan, "Tough Conversations: Teaching Biblical Texts of Terror," *Shiloh Project* (blog), June 13, 2019, https://www.shilohproject.blog/tough-conversations-teaching-biblical-texts-of-terror/.
5. Trible, *Texts of Terror*, 3.
6. Sohaila Abdulali, *What We Talk About When We Talk About Rape* (New York: New Press, 2018), 4.
7. There is of course some debate, especially over how to read Dinah; I discuss this in detail in chapter 2.
8. Joseph J. Fischel, *Sex and Harm in the Age of Consent* (Minnesota: University of Minnesota Press, 2016).
9. Trible, *Texts of Terror*, 1.

Chapter 1

1. Coomi S. Vevaina, "Margaret Atwood and History," in *The Cambridge Companion to Margaret Atwood*, ed. Coral Ann Howells (New York: Cambridge University Press, 2006), 86–99, 89. *The Handmaid's Tale* is dedicated to Mary Webster.
2. Margaret Atwood, *The Handmaid's Tale* (New York: Anchor Books, 1985), 94.
3. Atwood, of course, is not so simple, especially with respect to questions of feminism. See, to begin, Madeleine Davis, "Margaret Atwood's Female Bodies," in Howells, *Cambridge Companion to Margaret Atwood*, 59–60.
4. On the significance of feeling, especially in accounts of sexual trauma, see Ann Cvetkovich, *An Archive of Feelings: Trauma, Sexuality, and Lesbian Public Cultures* (Durham, NC: Duke University Press, 2003). I apply Cvetkovich's work to biblical rape texts in chapter 5.

5. For a related exploration, see Johanna Stiebert, *Rape Myths, the Bible, and #MeToo*, Rape Culture, Religion and the Bible 1 (New York: Routledge, 2019).

6. Ann Cvetkovich, *Depression: A Public Feeling* (Durham, NC: Duke University Press Books, 2012), 4–5.

7. Chanel Miller, *Know My Name: A Memoir* (New York: Penguin, 2019), 340.

8. Gavey, *Just Sex?*, 157.

9. Gavey, *Just Sex?*, 161.

10. Gavey, *Just Sex?*, 159.

11. Gavey, *Just Sex?*, 136.

12. See Gavey, *Just Sex?*, 193–213.

13. Vanessa Grigoriadis, *Blurred Lines: Rethinking Sex, Power, and Consent on Campus* (Boston: Eamon Dolan/Houghton Mifflin Harcourt, 2017), 47. Grigoriadis describes *Blurred Lines* as an attempt to name the complexities that attend feminist conversations about sexual violence. Of course, *blurry* is closely related to *fuzzy*.

14. In addition, many institutions downplay the extent and severity of drinking on campus, including by underage students. For an analysis of the narratives institutions tell in response to rape on campus, see Meredith Minister, *Rape Culture on Campus* (Lanham, MD: Lexington Books, 2018), 52–62.

15. Sarah Hepola, "The Alcohol Blackout," *Texas Monthly*, October 29, 2015, https://www.texasmonthly.com/the-culture/the-alcohol-blackout/.

16. I discuss Lot and his daughters in detail in chapter 2.

17. "Kavanaugh Hearing: Transcript," *Washington Post*, transcript courtesy of Bloomberg Government, September 27, 2018, https://www.washingtonpost.com/news/national/wp/2018/09/27/kavanaugh-hearing-transcript/.

18. Often, as Grigoriadis comments, "the details behind the milquetoast descriptions of what [perpetrators] have done wrong are *fuzzy*," especially in official reports (*Blurred Lines*, 291; emphasis added; see also 260).

19. For a lucid description of this sort of messiness, see Jennifer Doyle, *Campus Sex, Campus Security*, Intervention Series 19 (South Pasadena, CA: Semiotext(e), 2015), passim.

20. In the United States, Title IX is the primary federal law used to address sexual violence and sexual harassment on college campuses. Part of the Educational Amendments in 1972, Title IX reads: "No person in the United States shall, on the basis of sex, be excluded from participation in, be denied the benefits of, or be subjected to discrimination under any education program or activity receiving Federal financial assistance." The 2011 "Dear Colleague" letter issued by the Office for Civil Rights (OCR) under the Obama administration specified that Title IX applied to sexual violence and sexual harassment on campus.

21. On this point, see further my chapter 5.

22. The survivor is typically gendered as female in discourses surrounding sexual violence; see further Doyle, *Campus Sex*, 42. In addition, my language in *Texts after Terror* reflects my focus on female victims and survivors.

23. Kate Manne, *Down Girl: The Logic of Misogyny* (New York: Penguin Books Limited, 2019), especially 225n8.

24. Minister, *Rape Culture on Campus*, 43–44.

25. Noel Clark, "The Etiology and Phenomenology of Sexual Shame: A Grounded Theory Study" (PhD dissertation, Seattle Pacific University, 2017), 83, 90; Christin P. Bowman, "Persistent Pleasures: Agency, Social Power, and Embodiment in Women's Solitary Masturbation Experiences" (PhD dissertation, City University of New York, 2017), 98–99.

26. And, of course, work environments of all kinds, including academic departments and conferences.

27. "Cat Person" first appeared in the December 11, 2017, issue of *The New Yorker* and was subsequently included in Kristen Roupenian's collection *You Know You Want This: "Cat Person" and Other Stories* (New York: Gallery/Scout Press 2019), 79–98. Quotations are taken from the book.

28. Roupenian, "Cat Person," 88.

29. Roupenian, "Cat Person," 92, emphasis original.

30. Larissa Pham notes that when the story first went viral, many people responding to it on Twitter did not realize it was a short story at all, "despite the 'fiction' tag at the top of the article." Larissa Pham, "Our Reaction to 'Cat Person' Shows That We Are Failing as Readers," *Village Voice*, December 15, 2017, https://www.villagevoice.com/2017/12/15/our-reaction-to-cat-person-shows-that-we-are-failing-as-readers/.

31. See Emilie Buchwald, Pamela Fletcher, and Martha Roth, eds., *Transforming a Rape Culture* (Minneapolis: Milkweed Editions, 1995); Melissa McEwan, "Rape Culture 101," *Shakesville* (blog), October 9, 2009, http://www.shakesville.com/2009/10/rape-culture-101.html; Rhiannon Graybill, Meredith Minister, and Beatrice Lawrence, "Introduction," in *Rape Culture and Religious Studies: Critical and Pedagogical Engagements*, ed. Rhiannon Graybill, Meredith Minister, and Beatrice Lawrence, Feminist Studies and Sacred Texts (Lanham, MD: Lexington Books, 2019), 11–12; Stiebert, *Rape Myths, the Bible, and #MeToo*, 54–55.

32. Harold C. Washington, "Violence and the Construction of Gender in the Hebrew Bible: A New Historicist Approach 1," *Biblical Interpretation* 5, no. 4 (1997): 353.

33. For a comprehensive account, see Susanne Scholz, *Sacred Witness: Rape in the Hebrew Bible* (Minneapolis: Fortress Press, 2010).

34. Adultery and rape are not clearly distinguished in biblical law (Deut 22:21–25).

35. Washington, "Violence and the Construction of Gender," 354.

36. The laws do offer an exception when a rape takes place in open country (Heb. *baśśādeh*; Deut 25:25), where the woman's protests would not be heard by others. In this case, only the man is punished (Deut 22:25–27).

37. Cynthia R. Chapman, *The Gendered Language of Warfare in the Israelite-Assyrian Encounter*, Harvard Semitic Monographs 62 (Winona Lake, IN: Eisenbrauns, 2004).

38. Ken Stone, "Gender and Homosexuality in Judges 19: Subject-Honor, Object-Shame?," *Journal for the Study of the Old Testament* 20, no. 67 (1995): 87–107, 92.

39. James Harding, "Homophobia and Masculine Domination in Judges 19–21," *The Bible and Critical Theory* 12, no. 2 (2016).

40. The list of "female perpetrators" most frequently includes Lot's daughters (though see my extended analysis in chapter 2) and Potiphar's wife (Gen 39), though Stiebert

raises the significant possibility that she is telling the truth. Johanna Stiebert, "The Wife of Potiphar, Sexual Harassment, and False Rape Allegation," in *The Bible and Gender Troubles in Africa*, ed. Joachim Kügler, Rosinah Gabaitse, and Johanna Stiebert (Bamberg: University of Bamberg Press, 2019), 73–114.

41. I have written about this topic elsewhere. See, to begin, Rhiannon Graybill, *Are We Not Men?: Unstable Masculinity in the Hebrew Prophets* (New York: Oxford University Press, 2016); Rhiannon Graybill, "Jonah 'Between Men': The Prophet in Critical Homosocial Perspective," in *Hebrew Masculinities Anew*, ed. Ovidiu Creangă, Hebrew Bible Monographs 79 (Sheffield, UK: Sheffield Phoenix Press, 2019), 210–28.

42. For a feminist analysis of the rape of men in biblical texts, see Chris Greenough, *The Bible and Sexual Violence against Men*, Rape Culture, Religion and the Bible 4 (New York: Routledge, 2020); Emma Nagouse, "'To Ransom a Man's Soul': Male Rape and Gender Identity in *Outlander* and 'The Suffering Man' of Lamentations 3," in *Rape Culture, Gender Violence, and Religion: Biblical Perspectives*, ed. Caroline Blyth, Emily Colgan, and Katie B. Edwards, Religion and Radicalism (Palgrave Macmillan, 2018), 143–58. On male rape more generally, Gavey's reflections in *Just Rape?*, 193–213, are instructive.

43. Gavey, *Just Rape?*, 194.

44. Audre Lorde, "The Master's Tools Will Never Dismantle the Master's House" (1984), in *Sister Outsider: Essays and Speeches*, reprint ed. (Berkeley, CA: Crossing Press, 2007), 110–14.

45. Donna J. Haraway, *Simians, Cyborgs, and Women: The Reinvention of Nature* (New York: Routledge, 1990); *Modest_Witness@Second_Millennium: FemaleMan©_Meets_OncoMouse™: Feminism and Technoscience* (New York: Routledge, 1997); *Staying with the Trouble: Making Kin in the Chthulucene* (Durham, NC: Duke University Press, 2016). For additional recent critiques of the innocent subject position see, to begin, Sarah Schulman, *Conflict Is Not Abuse: Overstating Harm, Community Responsibility, and the Duty of Repair* (Vancouver: Arsenal Pulp Press, 2016); Alexis Shotwell, *Against Purity: Living Ethically in Compromised Times* (Minneapolis: University of Minnesota Press, 2016).

46. Both of these essays are included in *Simians, Cyborgs, and Women*. Haraway continues to stress this point through her more recent work, including 2016's *Staying with the Trouble*.

47. Donna J. Haraway, *When Species Meet* (Minneapolis: University of Minnesota Press, 2008), 70.

48. Rhiannon Graybill, "When Bodies Meet: Fraught Companionship and Entangled Embodiment in Jeremiah 36," *Journal of the American Academy of Religion* 86, no. 4 (2018): 1046–71.

49. Haraway, *Staying with the Trouble*, 3.

50. I explore this question in detail in chapter 2.

51. Eve Kosofsky Sedgwick, *Touching Feeling: Affect, Pedagogy, Performativity*, Series Q (Durham, NC: Duke University Press, 2002).

52. Sedgwick, *Touching Feeling*, 130.

53. Sedgwick, *Touching Feeling*, 130.

54. Sedgwick, *Touching Feeling*, 137.

55. The same is true of LGBTQ scholarship, though to a lesser degree.

56. Sedgwick, *Touching Feeling*, 128.

57. Sara Ahmed, *The Promise of Happiness* (Durham, NC: Duke University Press, 2010).

58. Rhiannon Graybill, Meredith Minister, and Beatrice Lawrence, "Sexual Violence in and around the Classroom," *Teaching Theology & Religion* 20, no. 1 (2017): 74. Minister also describes attempts to "purify" the category of survivor; see Minister, *Rape Culture on Campus*, 43–44.

59. This is true, for example, of the protagonists of the novels I will discuss in chapter 4, as well as the main characters of Roupenian's "Cat Person."

60. Gayatri Chakravorty Spivak, "French Feminism Revisited: Ethics and Politics," in *Feminists Theorize the Political*, ed. Judith Butler and Joan W. Scott (New York: Routledge, 1992), 54–84, 55.

61. On this use of the term "stories," including when reading poetic texts, see the Introduction.

62. See, e.g. Susan Brooks Thistlethwaite, "You May Enjoy the Spoil of Your Enemies: Rape as a Biblical Metaphor for War," *Semeia*, no. 61 (1993): 59–75; Julia M. O'Brien, *Nahum*, Readings (London: Sheffield Academic Press, 2002), 84–103; Gerlinde Baumann, "Nahum," in *Feminist Biblical Interpretation: A Compendium of Critical Commentary on the Books of the Bible and Related Literature*, ed. Luise Schottroff and Marie-Theres Wacker (Grand Rapids, MI: Wm. B. Eerdmans Publishing, 2012), 433–42, 438; Wilda C. M. Gafney, *Nahum, Habakkuk, Zephaniah* (Collegeville, MN: Liturgical Press, 2017), 47–54.

63. The literature is extensive. See, to begin, Renita J. Weems, *Battered Love: Marriage, Sex, and Violence in the Hebrew Prophets* (Minneapolis: Fortress Press, 1995); Athalya Brenner, *A Feminist Companion to the Latter Prophets*, Feminist Companion to the Bible (Sheffield, UK: Sheffield Academic Press, 1995); Athalya Brenner, ed., *A Feminist Companion to Prophets and Daniel*, Feminist Companion to the Bible, 2nd ser. (Sheffield, UK: Sheffield Academic Press, 2002); Carleen Mandolfo, *Daughter Zion Talks Back to the Prophets: A Dialogic Theology of the Book of Lamentations*, rev. ed. (Atlanta: SBL Press, 2007); Scholz, *Sacred Witness*.

64. Sedgwick, *Touching Feeling*, 136.

65. "Though I have raped you, I will rape you no more": *wĕʿinnitik lōʾ ʾăʿannēk ʿôd.* NRSV translates with the more general "afflicted," thus, "though I have afflicted you, I will afflict you no more." On the translation of rape here, see O'Brien, *Nahum*, 144–45. I discuss *ʿinnâ* in chapter 2.

66. Roupenian, "Cat Person," 98. Emphasis, spelling, and punctuation original.

67. Roupenian, "Cat Person," 96, 79, 86, 97. Of course, Margot also worries that Robert might murder her. Though she carefully compartmentalizes her anxiety, it lingers, uneasily, in the text.

68. Patricia Lockwood, "Rape Joke," in *Motherland, Fatherland, Homelandsexuals*, Penguin Poets (New York: Penguin Books, 2014), 40–44. I discuss *Conversations with Friends, Supper Club,* and their representations of sexual violence in detail in chapter 4.

69. See further chapter 5.

70. Atwood, *Handmaid's Tale*, 87.

Chapter 2

1. Thus, consent is always specific and limited; giving consent once does not imply blanket consent, just like having a cup of tea once does not indicate an eternal and insatiable desire for tea. See Blue Seat Studios (2015). For a critique, see Rhiannon Graybill, "Critiquing the Discourse of Consent," *Journal of Feminist Studies in Religion* 33, no. 1 (2017): 175–76; Joseph J. Fischel, *Screw Consent: A Better Politics of Sexual Justice* (Oakland: University of California Press, 2019), 12–13; Abdulali, *What We Talk about*, 40–41.
2. And, as I will demonstrate, to our own contexts.
3. Fischel, *Screw Consent*, 3–4.
4. Fischel, *Screw Consent*, 3–4.
5. This image of consent as like a traffic signal is increasingly common. See, for example, http://greenlightgo.squarespace.com/. Red-Light, Green-Light consent games have been organized at universities such as George Washington University, the University of Calgary, and Washington State University. Grigoriadis provides a description and analysis (*Blurred Lines*, 118, 139). See also Miller, *Know My Name*, 263.
6. Sandie Gravett, "Reading 'Rape' in the Hebrew Bible: A Consideration of Language," *Journal for the Study of the Old Testament* 28, no. 3 (March 1, 2004): 279–99; Ken Stone, "'You Seduced Me, You Overpowered Me, and You Prevailed': Religious Experience and Homoerotic Sadomasochism in Jeremiah," in *Patriarchs, Prophets and Other Villains*, ed. Lisa Isherwood, Gender, Theology, and Spirituality (London: Equinox, 2007), 101–9.
7. For a critique of this approach (though not specifically Kawashima's article), see Susanne Scholz, "'Back Then It Was Legal': The Epistemological Imbalance in Readings of Biblical and Ancient Near Eastern Rape Legislation," *Journal of Religion & Abuse* 7, no. 3 (November 2, 2005): 5–35.
8. Robert S. Kawashima, "Could a Woman Say 'No' in Biblical Israel? On the Genealogy of Legal Status in Biblical Law and Literature," *AJS Review* 35, no. 1 (2011): 2–3, n4.
9. Though this is not to say that no wrong is done: The sexual culture has a system of adjudicating a sexual wrong with the woman as a central object and her male protector as the offended party. I thank Steed Davidson for this point.
10. Gravett, "Reading 'Rape,'" 280, 298.
11. Contrast Alison Joseph, who argues for the social shaming as the term's meaning. See Joseph, "Understanding Genesis 34:2: 'Innâ," *Vetus Testamentum* 66, no. 4 (2016): 663–68.
12. Kawashima, "Could a Woman Say 'No,'" 5.
13. Kawashima, "Could a Woman Say 'No,'" 21.
14. To this end, Kawashima titles his article "Could a Woman Say 'No' in Biblical Israel?," not "Could a Woman Say 'No' in the Hebrew Bible?" though he discusses the latter question as well.
15. Friedrich Nietzsche, *On the Genealogy of Morals and Ecco Homo*, ed. Walter Kaufmann (New York: Vintage Books, 1989), 15.

16. See Karmen MacKendrick, "Consent, Command, Confession," in *Querying Consent: Beyond Permission and Refusal*, ed. Jordana Greenblatt and Keja Valens (New Brunswick, NJ: Rutgers University Press, 2018), 11–26.

17. Minister, *Rape Culture on Campus*, 78.

18. Scholz, "Back Then It Was Legal."

19. Sara Ahmed, *Willful Subjects* (Durham, NC: Duke University Press, 2014), 55. Ahmed also specifically describes this situation as messy: "Tangles are messy, and accounts of the social will thus need to be messy in turn" (56).

20. For example, Roxane Gay, ed., *Not That Bad: Dispatches from Rape Culture* (New York: Harper, 2018); Shelly Oria, ed., *Indelible in the Hippocampus: Writings from the Me Too Movement* (San Francisco: McSweeney's, 2019); Grigoriadis, *Blurred Lines*; Jon Krakauer, *Missoula: Rape and the Justice System in a College Town* (New York: Doubleday, 2015).

21. Samuel L. Gaertner, John F. Dovidio, and Gary Johnson, "Race of Victim, Nonresponsive Bystanders, and Helping Behavior," *Journal of Social Psychology* 117, no. 1 (June 1, 1982): 69–77; Christine A. Gidycz, Lindsay M. Orchowski, and Alan D. Berkowitz, "Preventing Sexual Aggression among College Men: An Evaluation of a Social Norms and Bystander Intervention Program," *Violence Against Women* 17, no. 11 (2011): 730–42; Sidney Bennett, Victoria L. Banyard, and Lydia Garnhart, "To Act or Not to Act, That Is the Question? Barriers and Facilitators of Bystander Intervention," *Journal of Interpersonal Violence* 29, no. 3 (2013): 476–96.

22. Meredith Minister, "Sex and Alien Encounter: Rethinking Consent as a Rape Prevention Strategy," in Graybill, Minister, and Lawrence, *Rape Culture and Religious Studies*, 160–61.

23. Maria Bevacqua, *Rape on the Public Agenda: Feminism and the Politics of Sexual Assault* (Boston: Northeastern University Press, 2000); Crystal N. Feimster, *Southern Horrors: Women and the Politics of Rape and Lynching* (Cambridge, MA: Harvard University Press, 2009); Danielle L. McGuire, *At the Dark End of the Street: Black Women, Rape, and Resistance—A New History of the Civil Rights Movement from Rosa Parks to the Rise of Black Power* (New York: Vintage Books, 2011).

24. Already in the nineteenth century, Ida B. Wells described the ways in which the fear of rape of White women was used to justify the lynching of Black men. See Ida B. Wells, *Southern Horrors and Other Writings: The Anti-Lynching Campaign of Ida B. Wells, 1892–1900*, 2nd ed., ed. Jacqueline Jones Royster, Bedford Series in History and Culture (Boston: Bedford/St. Martin's, 2016), especially "Southern Horrors: Lynch Law in All Its Phases," 46–68.

25. Virtue ethics offers another possible way of responding to this critique, suggesting that consent is necessary for virtuous sex, or sex that enables us to flourish. I thank Caroline Blyth for this point.

26. Wendy Brown, *States of Injury: Power and Freedom in Late Modernity* (Princeton, NJ: Princeton University Press, 1995), 163.

27. On this point, see further Rhiannon Graybill, "Good Intentions Are Not Enough," in Graybill, Minister, and Lawrence, *Rape Culture and Religious Studies*, 183–85. See as well chapter 6.

28. Gayatri Chakravorty Spivak, "Can the Subaltern Speak?" in *Marxism and the Interpretation of Culture*, ed. Cary Nelson and Lawrence Grossberg (Champaign: University of Illinois Press, 1988), 271–314. On saving women, see as well chapter 6.

29. Spivak, "Can the Subaltern Speak?"; Jasbir Puar, *The Right to Maim: Debility, Capacity, Disability* (Durham, NC: Duke University Press, 2017), 98–99.

30. I also use this phrase ("Consent is a low bar") to critique consent in Graybill, "Critiquing the Discourse of Consent," 176. The analysis offered here expands upon that piece.

31. Kelly Oliver, "Party Rape, Nonconsensual Sex, and Affirmative Consent Policies," *Americana* 14, no. 2 (2015): n.p. See also Fischel, *Screw Consent*, 19.

32. Cf., Jordana Greenblatt, "Consensual Sex, Consensual Text: Law, Literature, and the Production of the Consenting Subject," in Greenblatt and Valens, *Querying Consent*, 44–62.

33. Rebecca Traister, "The Game Is Rigged: Why Sex That's Consensual Can Still Be Bad. And Why We're Not Talking About It," *The Cut*, October 20, 2015, http://www.thecut.com/2015/10/why-consensual-sex-can-still-be-bad.html.

34. Reading with the *qere* (na'ărā, "young woman"); the *ketiv* reads na'ar ("young man"). This occurs in both instances of the word in the verse. For an extended analysis, see Julie Kelso, "Reading the Silence of Women in Genesis 34," in *Redirected Travel: Alternative Journeys and Places in Biblical Studies*, ed. Roland Boer and Edgar W. Conrad, Journal for the Study of the Old Testament Supplement Series 382 (New York: T&T Clark, 2003), 93–95.

35. See Alison L. Joseph, "Redaction as Reception: The Case of Genesis 34," in *Reading Other Peoples' Texts: Social Identity and the Reception of Authoritative Traditions*, ed. Ken S. Brown, Alison L. Joseph, and Brennan Breed, Scriptural Traces 20 (New York: T&T Clark, 2020), 83–101.

36. Ellen van Wolde, "Does 'innâ Denote Rape? A Semantic Analysis of a Controversial Word," *Vetus Testamentum* 52, no. 4 (2002): 528–44, 543.

37. Joseph, "Understanding Genesis 34:2," 664.

38. Yael Shemesh, "Rape Is Rape Is Rape: The Story of Dinah and Shechem (Genesis 34)," *Zeitschrift für die alttestamentliche Wissenschaft* 119, no. 1 (2007): 2–21.

39. Goldberg's comments concerned director Roman Polanski. In 1977, Polanski was charged with drugging and raping a thirteen-year-old. He pled guilty to "unlawful sexual intercourse with a minor" but fled the United States before serving his sentence. In 2009, he was arrested in Switzerland. Commenting on the news of his arrest, Goldberg suggested that Polanski was not guilty of "rape-rape." Her comments were widely covered in the media; for example Maev Kennedy, "Polanski Was Not Guilty of 'Rape-Rape', Says Whoopi Goldberg," *Guardian*, September 29, 2009, http://www.theguardian.com/film/2009/sep/29/roman-polanski-whoopi-goldberg.   Polanski was not ultimately deported. Several years later, similar outrage arose over U.S. Representative Todd Akin's use of the term "legitimate rape" in discussing rape and unwanted pregnancy. See, e.g., John Eligon and Michael Schwirtz, "Senate Candidate Provokes Ire with 'Legitimate Rape' Comment," *New York Times*, August 19, 2012, sec. U.S. https://www.nytimes.com/2012/08/20/us/politics/todd-akin-provokes-ire-with-legitimate-rape-comment.html.

40. Anita Diamant, *The Red Tent*, 20th anniv. ed. (New York: Picador, 2007).

41. Todd Penner and Lilian Cates, "Textually Violating Dinah: Literary Readings, Colonizing Interpretations, and the Pleasure of the Text," *The Bible and Critical Theory* 3, no. 3 (2007): 37.1-37.18.

42. Musa W. Dube, "Dinah (Genesis 34) at the Contact Zone: Shall Our Sister Be Treated Like a Whore?" in *Feminist Frameworks and the Bible: Power, Ambiguity, and Intersectionality*, ed. L. Juliana Claassens and Carolyn J. Sharp, Library of Hebrew Bible/Old Testament Studies 630 (New York: T&T Clark), 39–58, 51.

43. "He forced himself on her and lay with her": *wayĕʿannehā wayyiškab ʾōtāh*. The same verbs are used, though in opposite order, with Dinah (Gen 34:2).

44. Alice A. Keefe, "Rapes of Women, Wars of Men: Women, War, Society, and Metaphoric Language in the Study of the Hebrew Bible," *Semeia* 61 (1993): 79–97.

45. William H. Propp, "Kinship in 2 Samuel 13," *Catholic Biblical Quarterly* 55, no. 1 (1993): 39–53, 39.

46. Note that Tamar refers to David as "the king" and not "my father," "your father," or "our father."

47. Ahmed, *Willful Subjects*, 55.

48. It is curious that the daughters express their belief that they are alone in the world, as they have just come from the small city of Zoar.

49. For a detailed examination, see Peter J. Sabo, "The Lot Complex" (PhD dissertation, University of Alberta, 2018).

50. Here, Fischel's analysis of incest in *Screw Consent* is instructive: It is age and power differentials, not consanguinity, that makes incest wrong (however icky "horizontal" incest [e.g., between adult cousins or siblings] might be). Thus, Lot's sexual relationship with his daughters is wrong not because of the blood relations between them but because of the power he holds over them: "power matters over blood" (24). See also *Screw Consent*, 78–81.

51. Ilona N. Rashkow, *Taboo or Not Taboo: Sexuality and Family in the Hebrew Bible* (Minneapolis: Fortress Press, 2000), 113.

52. J. Cheryl Exum, "Desire Distorted and Exhibited: Lot and His Daughters in Psychoanalysis, Painting, and Film," in *"A Wise and Discerning Mind": Essays in Honor of Burke O. Long*, ed. Saul M. Olyan and Robert C. Culley, Brown Judaic Studies 325 (Providence, RI: Brown University Press, 2000), 94–96.

53. Rhiannon Graybill and Peter J. Sabo, "Caves of the Hebrew Bible: A Speleology," *Biblical Interpretation* 26, no. 1 (2018): 1–22.

54. Though, as Fischel notes in *Screw Consent*, "Ickiness is a bad basis for regulating sex" (81).

55. Incest is often excluded from modern definitions of consensual sexual activity.

56. One of the most common questions posed to affirmative consent policies concerns the case where both parties are intoxicated and thus unable to consent. Consider also the question of sex and mental disability.

57. Mattias Rudolf, "Vulnerabilities: Consent with Pfizer, Marx, and Hobbes," in Greenblatt and Valens, *Querying Consent*, 212.

58. Haraway, *Simians, Cyborgs, and Women*, 188.

59. Haraway, *When Species Meet*, 70.

60. Haraway, *Staying with the Trouble*, 3.

61. Dube, "Dinah (Genesis 34) at the Contact Zone," 50.

62. J. Cheryl Exum, *Fragmented Women: Feminist (Sub)Versions of Biblical Narratives*, Journal for the Study of the Old Testament Supplement Series 163 (Sheffield, UK: JSOT Press, 1993).

63. Dube, "Dinah (Genesis 34) at the Contact Zone," 51.

64. Schulman, *Conflict Is Not Abuse*, 189–205.

65. Sedgwick, *Touching Feeling*, 130.

66. Jenny Holzer, *Abuse of Power Comes as No Surprise* (Installation at Walker Art Center, Minneapolis, 1983).

67. Sedgwick, *Touching Feeling*, 149.

68. Sedgwick adopts this idea of the paranoid and the reparative as positions from Melanie Klein.

69. Ahmed, *Promise of Happiness*, 120.

70. Sara Ahmed, *Queer Phenomenology: Orientations, Objects, Others* (Durham, NC: Duke University Press, 2006), 157–58.

71. Both names refer to the same series: *Xenogenesis* has been mostly replaced by *Lilith's Brood*. I follow Minister's usage here, as it is their reading of the novels that is my focus.

72. Minister, "Sex and Alien Encounter," 171.

73. For example, yesmeansyes.com defines consent as "Consent is a mutual verbal, physical, and emotional agreement that happens without manipulation, threats, or head games." See https://www.yesmeansyes.com/consent.

74. Minister, "Sex and Alien Encounter," 170.

75. Jeremy Posadas, "Teaching the Cause of Rape Culture: Toxic Masculinity," *Journal of Feminist Studies in Religion* 33, no. 1 (2017): 177–79.

76. Graybill, *Are We Not Men?*

77. See Stone, " 'You Seduced Me,' " 101–9; cf. Graybill, *Are We Not Men?*, 89–91.

78. I thank Gwynn Kessler for this point.

79. See further Beatrice Lawrence, "Rape Culture and the Rabbinic Construction of Gender," in Graybill, Minister, and Lawrence, *Rape Culture and Religious Studies*, 137–56.

80. Fischel, *Screw Consent*, 136, 157–71.

81. Minister, "Sex and Alien Encounter," 170.

Chapter 3

1. Hemmings, *Why Stories Matter*, 158.

2. For a history of feminist engagements with biblical studies, see Jennifer L. Koosed, "Reading the Bible as a Feminist," *Brill Research Perspectives in Biblical Interpretation* 2, no. 2 (2017): 1–75.

3. Nietzsche, *On the Genealogy of Morals*.

4. For example, activist Rachael Denhollander has set forth this reading in her book and her tweets. Denhollander was one of the gymnasts who exposed serial abuser Larry Hasser. Denhollander, *What Is a Girl Worth?: My Story of Breaking the Silence and Exposing the Truth about Larry Nassar and USA Gymnastics* (Carol Stream, IL: Tyndale Momentum, 2019), 89–90.

5. Fischel, *Sex and Harm*, 135, italics original.

6. I adopt this phrase from Fischel, *Sex and Harm*, 149.

7. The speaker is unspecified.

8. Menachem Perry and Meir Sternberg, "The King through Ironic Eyes: Biblical Narrative and the Literary Reading Process," *Poetics Today* 7, no. 2 (1986): 275–79.

9. Gale A. Yee, "'Fraught with Background': Literary Ambiguity in II Samuel 11," *Union Seminary Review* 42, no. 3 (1988): 240–53. For another use of Auerbach to read the passage, see George G. Nicol, "The Alleged Rape of Bathsheba: Some Observations on Ambiguity in Biblical Narrative," *Journal for the Study of the Old Testament* 73 (1997): 43–54.

10. Robert Alter, *The David Story: A Translation with Commentary of 1 and 2 Samuel* (New York: W. W. Norton & Company, 2009), 249n.

11. Consent is not always verbal (see Minister, "Sex and Alien Encounter," 161–62). There are likewise no signs in 2 Sam 11 that Bathsheba *nonverbally* consents: It is a mistake to read "she came" as signaling consent; see Richard M. Davidson, "Did King David Rape Bathsheba? A Case Study in Narrative Theology," *Journal of the Adventist Theological Society* 17, no. 2 (2006): 87; Jennifer Andruska, "'Rape' in the Syntax of 2 Samuel 11:4," *Zeitschrift für die alttestamentliche Wissenschaft* 129, no. 1 (2017): 103–4. Furthermore, the difficulties of appealing to consent discourses should of course already be clear to the reader; see further my chapter 2.

12. Bathing on the roof is much discussed in the scholarly literature. For a representative argument that she is trying to seduce David, see Nicol, "Alleged Rape of Bathsheba," 44. For a critique of this position, see Davidson, "Did King David Rape Bathsheba?," 83–85. On the literary motif of roof bathing, see Caryn Tamber-Rosenau, "Biblical Bathing Beauties and the Manipulation of the Male Gaze: What Judith Can Tell Us about Bathsheba and Susanna," *Journal of Feminist Studies in Religion* 33, no. 2 (2017): 55–72. On the motif of bathing more broadly, see Anne Létourneau, "Beauty, Bath and Beyond: Framing Bathsheba as a Royal Fantasy in 2 Sam 11, 1–5," *Scandinavian Journal of the Old Testament* 32, no. 1 (2018): 72–91.

13. Davidson, "Did King David Rape Bathsheba?," 81–95.

14. Here, one divergent reading comes from Leah Rediger Schulte, who argues that the absence of God is a defining feature of biblical rape stories. Because Yahweh is mentioned in 2 Sam 11:27, Bathsheba's story fails to meet the standards for a rape narrative. See Leah Rediger Schulte, *The Absence of God in Biblical Rape Narratives*, Emerging Scholars (Minneapolis: Fortress Press, 2017), 134.

15. Perry and Sternberg, "The King through Ironic Eyes," 292–305.

16. See, e.g., Perry and Sternberg, "The King through Ironic Eyes," 289; Alter, *David Story*, 251. The NRSV translates the phrase *wĕhîʾ mitqaddešet miṭṭumʾātāh* in 2 Sam 11:4 as "Now she was purifying herself after her period," which is placed in parentheses in the verse, suggesting an explanatory aside.

17. Note that this does not reflect contemporary medical understanding. It is possible to have bleeding that resembles a menstrual period while pregnant.

18. This is a reading that I find forced, for reasons that Tamber-Rosenau ("Biblical Bathing Beauties") sets forth and that I discuss further later in the chapter.

19. For a discussion of the loss of the ordinary as experienced by victims/survivors, see Miller, *Know My Name*, 250, 260–63.

20. For readings of Bathsheba as a victim, see, e.g., Exum, *Fragmented Women*; Scholz, *Sacred Witness* 84–85; Davidson, "Did King David Rape Bathsheba?".

21. E.g., Nicol, "Alleged Rape of Bathsheba"; Kristine Henriksen Garroway, "Was Bathsheba the Original Bridget Jones?: A New Look at Bathsheba on Screen and in Biblical Scholarship," *Nashim* 24 (Spring 5773/2013): 53–73.

22. "Staying with the trouble" comes from Donna Haraway; see further my chapter 1.

23. Scholz, *Sacred Witness*, 100.

24. Exum, *Fragmented Women*, 172–73. Davidson reads both the rapid narrative pace and the specific sequence of verbs as indicating "power rape." Davidson, "Did King David Rape Bathsheba?," 88.

25. Exum, *Fragmented Women*, 174–75. See as well J. Cheryl Exum, *Plotted, Shot, and Painted: Cultural Representations of Biblical Women* (Sheffield, UK: Sheffield Academic Press, 1996).

26. Tamber-Rosenau, "Biblical Bathing Beauties." See as well Létourneau, "Beauty, Bath, and Beyond."

27. Andruska, " 'Rape' in the Syntax of 2 Samuel 11:4," 106. Andruska also notes a difference in wording between 2 Sam 11:4 and 2 Sam 12:24, when David next has sex with Bathsheba: The word "take" (Heb. *laqaḥ*) is used in the former case (as it is in the account of Shechem and Dinah) but not the latter.

28. The scholarly debate goes into remarkable detail about whether roofs are a typical, unusual, or extraordinary place to bathe. The timing of Bathsheba's bath is also subjected to detailed scrutiny. See my discussion later in the chapter.

29. Nicol, "Alleged Rape of Bathsheba," 53. See as well Nicol's earlier article "Bathsheba, A Clever Woman?," *Expository Times* 99 (1988): 360–63, and Exum's critique in *Fragmented Women*, 173–74.

30. Garroway, "Was Bathsheba the Original Bridget Jones?," 65. I find this "postfeminist" reading problematic; see further Caroline Blyth, "Lost in the 'Post': Rape Culture and Postfeminism in Admen and Eve," *The Bible and Critical Theory* 10, no. 2 (2014): 1–10.

31. For a discussion, see Exum, *Plotted, Shot, and Painted*, 22–23. This is a common representation in film; see Johanna Stiebert, "The Eve-ing of Bathsheba in Twentieth Century Film," *The Bible and Critical Theory* 10, no. 2 (2014): 22–31.

32. For example, Alice Bach, "Signs of the Flesh: Observations on Characterization in the Bible," in *Women in the Hebrew Bible: A Reader*, ed. Alice Bach (New York: Routledge, 1999), 362; David J. Zucker and Moshe Reiss, "David's Wives: Love, Power, and Lust," *Biblical Theology Bulletin* 46 (2): 70–78, 75. Note, however, that neither Bach nor Zucker and Reiss use the specific language of "survivor."

33. Zucker and Reiss, "David's Wives," 75.

34. Exum, *Fragmented Women*, 171.

35. Exum, *Fragmented Women*, 171. Exum doubles down on this reading in *Plotted, Shot, and Painted*, a follow-up to *Fragmented Women*.

36. Exum, *Fragmented Women*, 173–74.

37. Exum, *Fragmented Women*, 172–74.

38. Sara M. Koenig, *Isn't This Bathsheba?: A Study in Characterization*, Princeton Theological Monographs 177 (Eugene, OR: Pickwick Publications, 2011), 62–65; Jeremy Schipper, "Did David Overinterpret Nathan's Parable in 2 Samuel 12:1-6?," *Journal of Biblical Literature* 126, no. 2 (2007): 383–91.

39. Ken Stone, "Animal Difference, Sexual Difference, and the Daughter of Jephthah," *Biblical Interpretation* 24, no. 1 (January 12, 2016): 1–16, 6.

40. David's first appearance is a chapter prior, in 1 Sam 16, where he plays music for Saul—seemingly a less predatory action, though given how David infiltrates Saul's household and eventually gains the throne for himself, it may also be read as initiating a more subtle, long-term act of predation.

41. Both Brueggemann and Sharp use "predator" in reference to the events with Bathsheba; Halpern refers to David's general mercenary and "brigand" activity. In Brooks's novel, it is part of a reflection on the complexity of David's character. See Walter Brueggemann, *David's Truth in Israel's Imagination and Memory*, 2nd ed. (Minneapolis: Fortress Press, 2002), 24; Carolyn J. Sharp, *Irony and Meaning in the Hebrew Bible* (Bloomington: Indiana University Press, 2008), 344; Baruch Halpern, *David's Secret Demons: Messiah, Murderer, Traitor, King* (Grand Rapids, MI: Wm. B. Eerdmans Publishing, 2003), 344; Geraldine Brooks, *The Secret Chord* (New York: Penguin, 2016), 76.

42. Nicol, "Alleged Rape of Bathsheba," 53; Garroway, "Was Bathsheba the Original Bridget Jones?," 65.

43. Exum, *Fragmented Women*, 9.

44. Nietzsche, *On the Genealogy of Morals*, 44–45.

45. An especially dramatic example of these dynamics can be found in the television series *To Catch a Predator*, as Fischel draws out; *Sex and Harm*, 27–37.

46. See, for example, Miller, *Know My Name*, vii, 9, 66. The category of "survivor" is also criticized on similar grounds, as I discuss in the next chapter.

47. To summarize Fischel's argument: The child is assumed to be innocent, vulnerable, and unable to consent to sex of any kind before the age of eighteen (hence, legally "incompetent"); the sex offender is constructed as recidivistic, predatory, "especially heinous" (a phrase made popular by *CSI: SVU*), and immediately and clearly distinguishable from the good and proper sexual citizen; the homosexual, though once considered a threat, is now an example of appropriate sexual citizenship; correct sex is determined not by the sex or gender identity of its participants, but by being consensual, private, and between adults. Our sexual politics, and our sociolegal framing of sex and sexual harm, assume these fictions.

48. Fischel, *Sex and Harm*, 57.

49. Fischel, *Sex and Harm*, 99.

50. Fischel, *Sex and Harm*, 132, italics original.

51. Fischel, *Sex and Harm*, 14.

52. Fischel, *Sex and Harm*, 136. The "doer behind the deed" comes originally from Nietzsche, *On the Genealogy of Morals*, 45.

53. Fischel, *Sex and Harm*, 14. The three films are *Doubt* (2008, dir. John Patrick Shanley), *Thirteen* (2003, dir. Catherine Hardwicke), and *Superbad* (2007, dir. Greg Mottola).

54. Fischel, *Sex and Harm*, 117, italics original.

55. Fischel, *Sex and Harm*, 152.

56. John Patrick Shanley, *Doubt* (Burbank, CA: Miramax, 2008), DVD. Shanley also adapted the screenplay from his play.

57. Fischel, *Sex and Harm*, 151–52. The internal quote is from Elizabeth Cullingford, "*Evil, Sin*, or *Doubt?* The Dramas of Clerical Child Abuse," *Theatre Journal* 62, no. 2 (2010): 245–63, 260.

58. Fischel, *Sex and Harm*, 152.

59. The term was coined by film critic Nathan Rabin in a review of Cameron Crowe's film *Elizabethtown*. For a discussion of the trope, see Anita Sarkeesian, "Tropes vs. Women: #1 The Manic Pixie Dream Girl," *Feminist Frequency* (blog), March 24, 2011, https://feministfrequency.com/video/tropes-vs-women-1-the-manic-pixie-dream-girl/.

60. Stiebert, "Eve-ing of Bathsheba."

61. An often-cited text remains David J. A. Clines's essay "David the Man: The Construction of Masculinity in the Hebrew Bible," included in his *Interested Parties: The Ideology of Writers and Readers of the Hebrew Bible* (Sheffield, UK: Sheffield Academic Press, 1995), 212–43; more recently, Sara M. Koenig, "Make War Not Love: The Limits of David's Hegemonic Masculinity in 2 Samuel 10–12," *Biblical Interpretation* 23, no. 4–5 (2015): 489–517; Stephen Wilson, *Making Men: The Male Coming-of-Age Theme in the Hebrew Bible* (New York: Oxford University Press, 2015), 97–107; Kevin M. McGeough, "The Problem with David: Masculinity and Morality in Biblical Cinema," *Journal of Religion & Film* 22, no. 1 (2018): 33.

62. On this issue in masculinity studies, see further Kelly J. Murphy, *Rewriting Masculinity: Gideon, Men, and Might* (New York: Oxford University Press, 2019), 40–41.

63. Samuel's masculinity is clearly important to the books of Samuel, and to the articulation of Saul's masculinity as well. However, it only plays a limited role vis-à-vis David, which is why I do not stress it here.

64. A very concise treatment of the relevant issues is Ken Stone, "1 and 2 Samuel," in *The Queer Bible Commentary*, ed. Deryn Guest, Robert E. Goss, Mona West, and Thomas Bohache (London: SCM, 2006), 195–221, esp. 205–8. There are many sources on David and Jonathan; James E. Harding, *The Love of David and Jonathan: Ideology, Text, Reception*, Bible World (New York: Routledge, 2014) offers a long view of the text and its reception. On David and Yahweh (as well as Jonathan and Saul), see as well Theodore W. Jennings, *Jacob's Wound: Homoerotic Narrative in the Literature of Ancient Israel* (New York: Continuum, 2005), 3–67. Many introductions to LGBTQ biblical interpretation also discuss David and his various relationships.

65. For an analysis of a similar function of masculinity in the Jonah story, see Graybill, "Jonah 'Between Men,'" 210–28.

66. For an overview, see Harding, *Love of David and Jonathan*. Notable readings include Jennings, *Jacob's Wound*, which stresses the lover perspective; David M. Halperin, "Heroes and Their Pals," in *One Hundred Years of Homosexuality: And Other Essays on Greek Love*, New Ancient World (New York: Routledge, 1989), 75–87, which emphasizes the "hero and pal" relationship; and Roland Boer's reading in *Knockin' on Heaven's Door: The Bible and Popular Culture*, Biblical Limits (New York: Routledge, 1999), which describes David as "cock collector" (18).

67. On ethnicity as a sticky category, especially when intertwined with sexuality, see Erin Runions, "From Disgust to Humor: Rahab's Queer Affect," in *Bible Trouble: Queer Reading at the Boundaries of Biblical Scholarship*, ed. Teresa J. Hornsby and Ken Stone, Semeia Studies (Atlanta: SBL Press, 2011), 45–74. On Uriah's ethnicity, see Koenig, "Make War Not Love," 511.

68. Tamar and Rahab are Canaanites; Ruth is a Moabite.

69. Keith Bodner, "Is Joab a Reader-Response Critic?," *Journal for the Study of the Old Testament* 27, no. 1 (2002): 19–35.

70. Adele Berlin, *Poetics and Interpretation of Biblical Narrative* (Winona Lake, IN: Eisenbrauns, 1994), 27.

71. Hebrew has grammatical gender marked verbs and so does not require a pronoun to signal whether a subject is "he" or "she," as English does.

72. Sara Maitland, "Siren Song," in *Angel Maker: The Short Stories of Sara Maitland* (New York: Henry Holt and Company), 11–20, 20.

73. Zucker and Weiss, *David's Wives*, 75.

74. Exum, *Fragmented Women*, 199.

75. Heb. *sōkenet*, used in the feminine only here and in 1 Kgs 1:4. The meaning seems to refer to some sort of servant, though the specific details are unclear. See discussion in Mercedes L. García Bachmann, "What Is in a Name?: Abishag the Shunammite as *sokenet* in 1 Kings 1:1–4," in *Out of Place: Doing Theology on the Crosscultural Brink*, ed. Jione Havea and Clive Pearson, Cross Cultural Theologies (Routledge, 2016), 240–41. The masculine *sōken* occurs in Isa 22:5.

76. "Lap" = Heb. *ḥêq*, used of the middle of the body, in both sexual and nonsexual senses. The term is used to refer to Abraham's sexual encounter with Hagar (Gen 16:5); for close or intimate friends in Deut 13:7 [13:6 Eng.], and for maternal embrace in Deut 28:56 and 1 Kgs 17:19). Tellingly, this is also where the poor man's beloved lamb lies in Nathan's parable (2 Sam 12:3).

77. García Bachmann in particular emphasizes the rape threat that Abishag faces. See "What Is in a Name?", 237.

78. Heb. *wayyābō' 'abšālôm 'el*, literally "Absalom entered into."

Chapter 4

1. These include self-defense classes, rape whistles, buddy systems, abstaining from alcohol, carrying your keys between your knuckles as an impromptu weapon, avoiding

parking garages, and generally fearing and avoiding men, especially male strangers and racial others.

2. Sharon Marcus, "Fighting Bodies, Fighting Words: A Theory and Politics of Rape Prevention," in *Feminists Theorize the Political*, ed. Judith Butler and Joan W. Scott (New York: Routledge, 1992), 385–403, 387.

3. Marcus, "Fighting Bodies," 392; 390.

4. Marcus, "Fighting Bodies," 393.

5. Rachel Hall, "'It Can Happen to You': Rape Prevention in the Age of Risk Management," *Hypatia* 19, no. 3 (2004): 1–18.

6. Doyle, *Campus Sex*, 42.

7. See further the discussion in Jennifer Patterson, ed., *Queering Sexual Violence: Radical Voices from within the Anti-Violence Movement* (Riverdale, NY: Riverdale Avenue Books, 2016), especially River Willow Fagan, "Fluctuations in Voice: A Genderqueer Response to Traumatic Violence," 17–21.

8. Marcus, "Fighting Bodies," 390.

9. Here, Luce Irigaray's work on relations between women is an important source; one iteration of the relationship between objects comes in the chapter "Commodities among Themselves" (the "commodities" are women) in Luce Irigaray, *This Sex Which Is Not One*, trans. Catherine Porter (Ithaca, NY: Cornell University Press, 1985), 192–97.

10. Two Hebrew words are used to refer to these women: *šipḥāh* and *'āmāh*, variously translated as "servant," "handmaid," or "slave." The term *šipḥāh* is used to refer to Hagar in Gen 16:1, 2, 3, 5, 6, 8 and 25:12 and to Bilhah and/or Zilpah in Gen 29:24 and 29; 30:4, 7, 9, 10, 12, and 18; 32:22; and 33:1, 2, 25, 26; *'āmāh* is used to refer to Hagar in Gen 21:10, 12, and 13 and to Bilhah and/or Zilpah in Gen 30:3 and 31:33. The difference in meaning between *šipḥāh* and *'āmāh* is unclear; it may have been lost by the time the text reached its final form, if not before.

11. The relationship between Bilhah and Zilpah is never described in the text, though it has attracted speculation from readers.

12. On reading this sex as rape, see, e.g., Scholz, *Sacred Witness*, 57–63, and Vanessa Lovelace, "'This Woman's Son Shall Not Inherit with My Son': Towards a Womanist Politics of Belonging in the Sarah-Hagar Narratives," *Journal of the Interdenominational Theological Center* 41, no. 1 (2018): 63–82, 73. There are other interpretations. One set of historicizing readings seeks evidence for ancient surrogacy via slaves; e.g., James C. Okoye, "Sarah and Hagar: Genesis 16 and 21," *Journal for the Study of the Old Testament* 32, no. 2 (2007): 163–75, 173. Some interpreters argue that the slaves or servants achieve the status of second wives, particularly after giving birth; e.g., Pnina Galpaz-Feller, "Pregnancy and Birth in the Bible and Ancient Egypt (Comparative Study)," *Biblische Notizen* no. 102 (2000): 42–53, 52, and Ginny Brewer-Boydston, "Sarah the *Gevirah*: A Comparison of Sarah and the Queen Mothers, of Matriarchs in the Dynastic Succession of Sons and Nations," *Review and Expositor* 115, no. 4 (2018): 500–512, 503. This does not necessarily mean they are equal or even roughly equivalent to the primary wives: According to a formula used in Old Babylonian marriage contracts, the second wife is a "wife" to the husband

but a "slave" to the first wife; Philip Y. Yoo, "Hagar the Egyptian: Wife, Handmaid, and Concubine," *Catholic Biblical Quarterly* 78, no. 2 (2016): 219. Comparative and ethnographic approaches often adapt frameworks from other family models. Dora R. Mbuwayesango reads the stories together with the Ndebele and Shona, while Janice Pearl Ewurama De-Whyte reads the text against Ashanti traditions. See Mbuwayesango, "Childlessness and Woman-to-Woman Relationships in Genesis and in African Patriarchal Society: Sarah and Hagar from a Zimbabwean Woman's Perspective (Gen 16:1–16; 21:8–21)," *Semeia* no. 78 (1997): 27–36, and De-Whyte, *Wom(b)an: Cultural-Narrative Reading of the Hebrew Bible Barrenness Narratives* (Leiden: Brill, 2018). See also Solomon O. Ademiluka, "Sexual Exploitation or Legitimate Surrogacy: Reading the Hagar Narrative (Gn 16:1–4a) in African Context," *Theologia Viatorum* 43, no. 1 (2019): 1–10. Still another contemporary trend in interpretation treats the stories of Hagar, Bilhah, and Zilpah through and against the contemporary institution of gestational surrogacy; e.g., Marianne Bjelland Kartzow, "Navigating the Womb: Surrogacy, Slavery, Fertility—and Biblical Discourses," *Journal of Early Christian History* 2, no. 1 (2012): 38–54, and Gil Rosenberg, *Ancestral Queerness: The Normal and the Deviant in the Abraham and Sarah Narratives*, Hebrew Bible Monographs 80 (Sheffield: Sheffield Phoenix Press, 2019), 146–70.

13. Doyle, *Campus Sex*, 42.

14. Marcus, "Fighting Bodies," 393.

15. Marcus, "Fighting Bodies," 390.

16. Marcus, "Fighting Bodies," 397.

17. On the relationship between literature, feminism, and theology, and the disruptive power of literature for feminist critique, see as well Dawn Llewellyn, *Reading, Feminism, and Spirituality: Troubling the Waves* (New York: Palgrave Macmillan, 2015).

18. Virginia Woolf, *A Room of One's Own* (New York: Harcourt Brace, 1975 [1929]), 82.

19. Elena Ferrante, *The Neapolitan Novels by Elena Ferrante*, trans. Ann Goldstein (New York: Europa, 2015).

20. Rachel B. Glaser, *Paulina & Fran* (New York: Harper Perennial, 2015); Sally Rooney, *Conversations with Friends* (London: Hogarth, 2017); Julie Buntin, *Marlena* (New York: Henry Holt and Co., 2017); Ottessa Moshfegh, *My Year of Rest and Relaxation* (New York: Penguin Press, 2018); Tara Isabella Burton, *Social Creature* (New York: Doubleday, 2018); Lara Williams, *Supper Club* (New York: G.P. Putnam's Sons, 2019); Susan Choi, *Trust Exercise* (New York: Henry Holt and Co., 2019).

21. Gavey, *Just Sex?*, 2.

22. Rooney, *Conversations with Friends*, 201.

23. Rooney, *Conversations with Friends*, 201.

24. On this theme in Rooney's works, see as well Madeleine Schwartz, "How Should a Millennial Be?," *New York Review of Books*, April 18, 2019, https://www.nybooks.com/articles/2019/04/18/sally-rooney-how-should-millennial-be/.

25. Rooney, *Conversations with Friends*, 235.

26. Alexandra Schwartz, "A New Kind of Adultery Novel," *The New Yorker*, July 31, 2017, https://www.newyorker.com/magazine/2017/07/31/a-new-kind-of-adultery-novel. The print edition of the article was titled "Talk to Me."

27. Williams, *Supper Club*, 66.

28. Williams, *Supper Club*, 67.

29. Williams, *Supper Club*, 286.

30. Williams, *Supper Club*, 286.

31. Williams, *Supper Club*, 288.

32. Williams, *Supper Club*, 288.

33. On this point, see Jayme R. Reaves, "Sarah as Victim and Perpetrator: Whiteness, Power, and Memory in the Matriarchal Narrative," *Review & Expositor* 115, no. 4 (2018): 483–99; Elizabeth Durant, "It's Complicated: Power and Complicity in the Stories of Hagar and Sarah," *Conversations with the Biblical World* 35 (2015): 78–93. See as well Phyllis Trible, "Genesis 22: The Sacrifice of Sarah" in *"Not in Heaven": Coherence and Complexity in Biblical Narrative*, ed. Jason P. Rosenblatt and Joseph C. Sitterson, Jr., Indiana Studies in Biblical Literature (Bloomington: Indiana University Press, 1991), 28–57.

34. See Jennifer C. Nash, *Black Feminism Reimagined: After Intersectionality* (Durham, NC: Duke University Press, 2018), 106–7.

35. Kimberlé Crenshaw, "Demarginalizing the Intersection of Race and Sex: A Black Feminist Critique of Antidiscrimination Doctrine, Feminist Theory and Antiracist Politics," *University of Chicago Legal Forum* 1989 (1989): 139. While Crenshaw coined the term "intersectionality" in 1989, Black and woman of color feminist critique includes a healthy genealogy of work *avant la lettre*. For a detailed history, see Nash, *Black Feminism Reimagined*, 6–11.

36. Nash, *Black Feminism Reimagined*, 106–7.

37. Judith Butler, *Undoing Gender* (New York: Taylor and Francis, 2004), 19.

38. Juliana Claassens, "Just Emotions: Reading the Sarah and Hagar Narrative (Genesis 16, 21) through the Lens of Human Dignity," *Verbum et Ecclesia* 34, no. 2, Art. 787 (2013): 3.

39. Claassens, "Just Emotions," 3.

40. See also Claassens, "Just Emotions," 4.

41. E.g., Reaves, "Sarah as Victim and Perpetrator"; Durant, "It's Complicated."

42. Though Sara Maitland's treatment in her short story "Triptych" is a notable counterexample. The story is included in her collection *Angel Maker*. Phyllis Trible also criticizes Abraham in "Sacrifice of Sarah."

43. Susan M. Pigott, "Hagar: The M/Other Patriarch," *Review & Expositor* 115, no. 4 (2018): 513–28, 518–19.

44. Nash, *Black Feminism Reimagined*, 107, 106.

45. For the argument that Sarah does not desire a child or consent to her pregnancy, see Rosenberg, *Ancestral Queerness*, 126.

46. Williams, *Supper Club*, 291–92.

47. Maitland, "Triptych," 184.

48. Maitland, "Triptych," 185–86.

49. Maitland, "Triptych," 188–89.

50. Maitland, "Triptych," 200.

51. Maitland, "Triptych," 201.

52. Trible, "The Sacrifice of Sarah," 189.

53. In the New Testament, Hagar reappears in Gal 4:24–25.

54. Lynne Huffer, *Are the Lips a Grave?: A Queer Feminist on the Ethics of Sex* (New York: Columbia University Press, 2013), 142.

55. For example, Rebecca Alpert, "Finding Our Past: A Lesbian Interpretation of the Book of Ruth," in *Reading Ruth: Contemporary Women Reclaim a Sacred Story*, ed. Judith A. Kates and Gail Twersky Reimer (New York: Ballantine Books 1994), 91–96; Celena M. Duncan, "The Book of Ruth: On Boundaries, Love, and Truth," in *Take Back the Word: A Queer Reading of the Bible*, ed. Robert E. Goss and Mona West (Cleveland, OH: Pilgrim Press, 2000), 92–102.

56. Stephanie Day Powell, *Narrative Desire and the Book of Ruth*, LHB/OTS 662 (New York: T&T Clark, 2018).

57. Here I summarize several lines of argument from Rhiannon Graybill, "'Even unto This Bitter Loving': Unhappiness and Backward Feelings in the Book of Ruth," *Biblical Interpretation* (2020), online advance publication at https://brill.com/view/journals/bi/aop/article-10.1163-15685152-00284P11/article-10.1163-15685152-00284P11.xml.

58. E.g., César Melgar, "Ruth and the Unaccompanied Minors from Central America: Ethical Perspectives on a Socio-Economic Problem," *Review and Expositor* 112 (2015): 269–79, and Fulata Lusungu Moyo, "'Traffic Violations': Hospitality, Foreignness, and Exploitation: A Contextual Biblical Study of Ruth," *Journal of Feminist Studies in Religion* 32 (2016): 83–94. See further Graybill, "Even unto This Bitter Loving."

59. Elsewhere I explore reading Ruth and Naomi through Radclyffe Hall's classic lesbian novel *The Well of Loneliness* (Hertfordshire, UK: Wordsworth Editions Ltd., 2014; originally published 1928). See Graybill, "Even unto This Bitter Loving."

60. Huffer, *Are the Lips a Grave?*, 149.

61. Huffer, *Are the Lips a Grave?*, 149.

62. Huffer, *Are the Lips a Grave?*, 149–50.

63. Hagar's Blackness is often treated as self-evident by interpreters working in these traditions, as well as by many readers (especially, I suspect, readers in the American context). But as Nyasha Junior demonstrates, the Blackness of the biblical Hagar is a recent development, associated in particular with Delores S. Williams's *Sisters in the Wilderness* and uncritically reproduced by a wide swath of interpreters. See Junior, *Reimagining Hagar: Blackness and Bible* (New York: Oxford University Press, 2019) and Williams, *Sisters in the Wilderness: The Challenge of Womanist God-Talk* (Maryknoll, NY: Orbis Books, 2013).

64. Huffer, *Are the Lips a Grave?*, 144.

65. Huffer, *Are the Lips a Grave?*, 148.

66. Huffer, *Are the Lips a Grave?*, 153–54.

67. The Italian title is *L'amica geniale*.

68. Huffer, *Are the Lips a Grave?*, 158.

69. Roupenian, "Cat Person," 96–98.

Chapter 5

1. Susan Brownmiller, *Against Our Will: Men, Women, and Rape* (New York: Fawcett Columbine, 1993 [1976]); Ellen Bass and Laura Davis, *The Courage to Heal: A Guide for Women Survivors of Child Sexual Abuse*, 20th anniv. ed. (New York: William Morrow, 2008); Judith Lewis Herman, *Trauma and Recovery: The Aftermath of Violence, from Domestic Abuse to Political Terror* (New York: Basic Books, 2015 [1992]); Andrea Dworkin and Catharine A. MacKinnon, *Pornography and Civil Rights: A New Day for Women's Equality* (Minneapolis: Organizing Against Pornography, 1988). The discussion of pornography (following Dworkin and MacKinnon) and biblical literature often travels under the moniker of "pornoprophetics."

2. Patterson, *Queering Sexual Violence*; Leah Lakshmi Piepzna-Samarasinha, *Care Work: Dreaming Disability Justice* (Vancouver: Arsenal Pulp Press, 2018); Carmen Maria Machado, *In the Dream House: A Memoir* (Minneapolis: Graywolf Press, 2019).

3. While the other two texts have single authors, *Queering Sexual Violence* is an anthology, whose contributors reflect a range of experiences with sexual violence and relationships to the category "survivor" and "victim."

4. See Cvetkovich, *Archive of Feelings*.

5. On the translation of *bat zion*, see William Franklin Stinespring, "No Daughter of Zion: A Study of the Appositional Genitive in Hebrew Grammar," *Encounter* 26, no. 13 (1965): 3–41; Michael H. Floyd, "Welcome Back, Daughter of Zion!," *Catholic Biblical Quarterly* 70, no. 3 (2008): 484–504; J. Andrew Dearman, "Daughter Zion and Her Place in God's Household," *Horizons in Biblical Theology* 31, no. 2 (2009): 144–59.

6. Anne Carson, "The Gender of Sound" in *Glass, Irony and God* (New York: New Directions, 1995), 119–42; Graybill, *Are We Not Men?*, 78–80; Elaine T. James, *A Handbook of Biblical Poetry. Essentials of Biblical Studies* (New York: Oxford University Press, 2021).

7. Peter J. Sabo, "Poetry amid Ruins," in *Poets, Prophets, and Texts in Play: Studies in Biblical Poetry and Prophecy in Honour of Francis Landy*, ed. Ehud Ben Zvi, Claudia V. Camp, David M. Gunn, and Aaron W. Hughes, LHB/OTS 597 (New York: T&T Clark, 2015), 141–58.

8. The anxiety that Lam 1–2 generates is chiefly (though not exclusively) theological; as Linafelt points out, it is often motivated by a desire "to move quickly through chapters 1 and 2 in order to light upon chapter 3." Tod Linafelt, *Surviving Lamentations: Catastrophe, Lament, and Protest in the Afterlife of a Biblical Book* (Chicago: University of Chicago Press, 2000), 2.

9. Heb. *nîydāh*; read as *niddāh*, whose meaning encompasses "menstrual bleeding" (e.g., Lev 15:19–33) and, metaphorically, "impurity" or "defilement" (e.g., Zech 13:1; Ezra 9:11). *niddāh* also occurs in Lam 1:17. While *niddāh* could also be translated as "menstrual impurity" or even "menstruation," these terms are not used with the same pejorative sense in contemporary English (and, indeed, are mostly reserved for formal or commercial language, as in the phrase "menstrual products"). The Hebrew uses a noun but I have translated it with a pair of adjectives ("bleeding and filthy") to better capture the sense.

10. F. W. Dobbs-Allsopp and Tod Linafelt, "The Rape of Zion in Thr 1, 10," *Zeitschrift für die Alttestamentliche Wissenschaft* 113, no. 1 (2001): 77–81.

11. Alan Mintz notes the analogical "correspondence" between body and temple and between genitals and "inner sanctuary." Mintz, "The Rhetoric of Lamentations and the Representation of Catastrophe," *Prooftexts* 2, no. 1 (1982): 4.

12. Heb. *kol-rōdĕpêhā hiśśîgûhā bên hammĕṣārîm.*

13. Furthermore, the word I have translated "distress," *mĕṣārîm*, is an uncommon noun, from the root *ṣrr*, which also has a meaning of narrowness. Guest proposes translating "between the narrow places," noting "the pursuit of her and the taking of her between 'narrow confines' may well imply sexual overtaking in a rape context." Deryn Guest, "Hiding behind the Naked Women in Lamentations: A Recriminative Response," *Biblical Interpretation* 7, no. 4 (1999): 413–48, 418.

14. This is a widespread convention in ancient Near Eastern literature, including the Hebrew Bible.

15. The "uncleanness" (*ṭum'āh*) in Zion's skirts is associated with menstruation (Lev 15:25–30; 18:19; Ezek 36:17), though the word can also be used for other forms of uncleanness, including some that apply to men as well as women, such as impurity from touching a corpse (Lev 5:3) or eating unclean animals (Lev 7:2). The term *ṭum'āh* is also used in the story of Bathsheba, where it is the immediate cause of Bathsheba's self-purification (2 Sam 11:4). The term *niddāh* specifically refers to a menstruating woman and/or menstrual impurity (Lev 12:2–5, 15:19–33), though like *ṭum'āh* it can also be used as a more general or metaphorical term for impurity.

16. Kathleen M. O'Connor, *Lamentations and the Tears of the World* (Maryknoll, NY: Orbis Books, 2002), 29. Emphasis added. The inset quote is from Mintz, "Rhetoric of Lamentations," 3.

17. Dobbs-Allsopp and Linafelt, "Rape of Zion," 81, emphasis added.

18. O'Connor, *Lamentations and the Tears*, xiv, xiii.

19. Guest, "Hiding behind the Naked Women," 427, italics added.

20. Mandolfo, *Daughter Zion Talks Back*, 83, italics added (*with* and *toward* italicized in the original).

21. Hugh Pyper also speaks of "the responsibility of the author and indeed the readers of the book" in "Reading Lamentations," *Journal for the Study of the Old Testament* 95 (2001): 55–69, 56.

22. Barbara Johnson, "The Critical Difference," in *The Barbara Johnson Reader: The Surprise of Otherness*, ed. Melissa Feuerstein, Bill Johnson González, Lili Porten, and Keja L. Valens (Durham, NC: Duke University Press, 2014), 3.

23. Lee Edelman, *No Future: Queer Theory and the Death Drive*, Series Q (Durham, NC: Duke University Press), 67ff. On the logic of compassion, Edelman observes, "that logic, in turn, as Kant insists, may hang on the formal abstraction of compassion's tender touch until it becomes the vise-like grip of duty's iron fist" (p. 68).

24. The "plight" of women—and, more recently, of LGBTQ people as well—is a frequent point of appeal used to justify intervention abroad. Women's rights (and, more recently, LGBTQ rights) provide a convenient cover for other forms of global intervention. Thus the seemingly blameless and unimpeachably feminist desire to help "save

women" conceals all sorts of other unspoken politics, many of which are strongly antifeminist in their implications. See further Partha Chatterjee, *The Nation and Its Fragments: Colonial and Postcolonial Histories* (Princeton, NJ: Princeton University Press, 1993); Puar, *Right to Maim*; Lena Salaymeh, "Imperialist Feminism and Islamic Law," *Hawwa* 17, no. 2–3 (2019): 97–134.

25. Samantha Barrick, "Infinity and the Construction of Safe Space," in Patterson, *Queering Sexual Violence*, 67.

26. The third verset of 1:9, "Look, Yahweh, at my affliction, for the enemy has triumphed!" is sometimes attributed to Daughter Zion as well.

27. Heb. *dāwāh*. The specific reference is to menstrual bleeding; cf. Lev 15:33, 20:18. In the same verse, *netānanî šōmēmāh* ("he left me all alone" or "he left me desolate") refers to both physical isolation and a state of shuddering or being appalled—suggesting either abandonment or shuddering (perhaps with cramps or menstrual pain) here.

28. Mandolfo, *Daughter Zion Talks Back*, 94–95.

29. The exception here is 1:17; however, that verse can also be read as an introjection by the lamenter, just as Zion's words interrupt his in 1:9c.

30. Dorothea Erbele-Küster, "A Response to Julie Claassens's 'A True Disgrace? The Representation of Violence against Women in the Book of Lamentations and in J.M. Coetzee's Novel *Disgrace*,'" in *Fragile Dignity: Intercontextual Conversations on Scriptures, Family, and Violence*, ed. L. Juliana Claassens and Klaas Spronk (Atlanta: SBL, 2013), 99–100, 96. In a similar vein, Maria Häusl titles her reading "Lamentations: Zion's Cry in Affliction" (in Schottroff and Wacker, *Feminist Biblical Interpretation*, 334–44).

31. On "very young girls," see Doyle, *Campus Sex*, 24. The shattered victim is assumed by many discourses of rape as "unimaginable"; see discussion in Marcus, "Fighting Bodies," and Abdulali, *What We Talk about*, 206. The survivor who overcomes trauma and is unmarked by it is discussed by Rousse Arielle, "Beyond the Binaries: Exclusive Dichotomies in the Anti-Sexual Violence Movement," in Patterson, *Queering Sexual Violence*, 39, and Piepzna-Samarasinha, *Care Work*, 229–30. See also Barrick, "Infinity and the Construction of Safe Space," 67.

32. The Hebrew here is *pěšāʿay běyādô*, literally "the offenses of my hand." The term *pešaʿ*, "offense," also has a sense of crime and of wantonness.

33. Familial cannibalism is also hinted at, though somewhat obliquely, in Lam 1:11, where "dear ones" (Heb. *maḥmād*) are traded for food.

34. Mandolfo, *Daughter Zion Talks Back*, 95.

35. See Francis Landy, "Lamentations," in *The Literary Guide to the Bible*, ed. Robert Alter and Frank Kermode (Cambridge, MA: Belknap Press of Harvard University Press, 1987); Charles William Miller, "Reading Voices: Personification, Dialogism, and the Reader of Lamentations 1," *Biblical Interpretation* 9, no. 4 (2001): 395, 402.

36. *Inter alia* Dobbs-Allsopp and Linalfelt, "Rape of Zion," 81; Gina Hens-Piazza, *Lamentations*, Wisdom Commentary 30 (Collegeville, MN: Liturgical Press, 2017), 53; Guest, "Hiding behind the Naked Women," passim; David A. Bosworth, "Daughter Zion and Weeping in Lamentations 1–2," *Journal for the Study of the Old Testament* 38, no. 2 (2013): 217–37, 227.

37. Pyper, "Reading Lamentations," 68; Sabo, "Poetry amid Ruins," 143.

38. On these descriptors, see Marcus, "Fighting Bodies," 387. See also my discussion of Marcus's essay in the previous chapter.

39. Mintz, "Rhetoric of Lamentations," 3; see also O'Connor, *Lamentations and the Tears*, 29.

40. Marcus, "Fighting Bodies," Hall, "It Could Happen to You"; Doyle, *Campus Sex*.

41. The alphabetic sequence shows slight variation: In Lam 2, 3, and 4, *peh* comes before *ayin*; in Lam 1, the order of *ayin* before *peh* is preserved. See Lam 1:16–17; 2:16–17; 3:46–51; 4:16–17.

42. O'Connor, *Lamentations and the Tears*, 12.

43. Elizabeth Boase, "Fragmented Voices: Collective Identity and Traumatization in Lamentations." In *Bible through the Lens of Trauma*, edited by Elizabeth Boase and Christopher G. Frechette, 49–66 (Atlanta: SBL Press, 2016), 49.

44. Elaine Scarry, *The Body in Pain: The Making and Unmaking of the World* (New York: Oxford University Press, 1987), 4–5.

45. Linafelt, *Surviving Lamentations*, 60; Scott Ellington, "De-Centering Lamentations: A Crisis of Hope, of Memory, and of Continued Presence," *Old Testament Essays* 31, no. 3 (2018): 494–505, 495.

46. Hens-Piazza, *Lamentations*, 35; Erbele-Küster, "Response to Julie Claassens," 97.

47. Mandolfo, *Daughter Zion Talks Back*, passim.

48. E.g., Häusl, "Lamentations," 335.

49. Cvetkovich, *Archive of Feelings*, 2.

50. Cvetkovich, *Archive of Feelings*, 7.

51. Cvetkovich, *Archive of Feelings*, 7.

52. Other well-known examples include Jack Halberstam's "Brandon archive" about Brandon Teena, collected in *In a Queer Time and Place: Transgender Bodies, Subcultural Lives* (New York: NYU Press, 2005), 22–46, and the "silly archive" of Halberstam's *The Queer Art of Failure* (Durham, NC: Duke University Press, 2011), 19. Sara Ahmed's work is also frequently organized around archives, including the "willfulness archive" of *Willful Subjects*, 67, 175, and the archives of both happiness and unhappiness in *Promise of Happiness*.

53. Cvetkovich, *Archive of Feelings*, 4.

54. Cvetkovich, *Archive of Feelings*, 7.

55. *Queering Sexual Violence* is published by Riverdale Avenue Books; *Care Work* by Arsenal Pulp Press; and *In the Dream House* by Graywolf Press (in the United States), Strange Light (in Canada), and Serpent's Tail (in the United Kingdom).

56. Cvetkovich, *Archive of Feelings*, 15.

57. Cvetkovich, *Archive of Feelings*, 8.

58. Reina Gossett, "Foreword," in *Queering Sexual Violence*, 1–3, 2, and Jennifer Patterson, "Introduction," in *Queering Sexual Violence*, 5–13, 11–12.

59. Cvetkovich, *Archive of Feelings*, 3.

60. O'Connor, *Lamentations and the Tears*, xiv.

61. See especially Arielle, "Beyond the Binaries," 39–47; Barrick, "Infinity and the Construction of Safe Space," 61–68; Patterson, "These Bones," 103–110; and Katherine Schott Nelson, "My Justice Is Her Justice: Toward a New Vision of Survivorhood," 251–56, all in Patterson, *Queering Sexual Violence*.

62. E.g., Patterson, "Introduction," 7; Fagan, "Fluctuations in Voice," 21. On the victim as gendered as female, see as well Doyle, *Campus Sex*, 42.

63. Patterson, "Introduction," 5–13, 6.

64. Arielle, "Beyond the Binaries," 41–42.

65. A particular concern is the way that the survivor identity is set up in opposition to the perpetrator, "excluding individuals whose narratives are more complicated than either of the strict oppositional identities" and "ignoring the fact that many individuals who commit sexual violence against others are themselves survivors of sexual violence" (Arielle, "Beyond the Binaries," 44).

66. Barrick, "Infinity and the Construction of Safe Space," 67.

67. Sassafras Lowrey, "Not a Good Survivor," in *Queering Sexual Violence*, 247–49, 247.

68. Nelson, "My Justice Is Her Justice," 254, 256.

69. Patterson, "These Bones," in *Queering Sexual Violence*, 103–10, 104.

70. To be clear, especially in light of the possible cross-cutting of the categories of "Survivor" and "Victim" with "Perpetrator": There are no indications in the text of Lamentations that Daughter Zion herself perpetrates sexual violence. On the overlap of victims and survivors with perpetrators, see Arielle, "Beyond the Binaries," 39–40, 44–46.

71. See Lowrey, "Not a Good Survivor," Barrick, "Infinity and the Construction of Safe Space," 67; Arielle, "Beyond the Binaries."

72. Piepzna-Samarasinha, *Care Work*, 164–65.

73. Piepzna-Samarasinha, *Care Work*, 166.

74. Sedgwick, *Touching Feeling*, 138.

75. Piepzna-Samarasinha, *Care Work*, 167.

76. See as well Page duBois, *Torture and Truth*, Routledge Revivals (New York: Routledge, 2016).

77. Piepzna-Samarasinha, *Care Work*, 226.

78. Piepzna-Samarasinha, *Care Work*, 225.

79. Piepzna-Samarasinha, *Care Work*, 235.

80. Rhiannon Graybill, Meredith Minister, and Beatrice Lawrence, "Critiquing Campus Efforts to Address Sexual Violence," in "Sexual Violence in and around the Classroom," *Teaching Theology & Religion* 20, no. 1 (2017): 74–75.

81. Piepzna-Samarasinha, *Care Work*, 232.

82. Eli Clare, *Brilliant Imperfection: Grappling with Cure* (Durham, NC: Duke University Press, 2017).

83. M. Cooper Minister, "Fuck the Survivor: Refusing the Future Promised by the Sanctified Cancer Patient," in *Lee Edelman and the Queer Study of Religion*, ed. Kent Brintnall, Rhiannon Graybill, and Linn Tonstad (New York: Routledge, forthcoming).

84. Brandy Daniels, "Sexual Violence and the 'End' of Subjectivity: Queer Negativity and a Theopolitics of Refusal" in Brintnall, Graybill, and Tonstad, *Lee Edelman and the Queer Study of Religion*, forthcoming.

85. I discuss and critique this interpretive tendency in Rhiannon Graybill, "Yahweh as Maternal Vampire in Second Isaiah: Reading from Violence to Fluid Possibility with Luce Irigaray," *Journal of Feminist Studies in Religion* 33, no. 1 (2017): 9–25.

86. Salters, *Lamentations*, 154, quoted in Hens-Piazza, *Lamentations*, 27.

87. Piepzna-Samarasinha, *Care Work*, 232.

88. At the same time, Machado's memoir received significantly more coverage in the mainstream media than the other two works, including reviews in the *New York Times*, *New Yorker*, and *Paris Review*, all three of which included it on the their "Best Books of the Year" lists.

89. An exception is the chapter "*Dream House at* Newton's Apple"; see Machado, *Dream House*, 214.

90. Machado, *Dream House*, 3–14.

91. Much like the early text-based computer games (and their analog predecessors), the *Choose Your Own Adventure* series presented readers with a series of choices, each producing a different narrative and outcome; many paths led to defeat or death. Machado's "Choose Your Own Adventure" sequence is a trap, impossible to escape without cheating; see 162–76. For the other chapters listed here, see 20, 69, 76–77, 45, and 28.

92. Machado, *Dream House*, 234, 134, 160–61.

93. Machado, *Dream House*, 30–35, 106, 112.

94. Machado, *Dream House*, 4.

95. Machado, *Dream House*, 59–60, 195.

96. Machado, *Dream House*, 37.

97. Machado, *Dream House*, 240n53.

98. Machado, *Dream House*, 112; see also 135–39.

99. Machado, *Dream House*, 239.

100. Machado, *Dream House*, 239–42.

101. Machado, *Dream House*, 239; see also 242.

102. Machado, *Dream House*, 176.

103. River Willow Fagan, "Fluctuations in Voice: A Genderqueer Response to Traumatic Violence," in *Queering Sexual Violence*, 17–21, 21; Avory Faucette, "Questions and Answers," in *Queering Sexual Violence*, 189–92, 192.

104. Julietta Singh, *No Archive Will Restore You*, 3Ecologies (Montreal: Punctum Books, 2018), 27.

Chapter 6

1. Ahmed, *Promise of Happiness*, 192–93.

2. The bibliography is extensive; I will mention only a few key examples here. A good starting point (including an overview of the extant scholarship) is Helen Paynter, *Telling Terror in Judges 19: Rape and Reparation for the Levite's Wife* (New York: Routledge, 2020). Beyond Paynter, significant feminist readings include Mieke Bal, *Death and Dissymmetry: The Politics of Coherence in the Book of Judges* (Chicago: University of Chicago Press, 1988); Exum, *Fragmented Women*; Koala Jones-Warsaw, "Toward a Womanist Hermeneutic: A Reading of Judges 19–21," in

A Feminist Companion to Judges, ed. Athalya Brenner, A Feminist Companion to the Bible, 1st ser. (Sheffield, UK: Sheffield University Press, 1993), 172–86; Scholz, *Sacred Witness*, 135–55; Sébastien Doane, "Gang Bang et Démembrement: Quatre Lectures de Juges 19," *Science et Esprit* 66, no. 2 (2014): 177–88; Isabelle Hamley, *Unspeakable Things Unspoken: An Irigarayan Reading of Otherness and Victimization in Judges 19–21* (Eugene, OR: Pickwick Publications, 2019). The question of rape is also engaged in detail by Frank M. Yamada, *Configurations of Rape in the Hebrew Bible: A Literary Analysis of Three Rape Narratives* (Bern: Peter Lang, 2008), 67–100; Leah Rediger Schulte, *The Absence of God in Biblical Rape Narratives* (Minneapolis: Fortress Press, 2017), 33–52. For a sensitive literary reading, see as well Francis Landy, "Between Centre and Periphery: Space and Gender in the Book of Judges in the Early Second Temple Period," in *Centres and Peripheries in the Early Second Temple Period*, ed. Ehud Ben Zvi and Christoph Levin, *Forschungen zum Alten Testament* 108 (Tübingen: Mohr Siebeck, 2016), 133–62. There is of course a substantial literature on Judg 19–21 that does not consider questions of gender, misogyny, or rape (remarkable as these omissions may seem); I do not engage those works here.

3. Trible, *Texts of Terror*, 2.

4. Trible authored two very important works of feminist biblical criticism: *God and the Rhetoric of Sexuality*, published in 1978, and *Texts of Terror*, published in 1984. The former, which expanded upon Trible's groundbreaking 1973 article "Depatriarchalizing in Biblical Interpretation," in many ways set the agenda for feminist biblical criticism. "Depatriarchalizing" and *God and the Rhetoric of Sexuality* are significantly more optimistic about the possibility of finding positive representations of women and gender in the biblical texts. *Texts of Terror*, in contrast, emphasizes those biblical stories that lie beyond redemption through feminist criticism (more on this later in the chapter). Although "Depatriarchalizing" and *God and the Rhetoric of Sexuality* played a foundational role in the discipline of feminist biblical criticism, it is *Texts of Terror* that is more widely cited in the discipline as a whole. In addition, while feminist analysis of the texts Trible discusses in *God and the Rhetoric of Sexuality* (Gen 1–3, the Song of Songs, the book of Ruth, female imagery for God) has continued to develop beyond the readings she offers (often building upon, but also sometimes opposing, her claims), scholarship on the so-called texts of terror remains dominated by the paradigm Trible sketched in 1984. This is especially true in the case of Judg 11 and 19 (Jepthah's daughter and the Levite's concubine), the two stories I will consider here. In addition, outside of feminist biblical studies, Trible's later work in *Texts after Terror* is more widely discussed and cited.

5. Trible, *Texts of Terror*, 3.

6. Trible, *Texts of Terror*, 1.

7. Trible's language here is also in keeping with the conventions of rhetorical criticism, which she discusses in detail in relation to feminist hermeneutics in *God and the Rhetoric of Sexuality*.

8. This is a point explored in detail by Hemmings in *Why Stories Matter*, e.g., 1, 73–80.

9. Trible, *Texts of Terror*, 1–2.

10. Trible, *Texts of Terror*, 2.

11. Trible, *Texts of Terror*, 3.

12. See as well Haraway's critique of salvation history in her "Manifesto for Cyborgs," *Simians, Cyborgs, and Women*, 149–81, esp. 151, 172.

13. There is likewise something paranoid in the second half of the verse that Trible omits, "because the days are evil."

14. Consider Nietzsche's "Truth is a woman" or Socrates' appeal to Diotoma for his theory of love in the Symposium. See as well Graybill, *Are We Not Men?*, 127–28.

15. For the examples listed in this paragraph, see my chapter 5, as well as Patterson, ed., *Queering Sexual Violence*; Piepzna-Samarsinha, *Care Work*; Minister, "Fuck the Survivor"; Daniels, "Sexual Violence and the 'End' of Subjectivity; Machado, *In the Dream House*, 162–76.

16. Shakespeare, *Richard II*, Act III, scene 2, line 155. Trible, *Texts of Terror*, 117. The "un-named woman" is the Levite's concubine.

17. Trible, *Texts of Terror*, 117.

18. It is also possible to interpret "*In Memoriam*" as signaling our contemporary distance from the stories described in the biblical text, whether or not the characters die in the course of the narrative (they are, after all, *characters* and not real people). At the same time, it is not typical scholarly practice to imagine monuments "in memoriam" of other, less tragic biblical figures (to begin, Jephthah, the Levite, Amnon, or even Abraham). I will return to this question of touching across the past in the conclusion to this chapter.

19. Note as well the resonances with Sedgwick's description of "weak theories" in contrast to the "strong theory" of paranoid reading. See *Touching Feeling*, 136, 145.

20. Johnson, "Nothing Fails Like Success," in *The Surprise of Otherness*, 332.

21. Ahmed, *Promise of Happiness*, 21–25.

22. Ahmed, *Promise of Happiness*, 90–94.

23. Ahmed, *Promise of Happiness*, 195.

24. Ahmed, *Promise of Happiness*, 193. The internal quotation is from Aldous Huxley, *Brave New World* (New York: Harper and Row, 1969 [1932]), 163.

25. Ahmed, *Promise of Happiness*, 195.

26. Frank Kermode, *The Sense of an Ending: Studies in the Theory of Fiction with a New Epilogue* (New York: Oxford University Press, 2000).

27. I discuss these issues in greater detail in chapter 4. A similar tension between identitarian reading and critique can be found in those readings that treat Hagar and Sarah as (pre)figurations of Muslim–Jewish relations.

28. These consequences also spill over into the book of Samuel, which follows Judges: significantly, Saul is a Benjaminite; the rape and murder of the Levite's concubine occur in Gibeah, located in Benjamin. Furthermore, the war in Judg 20–21 is between Benjamin and the other eleven tribes.

29. On this term, see Isabelle Hamley, "'Dis(re)membered and Unaccounted For': *Pilegesh* in the Hebrew Bible," *Journal for the Study of the Old Testament* 42, no. 4 (2018): 415–34. Also well-known is the analysis by Bal, *Death and Dissymmetry*, 81–89, though her argument that *pilegeš* means "patrilocal wife" (89) is not widely accepted. I will

translate *pileges* as "concubine" in my discussion, as it seems to be the least-bad English translation; I intend the general sense of a secondary or lower-status wife rather than the specific historical institution of concubinage. This translation also has the benefit of being familiar from the NRSV, KJV, and NJPS.

30. The phrase I have translated as "rape him" is *nēdā'ennû*, literally "know him," a first-person plural form from the root *yada'*. However, the sexual (and here sexually violent) implications are clear. The same verb is used in the story of the divine messengers in Sodom in Gen 19:5. On the relationship between these two stories, see Stuart Lasine, "Guest and Host in Judges 19: Lot's Hospitality in an Inverted World," *Journal for the Study of the Old Testament* 9, no. 29 (1984): 37–59. The entanglement of masculinity, xenophobia, and homophobia is also clearly *fuzzy*, *messy*, and *icky*; for an analysis of these themes, see James Harding, "Homophobia and Masculine Domination in Judges 19–21," *The Bible and Critical Theory* 12, no. 2 (2016).

31. Heb. *wayyēdě'û*, from the root *yd'*, often used with a sexual sense. The rape meaning is clear here; compare also Gen 19:5.

32. "Her body": *'ăṣāmêhā*, from feminine plural noun *'ăṣāmôt*, "bones, skeletal remains, body" with feminine possessive suffix. The noun is used for both living and dead bodies.

33. Gk. *kai ouk apekrithē autǭ, alla tethnēkei*. The Septuagint's addition is clearly a gloss.

34. On this point, see further Trible, *Texts of Terror*, 81.

35. Bal in particular draws out the intertextuality between this death and the death of Jephthah's daughter; see *Death and Dissymmetry*, 80–93, 119, 184.

36. On the affective pull of the story, see Paynter, *Telling Terror*, 53–54.

37. Sedgwick, Touching Feeling, 133–36.

38. Abdulali, *What We Talk About*, 174.

39. E.g., Paynter, *Telling Terror*, 8–21; Hamley, *Unspeakable Things Unspoken*, 90–101.

40. Though with some exceptions: most notably Jones-Warsaw, "Toward a Womanist Hermeneutic." See as well Patrick S. Cheng, "Multiplicity and Judges 19: Constructing a Queer Asian Pacific American Biblical Hermeneutic," Semeia, no. 90/91 (2002): 119–33. While both Jones-Warsaw and Cheng are widely cited, it is Trible's paradigm, along with Bal's *Death and Dissymmetry* and Exum's *Fragmented Women*, that continues to dominate. As I draw out in the following, while both Bal and Exum dispute Trible on various specific points, their readings share a basic orientation toward "telling sad stories." Some recent feminist work has also foregrounded masculinity as a category of analysis in Judg 19–21; see, e.g., Harding, "Homophobia and Masculine Domination."

41. Trible, *Texts of Terror*, 80–81.

42. "Greater love has no man than this, that a man lay down his life for his friends," in the RSV translation; *Texts of Terror* preceded the NRSV by five years.

43. See Bal, *Death and Dissymmetry*, 90; Exum, *Fragmented Women*, 176; Paynter, *Telling Terror*, 3, 59. "Beth" means "house" and reflects Bal's larger arguments about houses

and locality in Judges. "Bath Sheber" means "daughter of breaking"; it also sets up a contrast with "Bathsheba" in Exum's reading. "Beli-Fachad" is a Hebrew translation of "Nirbhaya" or "Fearless One," the name given to Jyoti Singh in the Indian press after her 2013 gang rape. Singh testified to the police prior to her death from her injuries. Trible herself does not name the woman in Judg 19.

44. This is demonstrated most dramatically by Bal; see *Death and Dissymmetry*, 119–22; 271n24.

45. Bal, *Death and Dissymmetry*, 119.

46. Bal, *Death and Dissymmetry*, 124.

47. On "literary murder" and the responses of feminist criticism, see Exum, *Fragmented Women*, 16–18.

48. This is also a bad reading in the sense that it ignores literary ambiguity. Surely, the story could have been told in a way that made clear when the Levite's concubine died, just as it would have been possible to name the characters. I am grateful to Peter J. Sabo for this point.

49. Alice Bach, "Rereading the Body Politic: Women and Violence in Judges 21," *Biblical Interpretation* 6, no. 1 (1998): 1–19, 5–6. Bach also calls on readers to "examine narrative elements that aid the storyteller in the representation of rape."

50. Dora's persistent cough is one classic example. See Sigmund Freud, *Dora: An Analysis of a Case of Hysteria*, ed. Philip Rieff (New York: Collier, 1963). On somatic compliance and prophetic speech, see Graybill, *Are We Not Men?*, 85–86.

51. See Judg 19:2. The precise significance of this verse is debated by commentators.

52. Exum, *Fragmented Women*, 187.

53. Paynter, *Telling Terror*, 48.

54. Alice Bolin, *Dead Girls: Essays on Surviving an American Obsession* (New York: William Morrow, 2018), 14.

55. These examples come from Bolin, who provides a more substantial list in *Dead Girls*, 13–14.

56. *Veronica Mars*, for example, features a female detective, as does *Top of the Lake*. On "feminist Dead Girl shows," see Bolin, *Dead Girls*, 21.

57. Bolin, *Dead Girls*, 16.

58. Bolin, *Dead Girls*, 18.

59. Bolin, *Dead Girls*, 48, 55; Gillian Flynn, *Gone Girl* (New York: Broadway Books, 2014), 234.

60. For a feminist response to Lynch, see Diana Hume George, "Lynching Women: A Feminist Reading of Twin Peaks," in *Full of Secrets: Critical Approaches to Twin Peaks*, ed. David Lavery (Detroit: Wayne State University Press, 1995), 109–19.

61. Jephthah promises to sacrifice "whoever comes out of the doors of my house to meet me when I return in victory from the Ammonites" (11:31a). The crucial phrase is *whoever comes out* (*hayotse' 'asher yetse'*), which employs a masculine singular participle and an imperfect third-person masculine singular verb. The phrase could equally be translated as "whatever comes out"; nothing in the language indicates that it refers to a human and not, say, an animal. That Jephthah uses masculine verbal forms suggests

he is not thinking specifically of his daughter, as does his distress upon encountering her on his return (11:35); it does not, however, strictly exclude her from the category. Furthermore, his fulfillment of the vow indicates that he perceives his daughter as an appropriate object for sacrifice, if also a personally tragic one.

62. Trible, *Texts of Terror*, 108.

63. An early example of praising the daughter's bravery comes from Louisa Southworth in *The Woman's Bible*; see Elizabeth Cady Stanton, ed., *The Woman's Bible: A Classic Feminist Perspective* (Mineola, NY: Dover Publications, 2002 [1898]), 27. On the daughter as founder of a religious ritual, see Susan Ackerman, *Warrior, Dancer, Seductress, Queen: Women in Judges and Biblical Israel*, The Anchor Bible Reference Library (New York: Doubleday, 1998), 111. On queer community, see Theodore W. Jennings Jr., "Same-Sex Relations in the Biblical World," in *The Oxford Handbook of Theology, Sexuality, and Gender*, ed. Adrian Thatcher (New York: Oxford, 2014), 206–21, 211. An especially feisty reading is offered by Philip R. Davies, "Jephthah's Daughter to Her Father," in *Yours Faithfully: Virtual Letters from the Bible*, ed. Philip R. Davies, rev. ed. (London: Routledge, 2014), 41–43. Poets reimagining the text include Alicia Ostriker and J'Laine Robnolt; on these and other poetic responses that give the daughter a voice, see Johanna Stiebert, *Fathers and Daughters in the Hebrew Bible* (New York: Oxford University Press, 2013), 84. Many critics give the daughter a name, including "Bath," "Bat," or "Batya" (all variations on the Hebrew word for "daughter") or "Seila" or "Sheila" (from the name given in Pseudo-Philo, *Bib. Ant.* 40). See Bal, *Death and Dissymmetry*, 43; Beth Gerstein, "A Ritual Processed," in *Anti-Covenant: Counter-Reading Women's Lives in the Hebrew Bible*, ed. Mieke Bal, Bible and Literature 22 (Sheffield, UK: Sheffield Academic Press, 1989), 175–94; 179, 190; Davies, "Jephthah's Daughter to Her Father," 43; as well as the extended discussion in Stiebert, *Fathers and Daughters*, 81–83. I have also written about this story and critiqued the dominant feminist scholarship on it in Graybill, "No Child Left Behind: Reading Jephthah's Daughter with the Babylon Complex," *The Bible and Critical Theory* 11, no. 2 (2015): 36–50.

64. The father's reply between these two short speeches by the daughter is not documented; however, each is introduced with "she said," suggesting two separate speech acts.

65. On these and other poetic responses that give the daughter a voice, see Stiebert, *Fathers and Daughters*, 84.

66. Trible, *Texts of Terror*, 87; see also her footnote 66 on p. 91.

67. Trible quotes the summary from the *Times*; see "News Summary," *New York Times*, March 17, 1983, B1.

68. *The Accused*, dir. Jonathan Kaplan. Paramount Pictures, 1988.

69. Paynter, *Telling Terror*, 65. For a similar analysis, see Scholz, *Sacred Witness*, 155.

70. See Lynn S. Chancer, "New Bedford, Massachusetts, March 6, 1983–March 22, 1984: The 'Before and After' of a Group Rape," *Gender & Society* 1, no. 3 (1987): 239–60; Helen Benedict, *Virgin or Vamp: How the Press Covers Sex Crimes* (New York: Oxford University Press, 1993), 104–5.

71. Benedict, *Virgin or Vamp*, 141–46.

72. For reflection on this point, see Miller, *Know My Name*, 287–88.

73. Given the intensely gendered violence of Judg 19–21 and indeed the book as a whole, I have intentionally translated *'îš* as "man" and not "person" or "people." The NRSV opts for the gender-neutralizing "all the people did what was right in their own eyes"; however, this elides the fact that the violence described is decidedly masculine.

74. Here I differ from Paynter and her understanding of reparative reading, which she extends to include Trible's reading in *Texts of Terror*. See Paynter, *Telling Terror*, 1–2, 24–28.

75. Heather Love, *Feeling Backward: Loss and the Politics of Queer History* (Cambridge, MA: Harvard University Press, 2007), 51.

76. Here I diverge from Paynter's attempts at repair in reading Judg 19 and, to a certain degree, Sedgwick's own description of "reparative reading" in "Paranoid Reading and Reparative Reading." Note that I am not offering a strong repudiation of reparative reading as such—after all, that would be a rather paranoid position to take—but rather suggesting that it is not the best approach here. I also suggest that Sedgwick's original description of "reparative reading" is more flexible, and much less concerned with finding a suppressed moral voice in the text, than Paynter's.

77. Love suggests that "feeling backward" offers one way of describing our complex relationship to texts and histories we cannot save, and cannot free ourselves from. Backwardness is one alternative to the hope and future-orientedness that characterize many queer relations to history. The story of the Levite's concubine, unlike the queer histories that frame Love's argument, is not a historical account, but rather a literary story. I offer the language of "unhappy reading," rather than "feeling backward," as a way of centering the literary. My approach, however, complements Love's.

78. Some of the most interesting recent feminist readings of Judg 19–21 are interesting precisely because they insist on alternate ways of telling the story, such as Minenhle Nomalungelo Khumalo's pairing of the story with nonconsensual pornography in video games or Esther Brownsmith's critical engagement with the "women in refrigerators" trope from popular culture. Harding's work on masculinity and domination is another example. See Khumalo, "Judges 19 and Non Con," in *Rape Culture and Religious Studies: Critical and Pedagogical Engagements*, ed. Graybill, Minister, and Lawrence; Brownsmith, "The Woman in the Refrigerator: Consumption and Objectification in Judges 19," chap. 3 in "Inconspicuous Consumption: Conceptual Metaphors of Women as Food in the Deuteronomistic History," PhD diss., Brandeis University, 2020; Harding, "Homophobia and Masculine Domination in Judges 19–21" and "Homophobia and Rape Cultures in the Narratives of Early Israel."

Conclusion

1. Margaret Atwood, *The Testaments* (New York: Nan A. Talese, 2019).

2. Joanna Russ, *The Female Man* (Princeton, NJ: Beacon Press, 1975).

3. Miller's statement was first published online by BuzzFeed News: Kelly J. M. Baker, "Here's The Powerful Letter The Stanford Victim Read To Her Attacker," *BuzzFeed News*, June 3, 2016, https://www.buzzfeednews.com/article/katiejmbaker/heres-the-powerful-letter-the-stanford-victim-read-to-her-ra. The statement is reprinted in Miller's memoir, *Know My Name*, 333–57.

4. Miller, *Know My Name*, 308–10.

5. Margaret Atwood, *The Blind Assassin* (New York: Anchor Books, 2000), 450.

6. Russ, *Female Man*, 95.

Bibliography

Abdulali, Sohaila. *What We Talk About When We Talk About Rape.* New York: New Press, 2018.

Ackerman, Susan. *Warrior, Dancer, Seductress, Queen: Women in Judges and Biblical Israel.* Anchor Yale Bible Reference Library. New York: Doubleday, 1998.

Ademiluka, Solomon O. "Sexual Exploitation or Legitimate Surrogacy: Reading the Hagar Narrative (Gn 16: 1–4a) in African Context." *Theologia Viatorum* 43, no. 1 (2019): 1–10.

Ahmed, Sara. *The Promise of Happiness.* Durham, NC: Duke University Press, 2010.

Ahmed, Sara. *Queer Phenomenology: Orientations, Objects, Others.* Durham, NC: Duke University Press, 2006.

Ahmed, Sara. *Willful Subjects.* Durham, NC: Duke University Press, 2014.

Alpert, Rebecca. "Finding Our Past: A Lesbian Interpretation of the Book of Ruth." In *Reading Ruth: Contemporary Women Reclaim a Sacred Story*, edited by Judith A. Kates and Gail Twersty Reimer, 91–96. New York: Ballantine Books, 1994.

Alter, Robert. *The David Story: A Translation with Commentary of 1 and 2 Samuel.* New York: W. W. Norton & Company, 2009.

Andruska, Jennifer. "'Rape' in the Syntax of 2 Samuel 11:4." *Zeitschrift für die alttestamentliche Wissenschaft* 129, no. 1 (2017): 103–9.

Arielle, Rousse. "Beyond the Binaries: Exclusive Dichotomies in the Anti-Sexual Violence Movement." In Patterson, *Queering Sexual Violence*, 39–47.

Atwood, Margaret. *The Blind Assassin.* New York: Anchor Books, 2000.

Atwood, Margaret. *The Handmaid's Tale.* New York: Anchor Books, 1985.

Atwood, Margaret. *The Testaments.* New York: Nan A. Talese, 2019.

Bach, Alice. "Rereading the Body Politic: Women and Violence in Judges 21." *Biblical Interpretation* 6, no. 1 (1998): 1–19.

Bach, Alice. "Signs of the Flesh: Observations on Characterization in the Bible." In *Women in the Hebrew Bible: A Reader*, edited by Alice Bach, 351–66. New York: Routledge, 1999.

Baker, Kelly J. M. "Here's the Powerful Letter the Stanford Victim Read to Her Attacker." *BuzzFeed News*, June 3, 2016. https://www.buzzfeednews.com/article/katiejmbaker/heres-the-powerful-letter-the-stanford-victim-read-to-her-ra.

Bal, Mieke. *Death and Dissymmetry: The Politics of Coherence in the Book of Judges.* Chicago: University of Chicago Press, 1988.

Barrick, Samantha. "Infinity and the Construction of Safe Space." In Patterson, *Queering Sexual Violence*, 61–68.

Bass, Ellen, and Laura Davis. *The Courage to Heal: A Guide for Women Survivors of Child Sexual Abuse.* 20th anniversary ed. New York: William Morrow, 2008.

Baumann, Gerlinde. "Nahum." In Schottroff and Wacker, *Feminist Biblical Interpretation*, 433–42.

Benedict, Helen. *Virgin or Vamp: How the Press Covers Sex Crimes.* New York: Oxford University Press, 1993.

Bennett, Sidney, Victoria L. Banyard, and Lydia Garnhart. "To Act or Not to Act, That Is the Question? Barriers and Facilitators of Bystander Intervention." *Journal of Interpersonal Violence* 29, no. 3 (2013): 476–96.

Berlin, Adele. *Lamentations: A Commentary*. The Old Testament Library. Louisville, KY: Westminster John Knox Press, 2002.

Berlin, Adele. *Poetics and Interpretation of Biblical Narrative*. Winona Lake, IN: Eisenbrauns, 1994.

Bernstein, Elizabeth. *Brokered Subjects: Sex, Trafficking, and the Politics of Freedom*. Chicago: University of Chicago Press, 2019.

Bevacqua, Maria. *Rape on the Public Agenda: Feminism and the Politics of Sexual Assault*. Boston: Northeastern University Press, 2000.

Bloomberg Government. "Kavanaugh Hearing: Transcript." *Washington Post*, September 27, 2018. https://www.washingtonpost.com/news/national/wp/2018/09/27/kavanaugh-hearing-transcript/.

Blue Seat Studios. *Tea Consent*. May 12, 2015, YouTube video. https://www.youtube.com/watch?v=oQbei5JGiT8. Accessed December 30, 2018.

Blyth, Caroline. "Lost in the 'Post': Rape Culture and Postfeminism in Admen and Eve." *The Bible and Critical Theory* 10, no. 2 (2014): 1–10.

Blyth, Caroline, and Emily Colgan. "Tough Conversations: Teaching Biblical Texts of Terror." *Shiloh Project* (blog), June 13, 2019. https://www.shilohproject.blog/tough-conversations-teaching-biblical-texts-of-terror/.

Blyth, Caroline, Emily Colgan, and Katie B. Edwards, eds. *Rape Culture, Gender Violence, and Religion: Biblical Perspectives*. Religion and Radicalism. Palgrave Macmillan, 2018.

Boase, Elizabeth. "Fragmented Voices: Collective Identity and Traumatization in Lamentations." In *Bible through the Lens of Trauma*, edited by Elizabeth Boase and Christopher G. Frechette, 49–66. Atlanta: SBL Press, 2016.

Bodner, Keith. "Is Joab a Reader-Response Critic?" *Journal for the Study of the Old Testament* 27, no. 1 (2002): 19–35.

Boer, Roland. *Knockin' on Heaven's Door: The Bible and Popular Culture*. Biblical Limits. New York: Routledge, 1999.

Bolin, Alice. *Dead Girls: Essays on Surviving an American Obsession*. New York: William Morrow, 2018.

Bosworth, David A. "Daughter Zion and Weeping in Lamentations 1–2." *Journal for the Study of the Old Testament* 38, no. 2 (2013): 217–37.

Bowman, Christin P. "Persistent Pleasures: Agency, Social Power, and Embodiment in Women's Solitary Masturbation Experiences." PhD diss., City University of New York, 2017.

Brenner, Athalya, ed. *A Feminist Companion to the Latter Prophets*. Feminist Companion to the Bible, 1st ser. Sheffield, UK: Sheffield Academic Press, 1995.

Brenner, Athalya, ed. *A Feminist Companion to Prophets and Daniel*. Feminist Companion to the Bible, 2nd ser. Sheffield, UK: Sheffield Academic Press, 2002.

Brewer-Boydston, Ginny. "Sarah the *Gevirah*: A Comparison of Sarah and the Queen Mothers, of Matriarchs in the Dynastic Succession of Sons and Nations." *Review & Expositor* 115, no. 4 (2018): 500–12.

Brintnall, Kent L., Rhiannon Graybill, and Linn Tonstad. *Lee Edelman and the Queer Study of Religion*. New York: Routledge, forthcoming.

Brooks, Geraldine. *The Secret Chord*. New York: Penguin, 2016.

Brown, Wendy. *States of Injury: Power and Freedom in Late Modernity*. Princeton, NJ: Princeton University Press, 1995.

Brownmiller, Susan. *Against Our Will: Men, Women, and Rape*. New York: Fawcett Columbine, 1993 [1975].

Brownsmith, Esther. "Inconspicuous Consumption: Conceptual Metaphors of Women as Food in the Deuteronomistic History." PhD diss., Brandeis University, 2020.

Brueggemann, Walter. *David's Truth in Israel's Imagination and Memory*. 2nd ed. Minneapolis: Fortress Press, 2002.

Buchwald, Emilie, Pamela Fletcher, and Martha Roth, eds. *Transforming a Rape Culture*. Minneapolis: Milkweed Editions, 1995.

Buntin, Julie. *Marlena*. New York: Henry Holt and Co., 2017.

Burton, Tara Isabella. *Social Creature*. New York: Doubleday, 2018.

Butler, Judith. *Undoing Gender*. New York: Routledge, 2004.

Butler, Judith, and Joan W. Scott. *Feminists Theorize the Political*. New York: Routledge, 1992.

Carson, Anne. "The Gender of Sound." In *Glass, Irony and God*, 119–42. New York: New Directions, 1995.

Chancer, Lynn S. "New Bedford, Massachusetts, March 6, 1983–March 22, 1984: The 'Before and After' of a Group Rape." *Gender & Society* 1, no. 3 (1987): 239–60.

Chapman, Cynthia R. *The Gendered Language of Warfare in the Israelite-Assyrian Encounter*. Harvard Semitic Monographs 62. Winona Lake, IN: Eisenbrauns, 2004.

Chatterjee, Partha. *The Nation and Its Fragments: Colonial and Postcolonial Histories*. Princeton, NJ: Princeton University Press, 1993.

Cheng, Patrick S. "Multiplicity and Judges 19: Constructing a Queer Asian Pacific American Biblical Hermeneutic." *Semeia*, no. 90/91 (2002): 119–33.

Choi, Susan. *Trust Exercise*. New York: Henry Holt, 2019.

Claassens, Juliana. "Just Emotions: Reading the Sarah and Hagar Narrative (Genesis 16, 21) through the Lens of Human Dignity." *Verbum et Ecclesia* 34, no. 2, art. 787 (2013): 1–6.

Clare, Eli. *Brilliant Imperfection: Grappling with Cure*. Durham, NC: Duke University Press, 2017.

Clark, Noel. "The Etiology and Phenomenology of Sexual Shame: A Grounded Theory Study." Dissertation, Seattle Pacific University, 2017.

Clendinen, Dudley. "Barroom Rape Shames Town of Proud Heritage." *New York Times*, March 17, 1983, A16.

Clines, David J. A. *Interested Parties: The Ideology of Writers and Readers of the Hebrew Bible*. Sheffield, UK: Sheffield Academic Press, 1995.

Crenshaw, Kimberlé. "Demarginalizing the Intersection of Race and Sex: A Black Feminist Critique of Antidiscrimination Doctrine, Feminist Theory and Antiracist Politics." *University of Chicago Legal Forum* 1989 (1989): 139–67.

Cullingford, Elizabeth. "*Evil, Sin*, or *Doubt*? The Dramas of Clerical Child Abuse." *Theatre Journal* 62, no. 2 (2010): 245–63.

Cvetkovich, Ann. *An Archive of Feelings: Trauma, Sexuality, and Lesbian Public Cultures*. Durham, NC: Duke University Press, 2003.

Cvetkovich, Ann. *Depression: A Public Feeling*. Durham, NC: Duke University Press, 2012.

Daniels, Brandy. "Sexual Violence and the 'End' of Subjectivity: Queer Negativity and a Theopolitics of Refusal." In Brintnall, Graybill, and Tonstad, *Lee Edelman and the Queer Study of Religion*, forthcoming.

Davidson, Richard M. "Did King David Rape Bathsheba? A Case Study in Narrative Theology." *Journal of the Adventist Theological Society* 17, no. 2 (2006): 81–95.

Davies, Philip R. "Jephthah's Daughter to Her Father." In *Yours Faithfully: Virtual Letters from the Bible*, edited by Philip R. Davies, revised ed., 41–43. London: Routledge, 2014.

Davis, Madeleine. "Margaret Atwood's Female Bodies." In Howells, *Cambridge Companion to Margaret Atwood*, 58–71.

Dearman, J. Andrew. "Daughter Zion and Her Place in God's Household." *Horizons in Biblical Theology* 31, no. 2 (2009): 144–59.

Denhollander, Rachael. *What Is a Girl Worth?: My Story of Breaking the Silence and Exposing the Truth about Larry Nassar and USA Gymnastics.* Carol Stream, IL: Tyndale Momentum, 2019.

De-Whyte, Janice Pearl Ewurama. *Wom(b)an: A Cultural-Narrative Reading of the Hebrew Bible Barrenness Narratives.* Leiden: Brill, 2018.

Diamant, Anita. *The Red Tent.* 20th anniversary ed. New York: Picador, 2007.

Doane, Sébastien. "Gang Bang et Démembrement: Quatre Lectures de Juges 19." *Science et Esprit* 66, no. 2 (2014): 177–88.

Dobbs-Allsopp, Frederick W., and Tod Linafelt. "The Rape of Zion in Thr 1, 10." *Zeitschrift für die alttestamentliche Wissenschaft* 113, no. 1 (2001): 77–81.

Doyle, Jennifer. *Campus Sex, Campus Security.* Intervention Series 19. South Pasadena, CA: Semiotext(e), 2015.

Dube, Musa W. "Dinah (Genesis 34) at the Contact Zone: Shall Our Sister Be Treated Like a Whore?" In *Feminist Frameworks and the Bible: Power, Ambiguity, and Intersectionality*, edited by L. Juliana Claassens and Carolyn J. Sharp, 39–58. Library of Hebrew Bible/Old Testament Studies 630. New York: T&T Clark, 2017.

duBois, Page. *Torture and Truth.* Routledge Revivals. New York: Routledge, 2016.

Duncan, Celena M. "The Book of Ruth: On Boundaries, Love, and Truth." In *Take Back the Word: A Queer Reading of the Bible*, edited by Robert E. Goss and Mona West, 92–102. Cleveland, OH: Pilgrim Press, 2000.

Durant, Elizabeth. "It's Complicated: Power and Complicity in the Stories of Hagar and Sarah." *Conversations with the Biblical World* 35 (2015): 78–93.

Dworkin, Andrea, and Catharine A. MacKinnon. *Pornography and Civil Rights: A New Day for Women's Equality.* Minneapolis: Organizing Against Pornography, 1988.

Edelman, Lee. *No Future: Queer Theory and the Death Drive.* Series Q. Durham, NC: Duke University Press, 2004.

Eligon, John, and Michael Schwirtz. "Senate Candidate Provokes Ire with 'Legitimate Rape' Comment." *New York Times*, August 19, 2012. https://www.nytimes.com/2012/08/20/us/politics/todd-akin-provokes-ire-with-legitimate-rape-comment.html.

Ellington, Scott. "De-Centering Lamentations: A Crisis of Hope, of Memory, and of Continued Presence." *Old Testament Essays* 31, no. 3 (2018): 494–505.

Erbele-Küster, Dorothea. "A Response to Julie Claassens's 'A True Disgrace? The Representation of Violence against Women in the Book of Lamentations and in J.M. Coetzee's Novel *Disgrace*.'" In *Fragile Dignity: Intercontextual Conversations on Scriptures, Family, and Violence*, edited by L. Juliana Claassens and Klaas Spronk, 99–100. Atlanta: SBL Press, 2013.

Exum, J. Cheryl. "Desire Distorted and Exhibited: Lot and His Daughters in Psychoanalysis, Painting, and Film." In *"A Wise and Discerning Mind": Essays in Honor of Burke O. Long*, edited by Robert C. Culley and Saul M. Olyan, 83–108. Providence, RI: Brown Judaic Studies 325, 2000.

Exum, J. Cheryl. *Fragmented Women: Feminist (Sub)Versions of Biblical Narratives.* Journal for the Study of the Old Testament Supplement Series 163. Sheffield, UK: JSOT Press, 1993.

Exum, J. Cheryl. *Plotted, Shot, and Painted: Cultural Representations of Biblical Women.* Sheffield, UK: Sheffield Academic Press, 1996.

Fagan, River Willow. "Fluctuations in Voice: A Genderqueer Response to Traumatic Violence." In Patterson, *Queering Sexual Violence*, 17–21.

Faucette, Avory. "Questions and Answers." In Patterson, *Queering Sexual Violence*, 189–92.

Feimster, Crystal N. *Southern Horrors: Women and the Politics of Rape and Lynching.* Cambridge, MA: Harvard University Press, 2009.

Ferrante, Elena. *The Neapolitan Novels by Elena Ferrante (Boxed Set).* Translated by Ann Goldstein. New York: Europa, 2015.

Fischel, Joseph J. *Screw Consent: A Better Politics of Sexual Justice.* Oakland: University of California Press, 2019.

Fischel, Joseph J. *Sex and Harm in the Age of Consent.* Minneapolis: University of Minnesota Press, 2016.

Floyd, Michael H. "Welcome Back, Daughter of Zion!" *Catholic Biblical Quarterly* 70, no. 3 (2008): 484–504.

Flynn, Gillian. *Gone Girl.* New York: Broadway Books, 2014.

Freud, Sigmund. *Dora: An Analysis of a Case of Hysteria.* Edited by Philip Rieff. New York: Collier, 1963.

Gaertner, Samuel L., John F. Dovidio, and Gary Johnson. "Race of Victim, Nonresponsive Bystanders, and Helping Behavior." *Journal of Social Psychology* 117, no. 1 (June 1, 1982): 69–77.

Gafney, Wilda C. M. *Nahum, Habakkuk, Zephaniah.* Wisdom Commentary Series 38. Collegeville, MN: Liturgical Press, 2017.

Galpaz-Feller, Pnina. "Pregnancy and Birth in the Bible and Ancient Egypt (Comparative Study)." *Biblische Notizen*, no. 102 (2000): 42–53.

García Bachmann, Mercedes L. "What Is in a Name?: Abishag the Shunammite as *sokenet* in 1 Kings 1:1–4." In *Out of Place: Doing Theology on the Crosscultural Brink*, edited by Jione Havea and Clive Pearson, 233–54. Cross Cultural Theologies. New York: Routledge, 2016.

Garroway, Kristine Henriksen. "Was Bathsheba the Original Bridget Jones? A New Look at Bathsheba on Screen and in Biblical Scholarship." *Nashim*, no. 24 (2013): 53–73.

Gavey, Nicola. *Just Sex?: The Cultural Scaffolding of Rape.* Women and Psychology. New York: Routledge, 2013.

Gay, Roxane, ed. *Not That Bad: Dispatches from Rape Culture.* New York: Harper, 2018.

George, Diana Hume. "Lynching Women: A Feminist Reading of *Twin Peaks*." In *Full of Secrets: Critical Approaches to* Twin Peaks, edited by David Lavery, 109–19. Detroit: Wayne State University Press, 1995.

Gerstein, Beth. "A Ritual Processed." In *Anti-Covenant: Counter-Reading Women's Lives in the Hebrew Bible*, edited by Mieke Bal, 175–94. Bible and Literature 22. Sheffield, UK: Sheffield Academic Press, 1989.

Gidycz, Christine A., Lindsay M. Orchowski, and Alan D. Berkowitz. "Preventing Sexual Aggression among College Men: An Evaluation of a Social Norms and Bystander Intervention Program." *Violence Against Women* 17, no. 11 (2011): 720–42.

Glaser, Rachel B. *Paulina & Fran.* New York: Harper Perennial, 2015.

Goss, Robert. *Jesus Acted Up: A Gay and Lesbian Manifesto.* San Francisco: HarperSanFrancisco, 1994.

Gossett, Reina. "Foreword." In Patterson, *Queering Sexual Violence,* 1–3.

Gravett, Sandie. "Reading 'Rape' in the Hebrew Bible: A Consideration of Language." *Journal for the Study of the Old Testament* 28, no. 3 (2004): 279–99.

Graybill, Rhiannon. *Are We Not Men?: Unstable Masculinity in the Hebrew Prophets.* New York: Oxford University Press, 2016.

Graybill, Rhiannon. "Critiquing the Discourse of Consent." *Journal of Feminist Studies in Religion* 33, no. 1 (2017): 175–76.

Graybill, Rhiannon. "'Even unto This Bitter Loving': Unhappiness and Backward Feelings in the Book of Ruth." *Biblical Interpretation* (2020), online advance publication at https://brill.com/view/journals/bi/aop/article-10.1163-15685152-00284P11/article-10.1163-15685152-00284P11.xml.

Graybill, Rhiannon. "Good Intentions Are Not Enough." In Graybill, Minister, and Lawrence, *Rape Culture and Religious Studies,* 175–204.

Graybill, Rhiannon. "Jonah 'between Men': The Prophet in Critical Homosocial Perspective." In *Hebrew Masculinities Anew,* edited by Ovidiu Creangă, 210–28. Hebrew Bible Monographs 79. Sheffield, UK: Sheffield Phoenix Press, 2019.

Graybill, Rhiannon. "No Child Left Behind: Reading Jephthah's Daughter with the Babylon Complex." *The Bible and Critical Theory* 11, no. 2 (2015): 36–50.

Graybill, Rhiannon. "When Bodies Meet: Fraught Companionship and Entangled Embodiment in Jeremiah 36." *Journal of the American Academy of Religion* 86, no. 4 (2018): 1046–71.

Graybill, Rhiannon. "Yahweh as Maternal Vampire in Second Isaiah: Reading from Violence to Fluid Possibility with Luce Irigaray." *Journal of Feminist Studies in Religion* 33, no. 1 (2017): 9–25.

Graybill, Rhiannon, Meredith Minister, and Beatrice Lawrence. "Sexual Violence in and around the Classroom." *Teaching Theology & Religion* 20, no. 1 (2017): 70–88.

Graybill, Rhiannon, Meredith Minister, and Beatrice Lawrence. "Introduction." In Graybill, Minister, and Lawrence, *Rape Culture and Religious Studies,* 1–20.

Graybill, Rhiannon, Meredith Minister, and Beatrice Lawrence, eds. *Rape Culture and Religious Studies: Critical and Pedagogical Engagements.* Feminist Studies and Sacred Texts. Lanham, MD: Lexington Books, 2019.

Graybill, Rhiannon, Meredith Minister, and Beatrice Lawrence. "Sexual Violence in and around the Classroom." *Teaching Theology & Religion* 20, no. 1 (2017).

Graybill, Rhiannon, and Peter J. Sabo. "Caves of the Hebrew Bible: A Speleology." *Biblical Interpretation* 26, no. 1 (2018): 1–22.

Greenblatt, Jordana. "Consensual Sex, Consensual Text: Law, Literature, and the Production of the Consenting Subject." In Greenblatt and Valens, *Querying Consent,* 44–62.

Greenblatt, Jordana, and Keja Valens, eds. *Querying Consent: Beyond Permission and Refusal.* New Brunswick, NJ: Rutgers University Press, 2018.

Greenough, Chris. *The Bible and Sexual Violence against Men.* Rape Culture, Religion and the Bible. New York: Routledge, 2020.

Grigoriadis, Vanessa. *Blurred Lines: Rethinking Sex, Power, and Consent on Campus.* Boston: Eamon Dolan/Houghton Mifflin Harcourt, 2017.

Guest, Deryn. "Hiding behind the Naked Women in Lamentations: A Recriminative Response." *Biblical Interpretation* 7, no. 4 (1999): 413–48.

Halberstam, Jack. *In a Queer Time and Place: Transgender Bodies, Subcultural Lives*. New York: NYU Press, 2005.

Halberstam, Jack. *The Queer Art of Failure*. Durham, NC: Duke University Press, 2011.

Hall, Rachel. "'It Can Happen to You': Rape Prevention in the Age of Risk Management." *Hypatia* 19, no. 3 (2004): 1–18.

Hall, Radclyffe. *The Well of Loneliness*. Hertfordshire, UK: Wordsworth Editions Ltd., 2014. Originally published 1928.

Halperin, David M. "Heroes and Their Pals." In *One Hundred Years of Homosexuality: And Other Essays on Greek Love*, 75–87. New Ancient World. New York: Routledge, 1989.

Halpern, Baruch. *David's Secret Demons: Messiah, Murderer, Traitor, King*. The Bible in Its World. Grand Rapids, MI: Wm. B. Eerdmans Publishing, 2003.

Hamley, Isabelle M. "'Dis(re)membered and Unaccounted For': *Pilegesh* in the Hebrew Bible." *Journal for the Study of the Old Testament* 42, no. 4 (2018): 415–34.

Hamley, Isabelle M. *Unspeakable Things Unspoken: An Irigarayan Reading of Otherness and Victimization in Judges 19–21*. Eugene, OR: Pickwick Publications, 2019.

Haraway, Donna J. *Modest_Witness@Second_Millennium: FemaleMan©_Meets_OncoMouse™: Feminism and Technoscience*. New York: Routledge, 1997.

Haraway, Donna J. *Simians, Cyborgs, and Women: The Reinvention of Nature*. New York: Routledge, 1990.

Haraway, Donna J. *Staying with the Trouble: Making Kin in the Chthulucene*. Durham, NC: Duke University Press Books, 2016.

Harding, James. "Homophobia and Masculine Domination in Judges 19–21." *The Bible and Critical Theory* 12, no. 2 (2016): 41–74.

Harding, James E. "Homophobia and Rape Cultures in the Narratives of Early Israel." In Blyth, Colgan, and Edwards, *Rape Culture, Gender Violence, and Religion*, 159–78.

Harding, James E. *The Love of David and Jonathan: Ideology, Text, Reception*. Bible World. New York: Routledge, 2014.

Häusl, Maria. "Lamentations: Zion's Cry in Affliction." In Schottroff and Wacker, *Feminist Biblical Interpretation*, 334–44.

Hemmings, Clare. *Why Stories Matter: The Political Grammar of Feminist Theory*. Durham, NC: Duke University Press, 2011.

Hens-Piazza, Gina. *Lamentations*. Wisdom Commentary 30. Collegeville, MN: Liturgical Press, 2017.

Hepola, Sarah. "The Alcohol Blackout." *Texas Monthly*, October 29, 2015. https://www.texasmonthly.com/the-culture/the-alcohol-blackout/.

Herman, Judith Lewis. *Trauma and Recovery: The Aftermath of Violence, from Domestic Abuse to Political Terror*. New York: Basic Books, 1992.

Holzer, Jenny. *Abuse of Power Comes as No Surprise*. Installation at Walker Art Center, Minneapolis, 1983.

Howells, Coral Ann. *The Cambridge Companion to Margaret Atwood*. New York: Cambridge University Press, 2006.

Huffer, Lynne. *Are the Lips a Grave?: A Queer Feminist on the Ethics of Sex*. New York: Columbia University Press, 2013.

Huxley, Aldous. *Brave New World*. New York: Harper and Row, 1969. Originally published 1932.

Irigaray, Luce. *This Sex Which Is Not One*. Translated by Catherine Porter. Ithaca, NY: Cornell University Press, 1985.

James, Elaine T. *A Handbook of Biblical Poetry*. Essentials of Biblical Studies. New York: Oxford University Press, 2021.

Jennings, Theodore W. *Jacob's Wound: Homoerotic Narrative in the Literature of Ancient Israel*. New York: Continuum, 2005.

Jennings, Theodore W. "Same-Sex Relations in the Biblical World." In *The Oxford Handbook of Theology, Sexuality, and Gender*, edited by Adrian Thatcher, 206–21. New York: Oxford University Press, 2014.

Johnson, Barbara. *The Barbara Johnson Reader: The Surprise of Otherness*, edited by Melissa Feuerstein, Bill Johnson González, Lili Porten, and Keja L. Valens. Durham, NC: Duke University Press, 2014.

Jones-Warsaw, Koala. "Toward a Womanist Hermeneutic: A Reading of Judges 19–21." In *A Feminist Companion to Judges*, edited by Athalya Brenner, 172–86. A Feminist Companion to the Bible (1st ser.). Sheffield, UK: Sheffield University Press, 1993.

Joseph, Alison L. "Redaction as Reception: The Case of Genesis 34." In *Reading Other Peoples' Texts: Social Identity and the Reception of Authoritative Traditions*, edited by Ken S. Brown, Alison L. Joseph, and Brennan Breed, 83–101. Scriptural Traces 20. New York: T&T Clark, 2020.

Joseph, Alison L. "Understanding Genesis 34:2: 'Innâ." *Vetus Testamentum* 66, no. 4 (2016): 663–68.

Junior, Nyasha. *Reimagining Hagar: Blackness and Bible*. New York: Oxford University Press, 2019.

Kaplan, Jonathan, dir. *The Accused*. Paramount Pictures, 1988.

Kartzow, Marianne Bjelland. "Navigating the Womb: Surrogacy, Slavery, Fertility—and Biblical Discourses." *Journal of Early Christian History* 2, no. 1 (2012): 38–54.

Kawashima, Robert S. "Could a Woman Say 'No' in Biblical Israel? On the Genealogy of Legal Status in Biblical Law and Literature." *AJS Review* 35, no. 1 (2011): 1–22.

Keefe, Alice A. "Rapes of Women, Wars of Men: Women, War, Society, and Metaphoric Language in the Study of the Hebrew Bible." *Semeia*, no. 61 (1993): 79–97.

Kelly, Liz. "The Everyday/Everynightness of Rape: Is It Different in War?" In *Gender, War, and Militarism: Feminist Perspectives*, edited by Laura Sjoberg and Sandra Via, 114–23. Santa Barbara, CA: Praeger, 2010.

Kelso, Julie. "Reading the Silence of Women in Genesis 34." In *Redirected Travel: Alternative Journeys and Places in Biblical Studies*, edited by Roland Boer and Edgar W. Conrad, 85–109. Journal for the Study of the Old Testament Supplement Series 382. New York: T&T Clark, 2003.

Kennedy, Maev. "Polanski Was Not Guilty of 'Rape-Rape', Says Whoopi Goldberg." *Guardian*, September 29, 2009, sec. Film. http://www.theguardian.com/film/2009/sep/29/roman-polanski-whoopi-goldberg.

Kermode, Frank. *The Sense of an Ending: Studies in the Theory of Fiction with a New Epilogue: Studies in the Theory of Fiction with a New Epilogue*. New York: Oxford University Press, 2000.

Khumalo, Minenhle Nomalungelo. "Judges 19 and Non Con." In Graybill, Minister, and Lawrence, *Rape Culture and Religious Studies*, 93–112.

Koenig, Sara M. *Isn't This Bathsheba?: A Study in Characterization*. Princeton Theological Monographs 177. Eugene, OR: Pickwick Publications, 2011.

Koenig, Sara M. "Make War Not Love: The Limits of David's Hegemonic Masculinity in 2 Samuel 10–12." *Biblical Interpretation* 23, no. 4–5 (2015): 489–517.

Koosed, Jennifer L. "Reading the Bible as a Feminist." *Brill Research Perspectives in Biblical Interpretation* 2, no. 2 (2017): 1–75.

Krakauer, Jon. *Missoula: Rape and the Justice System in a College Town*. New York: Doubleday, 2015.

Landy, Francis. "Between Centre and Periphery: Space and Gender in the Book of Judges in the Early Second Temple Period." In *Centres and Peripheries in the Early Second Temple Period*, edited by Ehud Ben Zvi and Christoph Levin, 133–62. *Forschungen zum Alten Testament* 108. Tübingen: Mohr Siebeck, 2016.

Landy, Francis. "Lamentations." In *The Literary Guide to the Bible*, edited by Robert Alter and Frank Kermode, 329–34. Cambridge, MA: Belknap Press of Harvard University Press, 1987.

Lasine, Stuart. "Guest and Host in Judges 19: Lot's Hospitality in an Inverted World." *Journal for the Study of the Old Testament* 9, no. 29 (1984): 37–59.

Lawrence, Beatrice. "Rape Culture and the Rabbinic Construction of Gender." In Graybill, Minister, and Lawrence, *Rape Culture and Religious Studies*, 137–56.

Létourneau, Anne. "Beauty, Bath and Beyond: Framing Bathsheba as a Royal Fantasy in 2 Sam 11, 1–5." *Scandinavian Journal of the Old Testament* 32, no. 1 (2018): 72–91.

Linafelt, Tod. *Surviving Lamentations: Catastrophe, Lament, and Protest in the Afterlife of a Biblical Book*. Chicago: University of Chicago Press, 2000.

Llewellyn, Dawn. *Reading, Feminism, and Spirituality: Troubling the Waves*. New York: Palgrave Macmillan, 2015.

Lockwood, Patricia. *Motherland Fatherland Homelandsexuals*. Penguin Poets. New York: Penguin Books, 2014.

Lorde, Audre. *Sister Outsider: Essays and Speeches*. Reprint ed. Berkeley, CA: Crossing Press, 2007.

Love, Heather. *Feeling Backward: Loss and the Politics of Queer History*. Cambridge, MA: Harvard University Press, 2007.

Lovelace, Vanessa. "'This Woman's Son Shall Not Inherit with My Son': Towards a Womanist Politics of Belonging in the Sarah–Hagar Narratives." *Journal of the Interdenominational Theological Center* 41, no. 1 (2018): 63–82.

Lowrey, Sassafras. "Not a Good Survivor." In Patterson, *Queering Sexual Violence*, 247–49.

Machado, Carmen Maria. *In the Dream House: A Memoir*. Minneapolis: Graywolf Press, 2019.

MacKendrick, Karmen. "Consent, Command, Confession." In Greenblatt and Valens, *Querying Consent*, 11–26.

Maitland, Sara. *Angel Maker: The Short Stories of Sara Maitland*. New York: Henry Holt and Company, 1996.

Mandolfo, Carleen. *Daughter Zion Talks Back to the Prophets: A Dialogic Theology of the Book of Lamentations*. Revised ed. Atlanta: SBL Press, 2007.

Manne, Kate. *Down Girl: The Logic of Misogyny*. New York: Penguin Books Limited, 2019.

Marcus, Sharon. "Fighting Bodies, Fighting Words: A Theory and Politics of Rape Prevention." In Butler and Scott, *Feminists Theorize the Political*, 385–403.

Mbuwayesango, Dora R. "Childlessness and Woman-to-Woman Relationships in Genesis and in African Patriarchal Society: Sarah and Hagar from a Zimbabwean Woman's Perspective (Gen 16: 1–16; 21: 8–21)." *Semeia* 78 (1997): 27–36.

McEwan, Melissa. "Rape Culture 101." *Shakesville* (blog), October 9, 2009. http://www. shakesville.com/2009/10/rape-culture-101.html.

McGeough, Kevin M. "The Problem with David: Masculinity and Morality in Biblical Cinema." *Journal of Religion & Film* 22, no. 1, art. 33 (2018).

McGuire, Danielle L. *At the Dark End of the Street: Black Women, Rape, and Resistance—A New History of the Civil Rights Movement from Rosa Parks to the Rise of Black Power.* New York: Vintage Books, 2011.

Melgar, César. "Ruth and the Unaccompanied Minors from Central America: Ethical Perspectives on a Socio-Economic Problem." *Review and Expositor* 112 (2015): 269–79.

Miller, Chanel. *Know My Name: A Memoir.* New York: Viking, 2019.

Miller, Charles William. "Reading Voices: Personification, Dialogism, and the Reader of Lamentations 1." *Biblical Interpretation* 9, no. 4 (2001): 393–408.

Minister, Meredith. "Fuck the Survivor: Refusing the Future Promised by the Sanctified Cancer Patient." In Brintnall, Graybill, and Tonstad, *Lee Edelman and the Queer Study of Religion,* forthcoming.

Minister, Meredith. *Rape Culture on Campus.* Lanham, MD: Lexington Books, 2018.

Minister, Meredith. "Sex and Alien Encounter: Rethinking Consent as a Rape Prevention Strategy." In Graybill, Minister, and Lawrence, *Rape Culture and Religious Studies,* 157–74.

Mintz, Alan. "The Rhetoric of Lamentations and the Representation of Catastrophe." *Prooftexts* 2, no. 1 (1982): 1–17.

Moshfegh, Ottessa. *My Year of Rest and Relaxation.* New York: Penguin Press, 2018.

Moyo, Fulata Lusungu. "'Traffic Violations': Hospitality, Foreignness, and Exploitation: A Contextual Biblical Study of Ruth." *Journal of Feminist Studies in Religion* 32 (2016): 83–94.

Murphy, Kelly J. *Rewriting Masculinity: Gideon, Men, and Might.* New York: Oxford University Press, 2019.

Nagouse, Emma. "'To Ransom a Man's Soul': Male Rape and Gender Identity in Outlander and 'The Suffering Man' of Lamentations 3." In Blyth, Colgan, and Edwards, *Rape Culture, Gender Violence, and Religion,* 143–58.

Nash, Jennifer C. *Black Feminism Reimagined: After Intersectionality.* Durham, NC: Duke University Press, 2018.

Nelson, Katherine Schott. "My Justice Is Her Justice: Toward a New Vision of Survivorhood." In Patterson, *Queering Sexual Violence,* 251–56.

Nicol, George G. "The Alleged Rape of Bathsheba: Some Observations on Ambiguity in Biblical Narrative." *Journal for the Study of the Old Testament* 73 (1997): 43–54.

Nicol, George G. "Bathsheba, a Clever Woman?" *Expository Times* 99, no. 12 (1988): 360–63.

Nietzsche, Friedrich. *On the Genealogy of Morals and Ecco Homo.* Edited by Walter Kaufmann. New York: Vintage Books, 1989.

O'Brien, Julia M. *Nahum.* Readings. London: Sheffield Academic Press, 2002.

O'Connor, Kathleen M. *Lamentations and the Tears of the World.* Maryknoll, NY: Orbis Books, 2002.

Okoye, James C. "Sarah and Hagar: Genesis 16 and 21." *Journal for the Study of the Old Testament* 32, no. 2 (2007): 163–75.

Oliver, Kelly. "Party Rape, Nonconsensual Sex, and Affirmative Consent Policies." *Americana* 14, no. 2 (2015): n.pag.

Oria, Shelly, ed. *Indelible in the Hippocampus: Writings from the Me Too Movement.* San Francisco: McSweeney's, 2019.

Patterson, Jennifer. "Introduction." In Patterson, *Queering Sexual Violence,* 5–13.

Patterson, Jennifer, ed. *Queering Sexual Violence: Radical Voices from within the Anti-Violence Movement*. Riverdale, NY: Riverdale Avenue Books, 2016.

Paynter, Helen. *Telling Terror in Judges 19: Rape and Reparation for the Levite's Wife*. Rape Culture, Religion, and the Bible. New York: Routledge, 2020.

Penner, Todd, and Lilian Cates. "Textually Violating Dinah: Literary Readings, Colonizing Interpretations, and the Pleasure of the Text." *The Bible and Critical Theory* 3, no. 3 (2007): 37.1–37.18.

Perry, Menachem, and Meir Sternberg. "The King through Ironic Eyes: Biblical Narrative and the Literary Reading Process." *Poetics Today* 7, no. 2 (1986): 275–322.

Pham, Larissa. "Our Reaction to 'Cat Person' Shows That We Are Failing as Readers." *Village Voice*, December 15, 2017. https://www.villagevoice.com/2017/12/15/our-reaction-to-cat-person-shows-that-we-are-failing-as-readers/.

Piepzna-Samarasinha, Leah Lakshmi. *Care Work: Dreaming Disability Justice*. Vancouver: Arsenal Pulp Press, 2018.

Pigott, Susan M. "Hagar: The M/Other Patriarch." *Review & Expositor* 115, no. 4 (2018): 513–28.

Posadas, Jeremy. "Teaching the Cause of Rape Culture: Toxic Masculinity." *Journal of Feminist Studies in Religion* 33, no. 1 (2017): 177–79.

Powell, Stephanie Day. *Narrative Desire and the Book of Ruth*. Library of the Hebrew Bible/Old Testament Studies 662. New York: T&T Clark, 2018.

Propp, William H. "Kinship in 2 Samuel 13." *Catholic Biblical Quarterly* 55, no. 1 (1993): 39–53.

Puar, Jasbir K. *The Right to Maim: Debility, Capacity, Disability*. Durham, NC: Duke University Press, 2017.

Pyper, Hugh S. "Reading Lamentations." *Journal for the Study of the Old Testament* 26, no. 1 (2001): 55–69.

Rashkow, Ilona N. *Taboo or Not Taboo: Sexuality and Family in the Hebrew Bible*. Minneapolis: Fortress Press, 2000.

Reaves, Jayme R. "Sarah as Victim and Perpetrator: Whiteness, Power, and Memory in the Matriarchal Narrative." *Review & Expositor* 115, no. 4 (2018): 483–99.

Rooney, Sally. *Conversations with Friends*. New York: Hogarth, 2017.

Rosenberg, Gil. *Ancestral Queerness: The Normal and the Deviant in the Abraham and Sarah Narratives*. Sheffield, UK: Sheffield Phoenix Press, 2019.

Roupenian, Kristen. "Cat Person." *New Yorker*, December 11, 2017. https://www.newyorker.com/magazine/2017/12/11/cat-person.

Roupenian, Kristen. *You Know You Want This: "Cat Person" and Other Stories*. New York: Gallery/Scout Press, 2019.

Rudolf, Mattias. "Vulnerabilities: Consent with Pfizer, Marx, and Hobbes." In Greenblatt and Valens, *Querying Consent*, 205–21.

Runions, Erin. "From Disgust to Humor: Rahab's Queer Affect." In *Bible Trouble: Queer Reading at the Boundaries of Biblical Scholarship*, edited by Teresa J. Hornsby and Ken Stone, 45–74. Semeia Studies. Atlanta: SBL Press, 2011.

Russ, Joanna. *The Female Man*. Princeton, NJ: Beacon Press, 1975.

Sabo, Peter J. "The Lot Complex." PhD diss., University of Alberta, 2018.

Sabo, Peter J. "Poetry amid Ruins." In *Poets, Prophets, and Texts in Play: Studies in Biblical Poetry and Prophecy in Honour of Francis Landy*, edited by Ehud Ben Zvi, Claudia V. Camp, David M. Gunn, and Aaron W. Hughes, 141–58. Library of Hebrew Bible/Old Testament Studies 597. New York: T&T Clark, 2015.

Salaymeh, Lena. "Imperialist Feminism and Islamic Law." *Hawwa* 17, no. 2–3 (2019): 97–134.

Sarkeesian, Anita. "Tropes vs. Women: #1 The Manic Pixie Dream Girl." *Feminist Frequency* (blog), March 24, 2011. https://feministfrequency.com/video/tropes-vs-women-1-the-manic-pixie-dream-girl/.

Scarry, Elaine. *The Body in Pain: The Making and Unmaking of the World.* New York: Oxford University Press, 1987.

Schipper, Jeremy. "Did David Overinterpret Nathan's Parable in 2 Samuel 12:1–6?" *Journal of Biblical Literature* 126, no. 2 (2007): 383–91.

Scholz, Susanne. "'Back Then It Was Legal': The Epistemological Imbalance in Readings of Biblical and Ancient Near Eastern Rape Legislation." *Journal of Religion & Abuse* 7, no. 3 (2005): 5–35.

Scholz, Susanne. *Sacred Witness: Rape in the Hebrew Bible.* Minneapolis: Fortress, 2010.

Schottroff, Luise, and Marie-Theres Wacker. *Feminist Biblical Interpretation: A Compendium of Critical Commentary on the Books of the Bible and Related Literature.* Grand Lakes, IN: Wm. B. Eerdmans Publishing, 2012.

Schulman, Sarah. *Conflict Is Not Abuse: Overstating Harm, Community Responsibility, and the Duty of Repair.* Vancouver: Arsenal Pulp Press, 2016.

Schulte, Leah Rediger. *The Absence of God in Biblical Rape Narratives.* Minneapolis: Fortress Press, 2017.

Schwartz, Alexandra. "A New Kind of Adultery Novel." *New Yorker*, July 31, 2017. https://www.newyorker.com/magazine/2017/07/31/a-new-kind-of-adultery-novel.

Schwartz, Madeleine. "How Should a Millennial Be?" *New York Review of Books*, April 18, 2019. https://www.nybooks.com/articles/2019/04/18/sally-rooney-how-should-millennial-be/.

Sedgwick, Eve Kosofsky. *Touching Feeling: Affect, Pedagogy, Performativity.* Series Q. Durham, NC: Duke University Press Books, 2002.

Shanley, John Patrick, dir. *Doubt.* Burbank, CA: Miramax, 2008. DVD.

Sharp, Carolyn J. *Irony and Meaning in the Hebrew Bible.* Indianapolis: Indiana University Press, 2008.

Shemesh, Yael. "Rape Is Rape Is Rape: The Story of Dinah and Shechem (Genesis 34)." *Zeitschrift für die alttestamentliche Wissenschaft* 119, no. 1 (2007): 2–21.

Shotwell, Alexis. *Against Purity: Living Ethically in Compromised Times.* Minneapolis: University of Minnesota Press, 2016.

Singh, Julietta. *No Archive Will Restore You.* 3Ecologies Books. Montreal: Punctum Books, 2018.

Spivak, Gayatri Chakravorty. "Can the Subaltern Speak?" In *Marxism and the Interpretation of Culture*, edited by Cary Nelson and Lawrence Grossberg, 271–314. Champaign: University of Illinois Press, 1988.

Spivak, Gayatri Chakravorty. "French Feminism Revisited: Ethics and Politics." In Butler and Scott, *Feminists Theorize the Political*, 54–84.

Stanton, Elizabeth Cady, ed. *The Woman's Bible: A Classic Feminist Perspective.* Mineola, NY: Dover Publications, 2002. Originally published 1898.

Stiebert, Johanna. "The Eve-Ing of Bathsheba in Twentieth-Century Film." *The Bible and Critical Theory* 10, no. 2 (2014): 22–31.

Stiebert, Johanna. *Fathers and Daughters in the Hebrew Bible.* New York: Oxford University Press, 2013.

Stiebert, Johanna. *Rape Myths, the Bible, and #MeToo.* Rape Culture, Religion and the Bible 1. New York: Routledge, 2019.

Stiebert, Johanna. "The Wife of Potiphar, Sexual Harassment, and False Rape Allegation." In *The Bible and Gender Troubles in Africa*, edited by Joachim Kügler, Rosinah Gabaitse, and Johanna Stiebert, 73–114. Bamberg: University of Bamberg Press, 2019.

Stinespring, William Franklin. "No Daughter of Zion: A Study of the Appositional Genitive in Hebrew Grammar." *Encounter* 26, no. 13 (1965): 3–41.

Stone, Ken. "Animal Difference, Sexual Difference, and the Daughter of Jephthah." *Biblical Interpretation* 24, no. 1 (2016): 1–16.

Stone, Ken. "1 and 2 Samuel." In *The Queer Bible Commentary*, edited by Deryn Guest, Robert E. Goss, Mona West, and Thomas Bohache, 195–221. London: SCM, 2006.

Stone, Ken. "Gender and Homosexuality in Judges 19: Subject-Honor, Object-Shame?" *Journal for the Study of the Old Testament* 20, no. 67 (1995): 87–107.

Stone, Ken. "'You Seduced Me, You Overpowered Me, and You Prevailed': Religious Experience and Homoerotic Sadomasochism in Jeremiah." In *Patriarchs, Prophets and Other Villains*, edited by Lisa Isherwood, 101–9. Gender, Theology, and Spirituality. London: Equinox, 2007.

Tamber-Rosenau, Caryn. "Biblical Bathing Beauties and the Manipulation of the Male Gaze: What Judith Can Tell Us about Bathsheba and Susanna." *Journal of Feminist Studies in Religion* 33, no. 2 (2017): 55–72.

Thistlethwaite, Susan Brooks. "You May Enjoy the Spoil of Your Enemies: Rape as a Biblical Metaphor for War." *Semeia*, no. 61 (1993): 59–75.

Traister, Rebecca. "The Game Is Rigged: Why Sex That's Consensual Can Still Be Bad. And Why We're Not Talking About It." *The Cut*, October 20, 2015. http://www.thecut.com/2015/10/why-consensual-sex-can-still-be-bad.html.

Trible, Phyllis. "Depatriarchalizing in Biblical Interpretation." *Journal of the American Academy of Religion* 41 (1973): 30–48.

Trible, Phyllis. "Genesis 22: The Sacrifice of Sarah." In *Not in Heaven: Coherence and Complexity in Biblical Narrative*, edited by Jason P. Rosenblatt and Joseph C. Sitterson, 28–57. Bloomington: Indiana University Press, 1991.

Trible, Phyllis. *God and the Rhetoric of Sexuality*. Overtures to Biblical Theology. Philadelphia: Fortress Press, 1978.

Trible, Phyllis. *Texts of Terror: Literary-Feminist Readings of Biblical Narratives*. Overtures to Biblical Theology. Philadelphia: Fortress Press, 1984.

van Wolde, Ellen. "Does 'innâ Denote Rape? A Semantic Analysis of a Controversial Word." *Vetus Testamentum* 52, no. 4 (2002): 528–44.

Vevaina, Coomi S. "Margaret Atwood and History." In Howells, *Cambridge Companion to Margaret Atwood*, 86–99.

Washington, Harold C. "Violence and the Construction of Gender in the Hebrew Bible: A New Historicist Approach 1." *Biblical Interpretation* 5, no. 4 (1997): 324–63.

Weems, Renita J. *Battered Love: Marriage, Sex, and Violence in the Hebrew Prophets*. Minneapolis: Fortress Press, 1995.

Wells, Ida B. *Southern Horrors and Other Writings: The Anti-Lynching Campaign of Ida B. Wells, 1892–1900*. 2nd ed. Edited by Jacqueline Jones Royster. Bedford Series in History and Culture. Boston: Bedford/St. Martin's, 2016.

Williams, Delores S. *Sisters in the Wilderness: The Challenge of Womanist God-Talk*. 20th anniversary ed. Maryknoll, NY: Orbis Books, 2013.

Williams, Lara. *Supper Club*. New York: G. P. Putnam's Sons, 2019.

Wilson, Stephen. *Making Men: The Male Coming-of-Age Theme in the Hebrew Bible*. New York: Oxford University Press, 2015.

Woolf, Virginia. *A Room of One's Own*. New York: Harcourt Brace, 1975. Originally published 1929.

Yamada, Frank M. *Configurations of Rape in the Hebrew Bible: A Literary Analysis of Three Rape Narratives*. Bern: Peter Lang, 2008.

Yee, Gale A. "'Fraught with Background': Literary Ambiguity in II Samuel 11." *Union Seminary Review* 42, no. 3 (1988): 240–53.

Yoo, Philip Y. "Hagar the Egyptian: Wife, Handmaid, and Concubine." *Catholic Biblical Quarterly* 78, no. 2 (2016): 215–35.

Zucker, David J., and Moshe Reiss. "David's Wives: Love, Power, and Lust." *Biblical Theology Bulletin* 46, no. 2 (2016): 70–78.

Index

For the benefit of digital users, indexed terms that span two pages (e.g., 52–53) may, on occasion, appear on only one of those pages.